Memoirs
of a
Legal Courtesan

Memoirs
of a
Legal Courtesan

A Sex / Love Addict's
Journey to Sobriety

S.P. Owen

Feminine Collective Media
Los Angeles

Memoirs of a Legal Courtesan
A Sex/Love Addict's Journey to Sobriety

Book One - **Memoirs of a Legal Courtesan** (2001-2017)
Forthcoming:
Book Two - **Makings of a Legal Courtesan** (1979-1989)
Book Three - **Meditations of a Legal Courtesan** (1989 - 2001)

First Feminine Collective Media edition January 2018

Black & white author photo by Paul Morejón

All photos are property of the author. Contact www.spowen.com.

Disclaimer: I recount events, locales and conversations in these memoirs to the best of my recall. However, in order to protect the privacy of individuals and to account for memory foibles, I have changed most of the names as well as some of the occupations, nationalities, and places of residence.

Library of Congress Control Number: 2018931077

ISBN 978-0-692-99578-5

Dedication

I dedicate my memoirs to the wounded wombs of the world, be they biological wombs or spiritual wombs. We all have that womb, deep within our soul, which craves to give birth to love, joy, and happiness in this world. May we together gain strength, courage, and hope, that there is a way out of this sex/love addiction cycle. It took me over 50 years to see my addiction. It is never too late to heal.

Author's Foreword

Mid-life crisis gone wild? Remedy for 9/11 trauma? I began formulating my memoirs somewhere in the midst of my years of legal lust in New York City. Who knew the corporate world of law could offer such a sensual pool to fish from? I was a legal secretary in a highly prestigious law firm from 2002-2006. I worked for the senior partner and enjoyed my sexual liaisons with attorneys, clients, and even the boys in the mailroom. I was the unofficial social director, and everyone came to my desk for directions to the next fun after-work event. We worked together, played together, and sexed together - one big, happy, legal lump of lust!

I never knew turning 40 would be so much fun. The gals from *Sex and the City* were tame compared to me. I thought my sensual years as super model Patty Owen could never be trumped. Living on fame and fortune in the 80s was a nightly extravaganza with plenty of sensual liaisons to fuel the ride. Yet here I was after a decade of deep spiritual study to arrive in 2002, atop the ethereal twin towers. I was high and tripping on my drug of lust and love.

But it wasn't until the summer of 2008 when I left my life in law that I felt inspired to write down my sexcapades as a legal outlaw. Perhaps my inspiration was this escalating sensual life with my new boyfriend, Leonard. Escalating? How could my sex life possibly be escalating? Until I met Leonard, I thought I had hit the peak, or rather bottom, of my lust barrel. He made me look like a prude! Is that why I fell in love with him, finally feeling like a virgin again? Until meeting Leonard, I was naive about the world of kinky sex. With all his sex parties, craigslist personals, and BDSM (Bondage, Domination, Sadism and Masochism) equipment, I felt like a newbie. His extensive sexual experiences had the positive effect of minimizing all my promiscuous years.

My life with Leonard was a constant barrage of sex, sensuality, kink, love, and lust. I agreed to enter into a swinger lifestyle because Leonard's so-called lack of sexual experiences was all that stopped him from marrying me. Curious for sure about this swinger life but mostly, I wanted to please my man so I could keep him. Love addiction at its best. Thus a resistant swinger was born.

It was not long before the financial devastation of 2008 clawed at our empty tummies and wallets. So I saw nothing wrong with extending our swinger life into a more profitable activity: I became a prostitute at age 52.

When I originally began writing my memoirs I thought it would be a titillating romp through my sexcapades as a legal secretary when I was still single and wild. After a loveless and sexless seven-year marriage in the 90s (I know the seven-year itch!) I was ready for a good dose of lust. That is what I thought anyway. Little did I know I was on a journey deep into my sex/love addiction, a journey fraught with painful consequences that ended with me remarried, yet being paid to have sex with wealthy men. Yes, I wanted to believe it was legal. They were merely helping a lady who found herself in a difficult situation.

Until recently, few people recognized that sex/love addictions even existed, especially not for women, and least of all for me. Although I knew I had tremendous difficulty being alone for more than a few hours at a time, I had an even more difficult time coping outside the cocoon of a romantic relationship. When I was between relationships, I was absolutely miserable. Later on, I adopted the serial dating approach so I wouldn't have a moment to lament while desperately hoping to find the next Mr. Right. But I just told myself this was a fun adventure and for the most part, I did have fun, as long as the addiction was fed. I was never content though with my need to be in love and in a relationship. However, I preferred that to being in lust. I accepted lust only as a bad second to love, and I accepted it often.

Memoirs of a Legal Courtesan is about my zany, fun, sexy, dangerous, lonely, courageous, and painful life of longing, lust, and love. I hope that men and women who suffer from sex/love addictions, consciously or unconsciously, or know of those who do, will find insights, compassion, humor, hope, healing, and recovery from reading about my journey to sobriety.

--Shanti Patty Owen, September 2017, New York City.

Acknowledgments

I wish to thank all my teachers and their communities for always seeing, believing, and supporting the highest good in me, even when I couldn't see it myself. May we continue to make uplifting transformations within ourselves and inspire others on their journey.

A special thanks to my daughter, who gives me more love than I have ever known, receives the outpouring of love in my heart, and is a beacon of light in this world. May the deep love that fills her vessel to capacity protect her from following in my sex/love addiction footsteps. "Been there. Done that. Don't do it!"

Contents

Part I: Fantasy

Super model Patty Owen leaves her life of glitz and glamour on a deep spiritual quest to heal and becomes known as Shanti. Years later Shanti is hired by a prestigious law firm as a legal secretary and transforms quickly from yogini to office slut. Midlife-crisis mania?

Part II: Intrigue

Shanti continues to add men to her harem until she is accused of being a sex addict. If thirty is too many then is eight enough? She tries desperately to control her unmanageable sex life. The roller-coaster is exciting at times but it's making her nauseous.

Part III: **Monogamy**

Her heart wanted monogamy, but with Mike, Shanti picked a bird more broken than she. Make-up to break-up, that's all they did. Shanti's love addiction was in full flight. Therapy to the rescue as Shanti starts untangling this complex web of sex/love addiction.

Part IV: **Orgies**

When monogamy fails miserably, Shanti looks to Lenny to keep her from love withdrawal. When two alcoholics meet at a bar they end up drunk on the floor. When two sex addicts meet at a polyamorous workshop they end up at an orgy.

Part V: **Prostitution**

Can the end ever justify the means? Caring for her elderly parents and poverty stricken since 2008, Shanti decides to leave dumpster-diving to catch bigger fish. Sugar Daddies and Johns become her new food source, with plenty of leftovers.

Part VI: **Recovery!**

How did Shanti not see her sex/love addiction smashing her in the face all these years? After her mother's death in 2011, Shanti is finally able to remove the blinders of denial. Yet recovery is a slippery slope. Shanti only truly gets sober when she finds a sponsor, four years later.

Part I: **Fantasy**

Super model Patty Owen leaves her life of glitz and glamour on a deep spiritual quest to heal and becomes known as Shanti. Years later Shanti is hired by a prestigious law firm as a legal secretary and transforms quickly from yogini to office slut. Midlife-crisis mania?

Chapter 1

Frenching My Way into Law

I found myself at age 42 with a full-time position as the executive secretary to Mr. Tanner, the senior partner of an international law firm. Mr. Montenegro, the owner of the bilingual staffing agency who found me this position, invited me out for drinks in celebration.

Only four fearful weeks earlier I was crying in despair that I would never find a secretarial job in this post 9/11 economy. A super model in the 1980's I was now clamoring to be a legal secretary. I put myself through four years of college after my divorce hoping to become a documentary filmmaker. But the tragedy of 9/11 changed our physical, emotional, and financial landscape forever, especially for us here in New York City. We needed only to look up and see our lives were forever changed - our giant twins were gone. My glorified notion of filming this tragedy and its aftermath crumbled along with the Twin Towers. I had an eight-year-old daughter to feed. It was time to pay the bills and my enormous student loans.

Mr. Montenegro wanted to know my secret: "You have got to be the luckiest person I have met in years. Not only did you book back-to-back temp jobs in this horrendous economy, but you booked a full-time, high-paying, high-level staff position for the head of the firm. What is your secret?"

I had to laugh because I didn't have a secret, except my unusual past! As a fashion model living and working in Paris, I had become fluent in French. I explained, "I really missed speaking French and thought I'd check out jobs that required me to do so. I added fluent French to my resume and followed my French bliss!"

My new life began in April of 2002. I was having a blast making good steady income, brushing up on my rusty French,

1

and working in an environment of my peers. No more hanging out with 20-year-old college students, finally! My new co-workers were world travelers, like me, and I was soon to discover, world-class flirts, just like me. It's hard to say what came first, my flirting or their flirting. But I am guessing it came from them first for I would not have jeopardized my new position with marginal behavior. That came later.

Stuart Landau was the first to make his interests known.

"How fantastic you will be with us full time now!" he declared.

Then he looked over his shoulder and spoke more softly, "So, um, how is your Israeli boyfriend doing?"

While I was temping with the firm before being hired full time, Stuart asked many questions about my boyfriend, Yigal. Not dropping a beat, I caressed Stuart's wedding band and responded in an equally soft tone.

"Um, he's great. You want to speak with him? No wait, I have a better idea. Why don't we arrange for a double date with you and your wife?"

Stuart broke out laughing, "No, no she's really more of a homebody kind of gal."

"Ah, and let me guess. You are not."

Stuart's laughter escalated, "You got that right."

"Me thinks Mr. Landau is the bad boy in this office."

"Please, call me Stuart. I hate all that last name hierarchy crap. I'm more like a one-with-the-people kind of guy."

I smiled, "Indeed I see that you are. Well Mr. Stuart…"

He interrupts, "No, no, just Stuart"

"Okay just Stuart. Thank you for your warm welcome. I'll see you around the campfires."

"Oh yeah. Phew! Sure is getting hot in here."

Stuart's lurid smile grew ever wider as he walked away from my desk.

Within the next week nearly all the flirtatious players introduced themselves. One by one they congratulated me for landing this new position and each of them invited me out for drinks in celebration. Most of the fierce flirters were men but several were women who delighted in giving me the office back-stories. They too were deeply woven into this spicy story and eager to share their scandalous chapters.

Gloria, the executive secretary to another senior partner, was the ringleader of this social whirl. Gloria was born in Puerto Rico and moved to New York when she was five. She sounded like an all-American girl until she started cursing in Spanish. Gloria took me to lunch one afternoon and filled me in on the incestuous office antics.

I could barely speak, "My oh my this place is quite the soap opera isn't it?"

Gloria replied, "Oh you have no idea."

But I was soon to find out.

Raul was the head of the mailroom, six feet tall, dark and handsome, and incredibly sexy. He was born in the Dominican Republic but grew up in Harlem. At only 22 years of age he had a very responsible position and did his job well, very well. Whenever I needed a package sent out immediately he was at my desk before I could hang up the phone. I suppose it didn't hurt that our flirting was dangerously intense, great motivation for Raul to service me. But I would not allow myself to be with a guy 20 years my junior. Yigal, 15 years my junior, was bad enough. So I gave myself permission to flirt unabashedly with Raul, believing it would never go further than our daily dose of teasing.

My favorite pastime at the law firm was torturing Stuart Landau, one of their well-established attorneys. Stuart began flirting with me from day one and the tight gold band on his chubby ring finger was no deterrent to his lustful advances. I was equally attracted to him, chub and all. But I had a firm no married men policy in my personnel file. Just didn't make sense to be with a man who was unavailable to service me when needed, which was often. Then of course there would be the constant lies, which I abhorred, to camouflage the affair, not to mention the guilt I would surely feel if our affair destroyed their marriage. No thank you.

But I did so revel in running Stuart up my sensual flagpole by recounting to him all my sexual exploits with other men, other non-married men, I would reiterate. Monday morning brought Stuart to my desk as usual. He leaned in flirtatiously but not before looking over his shoulder to be sure my boss was not around.

"Hey Shanti, how was your weekend?"

I was delighted to reunite with my favorite office flirt. I replied, "Ah, good morning dear Stuart. My weekend? Where do I even begin? Well, I had a delicious Friday night sleep over with my young steady, Yigal. Then I hooked up with a new guy for dinner Saturday night. He's a handsome real estate agent from Greenwich, Connecticut that I met online."

"Is he married?" Stuart asked.

"Of course not. You know I don't do married men Stuart or you would be first in line."

"I like that," he responded with glee, "you're getting me hot. Whoosh! Did you sleep with him?"

Giving Stuart a coy smile I paused and then replied, "...but of course."

"Damn," he responded, while shaking his head.

"Then, for Sunday brunch, I banged a banker from Baltimore."

Stuart burst out, "No! My God you have the most exciting life!"

I replied, "You too could have an exciting life with me if you weren't married."

Stuart tried, "I could have an exciting life with you while I am married."

"Sorry buddy. No can do," I reminded him.

Stuart tried to build his case, "I can't believe that, with all the men you sleep with…"

Taunting him I said, "Don't forget the women."

"Yes and women, God damn it! Why can't you take on one married guy?"

"Sorry buddy," I replied, "my cardinal rule. It's Monday morning dude. Get cracking!"

Stuart walked away shaking his head as I laughed.

When my boss was out of town, which was often, Stuart would come skulking around my desk with his bedroom eyes.

"Oh the damage I could do with your body if you would only relax your no married men policy."

One morning, after just such a remark, I pulled him in close with my soft kitten whisper, "Stuart, though I have many lovers, alas my instincts tell me that they all pale in comparison to the fire we would create in bed."

Stuart straightened up and tucked in his shirt, "Now we are talking."

"The type of sensual attention I so desperately long for involve hours upon hours of foreplay."

"Yeah, with hot oil," he replied.

I pondered his addition to my fantasy and moved to one-up him.

"Hmmm, yes, maybe, but only after a heavy spanking session with wrist and ankle restraints."

Stuart's eyes widened, "Spanking? Oh wow, you really are wild!"

"I do hope you don't bruise easily though. Your wife might get suspicious."

"Wait, you want to spank me?" he asked.

Feeling his heat rising to a boil, I barked out loud in an abrasive tone, "The documents you are looking for are not here!"

Stuart jumped back like a crocodile had lunged at his balls, and his reaction threw me into a laughing fit.

"Who was there?" he whispered.

I giggled, "No one. I just wanted to see you jump!"

His sly grin expressed the amusement of my pleasurable torture.

By December of 2002, having already dug my heels and claws into some of the other office inhabitants, that old corporate Christmas party rolled around and with it, my massive blood lust, waiting to be born. This was my first corporate Christmas party. I had heard they could be boring, but some said it was the prelude to a night of sexual debauchery. Yum, just my style. The real players would meet up after the official party was over for some wild-side nightcaps. Our ongoing flirtation mixed with excessive alcohol beckoned Stuart into my sensual abode. I knew he wouldn't sleep over because he had to get home to his wife, so I was safe in that regard. But what was not safe was the heat and intense passion we felt for one another.

Hung over the next day and totally guilt-ridden, I understood the pull of a married man. He was starving for some kind of attention that his wife did not provide, be it sensual, emotional, spiritual, or intellectual. There was a void that craved deeply to be fulfilled and I felt Stuart's intense longing and gratitude that I could provide such an oasis. Made me feel all the more wanted. It was hot, very hot, sweet, and intense. I felt attached to Stuart immediately, but I berated myself the next day.

"Shit, now I have a big problem. I don't want to fall for a married guy. I just broke one of my cardinal rules, and I don't have many!"

In the ensuing weeks Stuart's light office flirting turned heavy and more serious.

"When can I see you again?" he asked. "I've had a small taste of the main course. Now I want the banquet."

His advances became more meaningful, laden with deep desire. It scared me. I really did not want to date a married man. But my heat for Stuart was growing after our holiday horniness opened way to pent-up passions.

"Stuart, I don't see how this can work. I have Rebecca on week nights, when you are in NYC and available, and you are with your family in New Jersey on weekends, when I am available."

"We'll figure it out. Let me work on it," Stuart insisted.

I managed to push Stuart away for a couple of months. But the cold, long nights of winter craved a warm blanket of sensual respite. Sure I had other men, plenty of them, but I wanted Stuart.

One day Stuart rushed by my desk and called me into my boss's office. My boss was out of town of course. He was sporting an uncharacteristically aggressive look. I felt something was up. But as soon as he closed the door, the only thing that was up was my dress, and down went his head. I did not resist. It was deliciously bad. Little did he know that my boss's office was scene to most of my naughty office liaisons. But I pretended this was terribly taboo of him, and his hard cock revealed the excitement of this risk.

Though I tried my best to resist Stuart in the weeks that followed, I fell to the mercy of our loins on a few more occasions.

As it became clear that I was starting to fall for him, and Stuart made it clear he would never leave his wife, I found myself at a difficult crossroads. This tryst would never lead to a monogamous relationship. However, was that what I really wanted? It is what my soul wanted, for sure, yet my loins begged to differ.

Since Stuart would never divorce and be totally available to me as my main man, I decided he should no longer be privileged with free visitations. He needed to pay rent. So at the end of the day, I removed my well-worn G-string panty and put it in an interoffice envelope with a note. However, I had to figure out how to by-pass Stuart's secretary. I knew her well and did not want her knowing that I was banging her boss. Of course some of my office compadres knew of the affair. That was half the fun. I needed to get one of my confidants to deliver the envelope to Stuart personally. Who better than Raul, head of the mailroom? Raul and I were both predators and appreciated each other's skills. I even showed Raul the panty and letter before closing the envelope.

> *Dearest Stuart,*
>
> *Sitting all day at my desk, feeling my intense heat for you, I wanted you to experience that heat first-hand with my moist panty in your stroking hand. I do hope that you will be able to remove my panties again in person. However, that will depend upon your good behavior.*
>
> *I have decided that since our relationship will never lead to marriage, per your admission, I am setting myself up for heartache and wasting my time when I should be looking for a proper suitor. However, if you make it worth my while, I will consider giving you regular visitations.*
>
> *Attached is a copy of my dental bill for two recent implants. Take care of this bill and I will take great care of you... ;o)*
>
> *In heated anticipation,*
>
> *Shanti*

Raul's eyes protruded his sockets when he finished reading the letter. He reeled in nervous laughter while sniffing my panty. I think I exceeded even his daring.

"Oh my God Shantz, you are mad crazy girl!" Raul exclaimed.

"Isn't that why you love me? Go ahead, give it to him."

No more than five minutes passed from the time Raul left my sight with the envelope until Stuart came rushing down the hallway. Quick response. I liked that. I had grown accustomed to Stuart's gait and started smiling even before he reached me, knowing he had such a strong response to my package that he couldn't wait another moment. At first his countenance was bright with turn-on and he looked over his shoulder to see if my boss was around. All clear.

Stuart spoke softly, "You're killing me. You know that right?"

Yes, I did know that yet I merely allowed my smile to convey my delight in that power.

Since it was the end of the workday, we had time to discuss my perfectly decent proposal. Stuart's demeanor became more serious.

He explained, "I don't make that kind of surplus income to keep you. I really wish I did."

Whether that was true or not, I was relieved that he could not afford to keep me because I could not afford the heartache. I knew that I had way more than just a sexual connection with Stuart and that we would be heading down a treacherous and painful path.

Disappointed, I replied, "That's okay Stuart. It's been sweet spending intimate time with you. Maybe we can reconnect in another life."

I never met with Stuart again in an intimate way. Yet I did so enjoy torturing him from time to time with the possibility of reconnecting.

Stuart was but one of a multitude of lovers during my years as a legal courtesan. Though many, each one of my lovers were like precious pearls that comprised my ever-expanding sensual necklace. I never once suspected that I could be hung by my own sensual creations, not until years later. I kept sex rolling like an alcoholic keeps a flask full. When full, all was good. But I made damn sure never to run even close to empty. An addict must always, at all times, keep the object of the addiction close at hand. In my case, I kept all my lovers close at the ready, even some of them that were low on the list. I never knew when a dry spell might occur therefore, I was constantly hunting, fishing, and sharpening my weapons. Starvation was never an option.

Chapter 2

My Young Israeli Heart-Rob

Never was there a lover that brought me such unbridled joy and yet such debilitating sorrow as Yigal. He was the love of my life and without him I had little to live for, except to mother my daughter, Rebecca. She is what kept me from suicide.

From 1999 to 2001 Yigal and I lived in total ecstasy together. Yigal lived only four blocks from my apartment on the Upper East Side of Manhattan. We often joked that it was like living together with a long hallway. I had never experienced intense passion with a man while getting along daily with such ease. That I was 15 years his senior was never a cause for concern, at least not initially.

However, when talk of marriage reached Yigal's family in Israel and they discovered I was not Jewish, his parents threatened to disown him. Yigal was not strong enough to go against them. The relationship ended abruptly. It was a Romeo and Juliet tragedy that nearly killed us both.

One night, after a torturous month apart, we reconnected. We were hopelessly in love. Yigal concocted a crazy scheme to continue to date others, but see one another once a month to recharge our broken hearts. We would agree never to share our dating experiences with one another, for that would be too hurtful.

The plan seemed utterly crazy to me but I was willing to do anything to stay connected to Yigal. Looking back, I can see my sex/love addiction starting to become apparent. It was not clear to me at the time, but I knew something was off about my accepting such relationship terms. Yet I couldn't live without Yigal, so I agreed.

Though I spent the summer of 2001 dating and having sex with various men, after the tragedy of 9/11, Yigal and I decided to stop the dating train. We both needed more emotional support after this crisis and we agreed not to venture out again until we both felt strong enough.

Yet once I was hired at the law firm and the months progressed, bringing with them the gift of financial security, I felt I could handle a little emotional insecurity. Therefore, I told Yigal that it was time for us to start dating other people again, to find "the suitable marriage partners." However, to my surprise, he flatly refused.

"No Shanti. I love you too much to share you and I have no need to see anyone else right now. Can't we just be together, just you and I?"

Then he broke into that song by Eddie Rabbitt and Crystal Gayle, repeating the refrain over and over again, "Just you and I. Just you and I..."

Yigal was a romantic goofball, a trait I absolutely adored about him. We were five months back together in monogamous bliss after my brief 9/11 romance with Randy. Randy had an issue with my baby clock, he said the runway was too short. Only time in my life I was ever too short! My heart was always with Yigal anyway, he was all I ever wanted. For Yigal to claim me in this way felt wonderful. But I was suspicious.

I pondered, "Hmmm, this is a long hiatus without dating others." I continued to surmise the possible reasons. "Maybe Yigal is entertaining the possibility of marrying me after all and letting go of his parent's approval? September 11th shook us all up. Maybe he is finally coming to his senses?"

That day after Yigal's insistence that we only see each other, he also insisted that we book a trip to Barbados for the end of July. I was a bit scared to ask Mr. Tanner for that time off when I had only been at the firm a few months. Yet my love addiction followed my man's desires nearly always. Luckily Mr. Tanner was happy to oblige, especially since he would be on vacation in France at that time and the workload would be light.

Mr. Tanner said, "Just promise me Shanti that you will come back."

Awweee, how cute is my boss? He wants me back. My job is secure!

"Oui, Monsieur Tanner! Absolutement!" I replied with great joy.

I did indeed come back from Barbados in late July of 2002. I was rested, tanned, happy, and pregnant. Yes, I did one of the most irresponsible teenage pranks I had ever done. I got myself pregnant, intentionally, to trap my man. I knew my menstrual and ovulation cycles like a Swiss clock. I used the rhythm method with Yigal and he would pull out before ejaculating if I was even near ovulation. With other lovers I always used condoms. It just so happened that I was ovulating on the full moon night of July 24th, while enjoying Barbados and the love of my life. For my purposes, it was the perfect time to get pregnant, so I lied to Yigal and gave him the "all systems go" sign. Sperm received.

I knew that Yigal truly loved me. I had no doubt about that. I was convinced that all he needed was a push to get him to marry me. I was 100% sure that Yigal would marry me if I got pregnant. Why else did he not want me to see anyone else at this time and take me on a romantic trip? He would surely do the "right thing." What could his parents argue now? I was pregnant. Of course I did not tell Yigal that I got pregnant intentionally. He would have been furious if he knew that. I didn't even tell any of my friends about my dastardly plan. I was afraid they would talk me out of it. Sign number one that a romantic plan is insane? Do not tell anyone about it. Love addiction 101.

By mid-August I took a pregnancy test and sure enough, that rabbit died. I was beyond delighted. I wasn't sure I could even get pregnant at age 43, and on the first try at that!

"Here's to you Randy, my 9/11 romance, and your fearful short runway. I am pregnant!"

I tried my best not to show Yigal the utter delight in my conquest. I kept my outer appearance on the concerned side even though I was dancing with glee on the inside. My concern became real, however, when Yigal showed little interest in becoming a father.

"Shanti, listen to me. I am only 28 years old. I am not ready to be a father. Can't you understand that? If you decide to keep this baby you will ruin my life. I cannot be a part of his life or my family will disown me. You don't understand."

I explained, "I understand sweetie but at my age, I am lucky to even get pregnant. This is most likely my last chance. It's now or never and I want this baby, your baby Yigal."

Negotiations were rough, extremely rough, with several calls to his family in Israel. Pregnant or not, they made it clear that they would never accept this baby -- or me. I was not Jewish and they would not accept a conversion to Judaism. I never much liked them after their initial rejection of me. Now, I absolutely despised them. I guess I was wrong about this pregnancy fallback plan. I was falling flat on my face. I was starting to lose all hope and cried profusely one night to Yigal.

"Shanti please, stop crying sweetie. You know I can't stand when you cry like that."

But I really couldn't stop. I had made a grave mistake by miscalculating the value of this pregnancy, because his family was as staunch as ever in their resistance. Now I had to make a decision. Keep the baby and lose my man, or lose the baby and keep my man, temporarily anyway.

For that next week I was clear that I should keep this baby no matter what. It felt additionally auspicious that this being was conceived on the full moon which made me believe more so that this being was magical and needed to be born, with or without Yigal's presence in my life. I made my decision clear to Yigal, who went back and forth from anger to elation over the notion of being a father without his family's consent and blessings.

Then, on August 16th, to my utter surprise and delight, Yigal agreed to be a father to this child and to marry me, with or without his family's blessings. My plan worked! I was ecstatic! I would marry my soulmate AND have his baby! The next day was my sister Janet's 40th birthday party in New Jersey. My parents drove in from Cape Cod and she had nearly 100 guests at her cookout. At some point towards the end of that celebration I took my parents inside to my sister's bedroom to announce my exciting news. They seemed delighted. I had already told Janet the news the day before; she was happy for me yet still had a lot of trepidation about my decision. Unbeknownst to me, my parents apparently were not at all delighted by my news. After I left they spoke with my sister for hours, about my situation.

My parents told my sister, "She might lose her steady job and this on-again off-again boyfriend might take off again and leave her strapped with a new baby and no money! Christ, this is a horrible decision!"

Yet no one in my family expressed these concerns to me, until the crash. A few days after I declared my pregnancy and imminent wedding plans to family and friends, Yigal had a complete change of heart, so severe that I completely crashed. Yigal's family declared that they would disown him if he married me and raised this child. They would never be in touch with Yigal ever again. He begged me to have an abortion and when I refused he got nasty like I'd never experienced before. He was as aggressive as a wild caged animal. He was kicking, screaming, raging, and reeling in fear as he pulled at the bars of my heart. For the first time I was actually physically afraid of Yigal.

However, I stood my ground for nearly a week with daily visits of rage-filled threats from him. I had never experienced Yigal in such a nasty and vindictive manner before. It was as if a demon had jumped into his body. But I held firm. It wasn't until he broke down in a torrent of tears that I softened my stance.

"Shanti please, I cannot lose my family. I love them too much and I know them so well. They will for sure never see me again. I just can't live without the love of my family. I just can't Shanti. You will eventually hate me because I will blame you for losing them and start to hate you and I don't want you to hate me. Look how terrible I have been treating you all week. This is not me. I am becoming a monster. Please, please, Shanti, I beg you with all my heart, don't keep this baby. You will completely destroy me!"

Yigal continued to sob and I cradled this six-foot-four giant in my slender arms.

As I sat holding my beloved I contemplated, "How many lives will I destroy by giving birth to this child?"

If my goal had been to have another child I would have held strong. But my goal was to have Yigal marry and adore me for the rest of my life and that didn't look like it would ever happen if I kept the baby. I surely wasn't in a financially stable place to care for another child without help.

The Catholic girl inside said, "Keep the baby. It is a sin to abort a child!"

But my broken heart said, "Let go of this manipulative plan and set Yigal and his family free. You don't need to bring this child into such an unhappy situation."

My broken heart won out and I decided to destroy our full-moon child and the hope that it would keep us together.

Teenage games are bad enough for teenagers. I never thought I would be desperate enough to play such a high-stakes entrapment game myself. But addiction is a life-and-death game and it often turns the addict into a criminal; stealing and manipulation are par for the course. We do whatever it takes to get our fix. I just never thought I would go that far. But Yigal was my love addiction fix and I would do anything to keep him. This was my last desperate effort and it failed completely. Not only was I losing all marital hope with Yigal, I was losing all hope of becoming a mother again. At my age, our chances would be over after this abortion and Yigal absolutely wanted children. He had made it clear that raising my daughter, Rebecca, would not be enough for him.

I knew I could never see Yigal again after the abortion. First I would be too angry that he pushed for the abortion. Second, knowing now with 100% clarity that he would never marry me, it felt totally pointless to be together. Before there was always that little ray of hope. But now, his parents had made their stance clear and Yigal chose them. My relationship hopes died forever. I felt no will to live either.

When I got clear what I needed to do I took Yigal out his misery. "Okay, I'll have the abortion. But if you jump up and kiss me I will smack you. Just sit up and listen and don't speak."

Yigal wiped his eyes and as I ordered, he did not speak.

I continued, "I will have this abortion and you and your twisted family can be happy again."

He didn't respond but he grumbled heavily.

Stopping his noises I said, "Ah ah, no talking! Once I have the abortion I will never, and I mean never, ever, ever, see you again. Destroying this child will totally destroy my heart and my hopes for us. Seeing you again will only put the final nail in my coffin."

I could see that he wasn't grasping the metaphor so I explained with more clarity. "If I ever see you again I will completely die of a broken heart knowing I can never have you. You will have to take me to the cemetery."

"Oh Shanti…" he replied.

"Shut up! I told you not to talk!"

My tears burst through my eyes like a geyser.

"You have no fucking idea how you are destroying my life. I will never be the same happy Shanti again. With this abortion a huge part of my soul will die along with this poor fetus. It is going to take me a lifetime to heal and seeing you will totally destroy me. So I need you to move."

"What do you mean move?" he asked.

"I mean you need to leave my neighborhood. I cannot see you on the street, in the grocery store, or with a new girlfriend. It will kill me. If you want me to have this abortion, you must agree to move."

Yigal's eyes fluttered and his face twitched. "But, I have a rent-stabilized apartment Shanti. It is a great deal. I'm not going to give that up. That would be stupid."

I laid into him, "Poor Yigal loses his cheap God damn fucking apartment. You think I give a shit? I'm losing my life here! Keep the apartment and I keep this baby. If you want me to give up this baby then you give up the apartment, period."

Yigal got quiet. I could see this was sinking in. He asked, "But... well, where do you want me to go?"

I replied, "Actually I would love you to move back to Israel. Go be with that family you love so much."

"Shanti come on now, they are good people."

Incensed I replied, "Good people? No Yigal, they are not good people. They are monsters and I cannot believe you were born of these creatures."

My tears began to flow again uncontrollably. The death of our relationship was beyond what I could handle. I vacillated between intense grief and heated rage as I continued to make my needs clear. In the end, Yigal agreed to move out of Manhattan: to New Jersey.

I went home and threw myself on the bed, sobbing for hours. Amelia called later that night. She was my dearest friend who recently graduated from Marymount Manhattan College with me. She knew Yigal well and everything I was going through.

She asked, "Honey, how are you?"

No words came out. All I could do was cry.

She said, "Shantz, I'm coming over. Don't leave."

When she arrived I told her of my tormented decision to have the abortion and she said she would come with me in the morning to the clinic. Such a sweetheart, she came for me the next morning in a taxi. But when we got to the clinic we were greeted by a group of pro-life protestors and I walked straight past the door.

"Shantz, where are you going?"

Crying with my heart racing, "Amelia, I can't go through with this. I just can't!"

Looking lost, Amelia did her best to take care of me.

"Well, okay honey. What do you want to do right now?"

"I don't know!" I screamed.

We eventually walked from midtown back to my tiny apartment on the Upper East Side and talked through all the options, over and over again. I came to the same conclusion. I wanted to terminate this pregnancy. But I couldn't handle those pro-life protestors because I did not really want to end the life of this being, our love child. So Amelia suggested I go to my private doctor and have Yigal pay for it.

When I spoke on the phone with Yigal, he was not at all happy to pay such a steep price for my private abortion.

I told him, "Too bad you have to pay such a high price for your freedom Yigal."

He replied, "Shanti, now you are the one turning into a monster!"

I blurt out, "Okay, then I'll keep the baby and you return to being the monster. Which do you prefer?"

Yigal said, "I don't prefer any of this. I wish..."

"What do you wish Yigal?"

"I...I don't know. I wish that we could stay together and my parents would accept you and this baby but..."

I broke the silence, "But that's never going to happen Romeo. How tragic that we can never be together again. It is beyond sad. I just want to die."

"Please Shanti, don't say that!"

"Why? You can't handle the truth of what your family has created? The truth is, if it weren't for my daughter I would probably kill myself right now."

"Shanti please stop!"

A few days later I met with the doctor that delivered my daughter eight years earlier. When he entered the room I began to cry.

He gave me the most loving hug and said, "Abortion is not an easy decision, especially at your age. I'm so sorry. Are you ready?"

And with that I nodded. The man who had delivered great life into my world eight years ago was about to remove a life from me now. It seemed so wrong, so tragic, and it broke my heart completely.

Amelia was waiting for me in the next room when the abortion was complete. I saw her sitting there so attentively like the great friend that she was, but I told her I didn't want to speak, I just wanted to go home and go to bed. She took me home in a taxi.

I slept all afternoon, got up briefly for a bowl of cereal and went back to bed for the night. I was hoping I would never wake up again. But of course I did. I called a few friends to tell them I was alive and make arrangements to have Rebecca picked up after school. Then I left a voicemail message on Yigal's phone when I knew he wouldn't answer, during his morning prayers.

I said, "It's done. I hope you and your family are happy now. Don't ever contact me again. You, like this fetus I aborted, are now dead to me."

My message was harsh. But I wanted him to feel some of the pain that I was feeling. For the next few days I did not listen to voicemails or read emails. I wanted to disconnect from the world. At work, everyone could see I was not myself but when asked I just told them that a relative had died. It was in fact true, an unborn relative. I never told anyone at work about my pregnancy, I didn't want to explain my tragedy. I was all business and no flirtation that week. But I knew I needed to reconnect with family and friends, so I let Friday night after work be that time.

I started by playing the voicemail messages, "Honey, I am so excited for you! I knew in the end he would do the right thing. Call me when you have a chance. When is the wedding date? When is the baby due?"

That is how my Friday night began. Voicemail after email messages congratulating me on my pregnancy and engagement. I couldn't take it any more. I called Rachel, my dear friend of twenty years, who knew most of my friends and family. I begged her to handle this.

Through a storm of tears and howls of pain I asked, "Rachel, can you please call everyone and tell them I had an abortion and left Yigal? There will be no wedding. There will be no baby. I cannot bear to get on the phone and speak with anyone and relive this nightmare or I will end up in the loony bin!"

Rachel replied, "God Shanti, I am not comfortable doing this."

"Rachel please! I am begging you to do this for me. I have never begged you to do anything before. I cannot have this conversation with thirty people. It will absolutely kill me! Please Rachel please I beg you!!"

And like the great friend that Rachel was, she called my list of thirty people. I told her to tell them not to contact me for a few weeks, to give me time to heal.

Everyone that Rachel called honored my request except my sister Janet. Not only did my sister not honor my request, she sent me a scathing email that very day.

The email read, "First of all, how fucking selfish of you to ruin my 40th birthday party with your pregnancy and wedding announcements to Mom and Dad. ALL they talked about for the next two days was you, you, you and what terrible decisions you were making to have this child and marry Yigal. Then you had the nerve to have your friend Rachel call us to do your dirty work?!"

She went on and on and brought up a lifetime of grievances against me. It felt like she was kicking me in the head while I was down and turning her stiletto heal into my ear until it pierced my brain. I sent her an equally scathing email in return.

I wrote, "Don't ever contact me again. For you to be so heartless during the lowest point in my life is cruel and intolerable. You've always been missing a compassionate gene but I won't put up with it any longer. I have all the pain I can handle. I've rid myself of my baby, my man, and now you my sister. Have a good life!"

Chapter 3

Self Destructive Sex

From the moment I agreed to the abortion and left Yigal that August of 2002, I entered into a course of complete destruction. It was destruction to anyone in my way, but mostly, complete destruction of my own self. The years that followed were marked with a path of such intense promiscuity that knew few boundaries. I was about to embark upon my new life as a legal courtesan. I worked as a legal secretary by day but lived like a courtesan at night. Several of my victims were even those from the law firm.

"Don't shit where you eat Shanti!" I heard many warn.

"Why not? It's easy access and plenty for the taking!"

Screw anyone that had anything bad to say about my newfound path of promiscuity. Yes, screwing became my new medication and I needed it often to ease the ocean of grief to which I found myself drowning. As long I kept the sexcapades rolling, I felt high and happy. I actually believed I was truly happy and at peace, lest one of my lovers fell off the radar. Then I panicked and spent hours on the Internet finding a replacement.

"What's one down when I had twenty up?"

Don't tell an addict they have enough. There is never enough.

One day in mid September, after the one-year anniversary of 9/11, my flirtation game with Raul shifted into high gear. I guess I was feeling particularly vulnerable when Raul came to my desk looking very concerned.

"Is Mr. Tanner out of town today?"

I told Raul, "Yes he is. Why? Everything okay?"

"Shantz, can we go into his office for a minute. I need to talk to you about something private."

I felt a bit awkward about his request and asked, "What if someone sees us going into the closed office?"

Raul assured me, "No worries, I'll look both ways first. Okay?"

All my instincts were screaming "No!" But an undiagnosed sex/love addict with horrible boundaries cannot say "no," especially not to an object of desire. Within seconds we were behind closed doors.

Raul revealed to me, "One of the shorties I'm dating told me I have a small cock."

"What the heck is a shortie?" I asked.

His stern expression broke into a soft smile for a moment.

"You know, a girlfriend. They are shorter than men so we call them shorties."

I replied, "Guess I never heard of this term before because very few guys could possibly call me a shortie!"

"Shantz you are mad funny. But seriously, this girl made me feel really bad. Look at me. Have you ever seen me like this before?"

I had to admit, "No, never since I've known you."

Raul asked, "I have a huge favor to ask you. You've had a lot of sexual experiences before so I trust you. If I ask you something will you tell me the truth?"

"You know I will."

"Okay" Raul said, dropping his pants.

"What the fuck?" I burst out.

I had to cover my own mouth to moderate the volume. I was absolutely terrified that someone might come in. I started sweating intensely as I envisioned this as my last day at the office. I was beyond freaking out.

Raul asked, "So tell me, do I have a small cock?"

Looking at his member I could truly say he had a huge hog but even if his cock was miniature-sized I would have lied. Anything to get him to put his pants back on!

I told him, "Raul, your dick is humongous, are you kidding me? Tell your shortie to call me and I'll straighten her out."

I started to open Mr. Tanner's closed door but Raul leaned up against it and started stroking his cock.

"It gets mad bigger when I touch it but if you touch it Shantz, gets crazy bigger."

Then Raul took my hand and put it on his cock saying, "Go ahead, try it."

Though I did not want to continue with this seduction, I gave his cock a few strokes. I thought I would appease him so that I could walk out.

"Raul, your cock is huge. Let's discuss this at my desk."

With that I burst out of Mr. Tanner's office. My heart was racing but for very different reasons than Raul's heart was racing. He soon followed me and stood by my desk, where I sat in terror and utter disbelief.

"So you think this girl was lying Shantz?" Raul asked with his head down.

I felt a combination of rage, fear, relief, and turn-on, all at the same time. I realized that this was a fabricated story to get me to check out his cock. If I didn't enjoy flirting with him so much, I might have allowed myself to tell him off. I probably should have anyway but instead I let him off the hook.

"Raul, do not do that again! I really thought you had a major problem like someone died or you got some girl pregnant or something. If we were caught in Mr. Tanner's office alone with the door shut, it would have been my ass that got fired, not yours."

Looking at me with his puppy dog eyes he asked, "Well, why you say that?"

I explained, "Because I'm the senior staff member, twenty years your senior as a matter of fact. I should have known better. I am the one responsible for allowing us into Mr. Tanner's office while he was away. If we had been caught I would have been fired on the spot, not you. Shit, don't ever do that again! I have a child to care for Raul and I need this job. You have to respect this boundary."

Raul dropped his head even lower. I knew he was only a young kid playing a sexy game but this game was dangerous.

I told him, "Listen, you know I still love you but you can't put my job at risk like that any more. Okay?"

21

"Okay," he replied sheepishly.

But then he flashed me that gorgeous and sexy Dominican smile. So I stood up and slapped his ass, really hard.

"Aw damn Shantz that was mad hard."

"Yeah good, like some other things around here. Now go back to the mail room bad boy!"

Raul left my desk with a huge grin.

Chapter 4

Lesbians and Other Lovers

"Show and tell" with Raul was my baptism into the wild times inside and outside the law firm. I no longer had the excuse that I could not play with others because I was with Yigal: Yigal was dead to me and so were most of my boundaries.

During this very difficult time of grieving and letting go of Yigal, I rejoined a female empowerment group and re-connected with a lesbian there, Adriana from Spain, ten years my junior. Although Adriana was attractive, bright, and gregarious, when I first met her a year earlier, I could not stand her. She was completely rah-rah about being lesbian and I found it repugnant. But when I rejoined the group I found her to be very subdued and quiet.

On the way out of our meeting one night she asked, "Do you need a ride home?"

I was surprised because we hadn't much connected before. But Adriana seemed particularly sincere and vulnerable that night.

I replied, "Sure, I could use a ride. Thanks."

As soon as we sat in her parked car she asked, "So how have you been? Haven't seen you in a while."

For some reason, perhaps because she seemed more down-to-earth, I decided to tell her the truth without candy-coating it.

"I am horrible. Most of the days it's all I can do to keep going. How are you?"

Adriana gasped, "Mamacita why?"

"I finally broke up with that Israeli guy I was off and on with and I can't find the joy in life any more. Nothing makes me smile."

She was so soft and vulnerable, I had never experienced her this way before.

Adriana replied, "I understand. I just broke up with my girlfriend of two years and I am depressed all the time. It's horrible isn't it?"

I replied, "Yes, heartache is the worst pain. I don't know how to heal from it. I'm afraid I never will."

We began to cry in unison. We must have sat in her car for over two hours sharing our heartache stories. Misery truly does love company. It has always been tough for me to be happy around people when I am that down. Faking any feeling was never much my forté. Then, right there, in Adriana's car, the woman I once despised turned into my best friend. We entered into a relationship that would change my life forever, about who I thought I was and how I viewed the world and myself. Adriana lived in the Bronx, so it was easy for her to drop me off on the Upper East Side; it was directly on her route home. That night our weekly car rides after our female empowerment group became my most joyful ritual.

After a few weeks into our bonding, I started to feel lighter, more hopeful, and joyous again. During one of our meetings the leader of the group asked everyone what we wanted next in our lives. The room was unusually quiet so she picked on Adriana, who was sitting next to me.

She asked, "Okay Adriana, you have been unusually quiet these days. What is it you want next in your life?"

Adriana squirmed in her chair as if looking for an answer, "I don't really know actually. I'm stuck."

Where upon the leader responded, "Oh that is such bull shit. You know exactly what you want. Come on, stop holding out on us. What do you want?!"

Adriana then looked at me with a sly smile and announced, "I want to suck Shanti's pussy!"

All eyes in the group were then on me and my sleepy eyes were now wide-awake.

The leader then addressed me. "Shanti? What do you have to say about this?"

I remember thinking, "It's been twenty years since I've been sexual with a woman. Why not? All boundaries are broken so whatever."

Then I turned to Adriana and responded, "Okay. But no kissing, no cuddling, and no sleeping over."

That was my new mantra for all the guys, why should she be any different.

The leader followed up and asked Adriana, "Does that work for you?"

With a huge gleeful smile she practically jumped out of her chair, "Oh definitely yes!"

I was completely neutral about this proposition, not at all giddy like Adriana. I truly wasn't sure how I felt. However I rarely if ever said No to someone who wanted to give me attention and an orgasm. That was my cocktail of choice, with or without a cock! A tongue and fingers are far more important for a female orgasm anyway, so the fact that she had no cock was irrelevant. She had ten deadly digits and that was what counted most for me. So off to my apartment we went after class to fulfill Adriana's desire, with my willing participation. Rebecca always stayed with her Dad on these female empowerment nights, so the apartment was ready for us.

We chilled at my place for over an hour before we got down to business as Adriana took in my decorations, photos, and all the stuff that made me feel most like me. She was genuinely interested in who I was. Hmmmm...is this what it's like to be in a lesbian relationship, lots of warm and fuzzy girl talk? That might have been fine if I wanted a relationship but all I wanted was sex. I cut off our chit-chat.

I told Adriana, "Okay Miss Rah-Rah Lesbian, show me what you've got."

I was surprised when Adriana got a bit shy. That's how I always got with a guy I was attracted to. She was clearly attracted to me so I understood it. I realized I needed to take control and be the man in this situation. Hey, as a heterosexual, I needed to translate this situation into what I could understand.

First order of business, discuss sexual disease history. I told Adriana, "I got tested for HIV/AIDS a few weeks ago and I am negative. "

Adriana responded, "That's good. But because you sleep with men and men carry diseases, I am still not comfortable going down on you without a dental dam."

"A dental dam?" I asked.

She explained, "It is a square of latex that dentists use, it lays perfectly across your divine pussy so I can lick you without exchanging germs."

This did not seem appealing. "Sorry to disappoint you my dear but I do not have such an apparatus. Guess I failed Lesbian 101? Fingers will have to do."

Adriana laughed, "I love your playful directness! Do you have latex gloves?"

What was with this chick and the latex fetish? I told her, "No, I do not. Wait, yes I do. I have a few pairs to dye my hair. Why?"

Adriana jumped out of her chair with joy. "It is safest to use gloves and when I feel safe I feel very horny."

She was a weird bird for sure. I told her, "Okay babe, whatever floats your boat."

There was practically no foreplay because I wasn't feeling it. She did suck my nipples a bit but I quickly directly her to my bed to get down to the main clitoral procedure. We gave each other hand/genital orgasms like a gynecologist gives an internal exam - gloves, lubrication, and precise technique. I was first to receive, then Adriana. Keeping to my specific boundaries, there was absolutely no kissing, no cuddling, and no sleeping over. It felt great to give and receive a good orgasm, get closer to my new friend, and cuddle up for a deep sleep, alone in my own bed. What an ideal situation.

In the morning I called the only friend I could talk to that might understand this new bizarre friendship and experience. Rachel, one of my oldest and very best friends, actually answered when I called, which was rare. I gave her the highlights.

Rachel asked in horror, "Shanti, you did what?!"

"Hey Rachel, you're a lesbian. Of all people I thought you would get this."

"No Shanti, you cannot play with a hard-core lesbian like you would a straight guy. I guarantee you that she is ready to move in with you. Look out the window. Is there a U-Haul out there?"

"Oh come on Rachel."

"No Shanti I am totally serious. Look out the window."

I actually did look out the window or she wouldn't talk to me further.

I reported, "Rachel, there is no U-Haul truck in front of my building."

"You've never heard this before about the U-Haul truck? Lesbians get attached in two seconds and move in together the same night."

Digesting this information I became frightened that Adriana might want to move in at any minute. Sure enough, Adriana called within the hour, spiking my paranoia.

"Hey Mamacita, how are you?"

Terrified Adriana was going to follow the typical lesbian protocol, I brought up my fear immediately.

"I'm good, I'm good. You give damn good orgasm, girl. But I was afraid that you might bring your U-Haul this morning to move in so I was sweating a bit."

Adriana began laughing. Her lighthearted response eased my anxiety. Clearly she understood the metaphor. Had to be a lesbian thang. Never heard of it before.

She said, "Oh no. I know you are not a lesbian even though you were masterful with my pussy last night. Meow!"

We both laughed.

Adriana went on to explain, "You and I are not ready for any kind of relationships right now. We are still healing. It is time for us to explore and have fun with one another and whomever else we want. We'll be like friends with benefits. Is that good for you Mamacita?"

Relieved, I took a huge deep breath, "That is *perfetto per me bella!*"

"That's Italian honey. I have to teach you Spanish. The real Spanish from Spain! But of course you can say whatever you want to me in whatever language you want. You're so hot!"

Never could get my Spanish and Italian sorted out. I welcomed a new language skill, especially since many of my boss's clients were from South America. I had a vested interest in keeping our clients happy...

When I called Rachel back later that day to tell her that Adriana had no intension of moving in with me, she wasn't buying any of it.

Rachel said, "This free-spirited shit is Adriana's way of easing you into a relationship. You got to know that, right?"

I heard what Rachel was saying but I really didn't care. I was finally feeling joy again and wasn't going to judge it.

I told Rachel, "Whatever happens, happens. I like the friendship with benefits that Adriana offers. It fits perfectly with my new care-free, no-boundaries lifestyle."

Except that I needed to keep a supply of latex gloves, the relationship worked perfectly for me. Adriana was an odd one for sure. I'd heard of lipstick lesbians before but a latex lesbian? This was a new one. I left this aspect of our relationship out of conversation when I spoke with Rachel. She was already critical. The latex would have pushed her over the edge.

That night I got a call from my tall, handsome Saudi, Karim. We had met on match.com two weeks after 9/11 but had never met in person. He lived between London and Riyadh so was rarely in New York City, the original location he had listed on match.com. However he recently moved, or so he said - people lie on dating sites. He probably just wanted a New York squeeze when he was in town on business. Whatever his reasoning, it worked for me.

When we originally started emailing, Karim avoiding my questions about his background and career. But one day I forced him to reveal his hand or I would stop communicating with him. Karim was standing outside a movie theater in Paris during our first phone conversation, when he revealed all to me.

"I'm a Saudi, a Muslim, and an airline pilot. You see why I have been avoiding your questioning? Not a great calling card right now."

I thought to myself, "Holy shit!"

I almost told him on the spot that I could not be in touch again. WTF? Hanging with a Muslim airline pilot? My friends would surely have me committed. But I felt this might be the perfect opportunity to heal my Muslim animosity. It was unlike me to be racist or prejudiced yet I could not deny how I felt about Muslims after 9/11.

"Hello, are you still there?" he asked.

"Yes, still here Karim but barely breathing. Well...promise me you won't fly me into a tall building on one of our joy rides, okay?"

My Saudi man chuckled softly and a post-9/11 friendship began. He would teach me much about Saudi and Muslim culture. It was fascinating.

On this night, the night after my first sensual encounter with Adriana, Karim called to see how I was doing. We hadn't spoken in months but periodically did check in with each other. He was clearly a hottie, at least by what I could gather from his photos, and I had a vested interest in keeping him in my safety net. Never knew when I would have an available opening. No one got exclusivity any longer.

Karim asked, "What have you been up to lately?"

I blurted out with great giddiness, "OMG I just had sex with a woman last night!"

"Excuse me. You did what?"

I wasn't trying to turn him on but I was truly excited about this new experience and he was only the second recipient of my news. Rachel had been the first to hear and was not at all supportive. I was afraid to tell my hetero girlfriends for fear they might think I would now come on to them. So Karim got all my pent-up enthusiasm. He was a very attentive listener indeed.

Karim asked, "Can you please explain to me how this all came to pass? Sleeping with a woman. That is radical for a heterosexual woman, isn't it? Does your boyfriend know about this?"

My well-educated Saudi was very proper. Most American guys would have jumped on this conversation with large buckets of drool. Maybe he had learned his manners in good London education, or perhaps Saudi men are very reserved. I didn't know but I found it terribly sweet. He was nothing like the evil images of Arab men that were being portrayed by the media.

I informed Karim, "I broke up with my boyfriend Yigal, never to return to him ever again."

"Oh, I'm sorry about that. I know that you loved him very much. Are you okay with it now?"

"Not really. He was the love of my life and I have been a total mess. But my new friendship with Adriana is helping ease the pain."

He asked, "Is she the woman you slept with last night?"

"Yes, Adriana is so cool, Karim. She is a wine distributor from Spain, attractive, smart, fun, and sexually open. Perfect friend for me right now."

"Does this mean that you are a lesbian now?" Karim asked with a slight hesitation in his voice.

I decided to show Karim my hand, "No Karim, I still love men. But she is a good friend and we can have sex sometimes. Maybe that makes me bisexual? I don't know. But I have plenty of room in my life for a tall, handsome, Saudi, that is for sure!"

I enjoyed hearing Karim's soft and deep chuckle on the phone. I purposely did not respond to the ensuing silence, my hand was clearly dealt. I was learning to be more brazen in communicating my desires - and enjoying the risks. When risk is often rewarded, it makes taking risks easier every time. And so I waited.

Karim broke the silence, "Hello, are you still there?"

"Yes my dear, I am very much still here. When will you come to New York to visit me? It has been a year. I believe it is time."

Karim opened his appointment calendar and revealed his schedule to me. "I have to return to Riyadh for a few weeks but I actually have a meeting in Boston to buy a new plane. I can make a stop in New York for a couple of days, if you would like."

I gasped, "New plane? Gotta tell you Karim, I don't know if I will ever get in a plane with you. The whole Muslim pilot thang keeps getting in my way."

Karim laughed. He had the sexiest laugh.

I continued, "However, there are other places we can spend time together for sure. Yes, absolutely yes, I would love to see you when you come to New York. Give me notice so I can clear my decks for you. Wow, we are finally going to meet!"

In the meantime I wasted not one breath waiting for my Saudi as I continued to collect other men, scoring a few on dance floors, at bars, on dating websites, and even in the subway. There was this really hot guy with a long salt-and-pepper ponytail that was clearly checking me out on the train. I sent him a brief smile in return. I imagined him to be a 40-something successful artist from Spain or Italy, his skin was of olive complexion and he wore a nice suit. I needed to start dating guys closer to my age so was happy about his grey hair. When I got out at my stop, lo and behold, he got out too. I was rolling my large briefcase to bring work home to my boss, who was recovering from foot surgery. Luckily I lived quite close to my boss. I could go to his home before and after work to drop off and pick up documents.

Mr. Ponytail wasted no time, "Can I help you with your luggage?"

I wasted no time in receiving his offer, "You absolutely can help me with my luggage. Thank you so much."

At the top of the stairs Mr. Ponytail remarked, "Hey, this bag is too heavy for a pretty lady like you to carry."

I smiled and thanked him again. Feeling that awkward moment when two people don't want to part but don't know what to say, I offered some dialog: "You have an accent. Where are you from, Spain?"

Mr. Ponytail responded, "No, but I get that sometimes. I am from Israel."

My smile melted onto the concrete, "What? You are from Israel?"

It has always been nearly impossible for me to hide my feelings, and I was sure he could see that I was not happy with his origins.

He asked, "What? You don't like Israelis?"

"No, I don't like Israelis."

I was shocked that I said it so abruptly. He began to laugh nervously, but my stern expression stuck.

"Wow, really? Why not?" he asked.

"It is a long horror story and I don't feel like telling it," I said.

"Tell you what. Let me take you to the coffee shop at the corner and you can tell me how horrible my people are. I will just listen. I might even agree with you."

He was so handsome, charming and sweet, just like Yigal, and I could not resist.

Nestled into my familiar coffee shop, I guess I felt comfortable because I spent the first ten minutes in a running monologue. This guy had said he wanted to listen so I gave it to him, full barrels. I told him all about my heart-wrenching relationship with Yigal, the short-lived wedding plans, my short-lived fetus, and Yigal's hateful Israeli family. He just sat there and listened with compassion, his eyes were soft and kind. When the full venom of my saga had been released and I stopped for a breath, Mr. Ponytail spoke.

"What an asshole is this guy! He had the most beautiful, sweetest women in the world and he had no balls to stand up to his family and bullshit culture. That's an asshole."

And with that, my months of excruciating pain was validated.

I apologized, "I am terribly sorry. I have been going on and on about my sad story and I never even asked for your name."

"That's okay. You were not sure you wanted to know me. My name is Elan."

"Oh that's a beautiful name. What does it mean?"

"It means Tree."

I burst out in uncontrollable laughter. I hate when I laugh at things when I am not sure the other person will find it funny. I was relieved that he laughed too.

"I know, my name is TREE! That's funny right?"

My laughter abruptly turned into tears.

"I'm so sorry, your name is not funny at all. I guess it is just a nervous laugh. You have been beyond kind to listen to all my woes. Elan is a most beautiful name and you are a most beautiful man."

"Hey, oh, wait a minute. Let me ask the waitress for more napkins."

I blew my nose on the new pile of paper napkins and felt extremely vulnerable, exposed, and uncomfortable. I wanted to take the attention away from me. I kept staring at his thick grey hair, but he didn't look older than me so I was curious.

I asked, "How old are you?"

"I am 30."

"You are what?" I gasped.

"I am 30 years old."

"Shit!" I exclaimed.

"No good?"

"No good at all!" I remarked.

"No Israelis. No 30-year-old guys."

"God damn it. What's with all that grey hair?" I asked.

"I know, so weird right? I started to get grey hair when I was 16."

"Listen Elan, you are the sweetest, most handsome guy but I cannot date you. You are too young for me."

"But I love older women. They are more beautiful and more wise."

"That's good for you and my cougar girlfriends. I'll take your number and give it to some of them."

"I don't want your girlfriends. I want you. We don't have to date. I never said anything about dating. We can be friends, right? Friends are okay?"

"Elan, I really have to get these papers to my boss and get home to my daughter. I have an eight-year-old daughter."

"Wow, you are blessed to have such a treasure."

His compassion was becoming too difficult to resist.

I told him, "You are making it impossible to throw you out."

"So that is good. How about I take you to dinner this weekend? Just a friend dinner, okay?"

"Okay, just a friend dinner," I made clear.

Elan smiled and gave me his number.

I asked, "You don't want my number?"

"No, you call if you want to have a meal with a good friend. I don't want to bother you if you don't want me to."

If Elan's behavior was an example of being killed with kindness, I was dead already.

I did call him a few days later and scheduled a luncheon; dinner would have been too romantic. I didn't want to fall for another young guy so I kept this relationship platonic. Though Elan was totally inappropriate for me, he gave me hope that I could find a loving partner again.

However, getting those loving and romantic hits from Elan was all I needed to start my sex/love addiction juices flowing again with great velocity. I really liked Elan and sad that he was so young and Israeli to boot. I couldn't afford another emotional crash and falling for Elan would surely lead to one. I was already feeling sad that I could not be with him. So I did what I recently learned would stop my pain, I grabbed onto another man as quickly as possible.

That very afternoon, after meeting Elan, I went on line for several hours, shopping for Mr. Right. I clearly liked Middle Eastern men but wanted one closer to my age, hopefully one who already had children and didn't want any more. I put my real age on the profile, expecting to deter any young ones. But sure enough, I connected with a tall, handsome Turkish man named Seref, a personal trainer who was only 31 years old. What the hell? Seref was balding and looked much older than 31! But my addiction would not let me be alone and since I did not have Rebecca for the weekend, I needed my fixes. I made plans to meet Seref.

Seref was a very dirty dancer and so after a night of clubbing with him I was horny as hell.

But I told myself, "It's okay, I can have fun once in a while. Just know that he will only be a boy toy, he's not relationship material."

I dragged Seref back to my lair and we had a super hot makeout. He even gave me an orgasm with his fabulously fine fingers. But then he stopped, just as I started to unbutton his pants.

"Too forward of me?" I thought to myself.

I guess sex on the first night was a bit forward but I wanted my fix. I no longer cared about social norms, just that my needs were being fulfilled.

"Hey, what's up hot stuff? Don't you want to cum too?" I asked.

His entire demeanor changed when I started undressing him. He was like Jekyll and Hyde.

Seref told me, "No, no, it's okay. I'm tired and have a client at 6 am so I have to go."

Watching him button his shirt I thought to myself, "Maybe he has a 'no sleeping over' policy like me?"

So I proposed to him, "Well you can cum and then go home right afterwards. How about that?"

Before I could get a response from Seref, he was at my front door with his coat on. Non-verbal answer received. At least I got an orgasm out of it.

That next day I met Elan for lunch. He came with a violet plant in hand and said, "Here, beautiful flowers for a beautiful lady."

My protective shield cracked, "Oh dear, you are too sweet. I must say you are the first guy to give me a plant instead of cut flowers."

Sitting down, Elan explained: "Well you see when you give cut flowers they die quickly. I want this plant to live a long life so every morning you wake up you think of me."

Elan was a total doll and if not for his age, I could have fallen for him. But he reminded me too much of Yigal and he brought up all the recent wounds. Therefore, I kept Elan at bay, for a while anyway.

Later that day I had drinks with some girlfriends, scoring a couple phone numbers from some hotties at the bar. Then I was off to dinner with a new potential lover and later a yummy bootie call with Philippe, my FBI agent from Martinique. I hadn't seen Philippe in a few years once I got serious with Yigal. But since Yigal was out of the picture Philippe was happy to keep my bed warm again and he did it while speaking French, *mais oui*! It was quite the perfect Saturday really.

But as always, I woke the next morning completely depressed, not wanting to greet the day. I was not in love, my ultimate drug, so all other activities were merely the means to an end of finding the next Mr. Right to fall in love with. The entire system I had concocted was quite exhausting, but I told myself it was a necessary path to finding The One. Otherwise, I would stay in bed all weekend crying. My intellect told me that the more men I surrounded myself with the better my chances of finding my Prince. Later I learned that that was the voice of a sex/love addict wanting to avoid pain at any cost.

But no matter how hard I tried, the pain did seep in and sometimes it poured in.

That Sunday morning Adriana called, "Hey Mamacita! What are you up to?"

Without censorship I told her, "Oh just laying here, trying to figure out how not to kill myself today."

"Oh my God stop that! I'm coming over."

Just like that, Adriana was at my house within 20 minutes. She might not have brought her U-Haul over to move in with me, but she was always there whenever I needed her. In so many ways she was the mother figure I always wanted and never had, even though she was ten years younger than me. On this day she listened to my relationship woes and my fears that I would never be in love again.

Adriana stopped me, "Okay, first of all, you have nothing to worry about. Everybody, and I mean everybody, wants you, including me. I've never seen anything like it. So it's really just about you picking the right person for you. Second of all, I totally adore you and you cannot leave me on this earth without you!"

I felt bad about telling Adriana how suicidal I felt, but I needed to be real with someone. We bonded in our realness.

I explained to her, "Adri, I would never actually kill myself. I could not do that to my daughter or to you. So you don't have to worry about that. But I feel like dying almost every morning. It goes away after a while but it is always unbearable in the morning."

Adriana had some great suggestions to help with this morning depression. She told me, "Jump out of bed as soon as you wake up. Do not stay in bed. Then do physical exercises right away for fifteen minutes. This really helped me get over my break-up. Next, and this is very important, masturbate after the exercises are over."

I burst into hysterical laughter.

She continued, "See, I knew I could get you to laugh again. But seriously, this really helps lift the depression. Come on, let me give you an orgasm right now and you will see."

One, two, three I pulled out the gloves, the lube, and she whirled me into ecstasy. Adriana gave me amazing orgasms. Guess there really is something to homosexual sex. We do know our own bodies the best.

Feeling great I exclaimed, "Okay, your turn now!"

"No, I'm good for now honey."

I asked, "What is going on? You are the second person this weekend who didn't want an orgasm from me. I'm starting to develop a complex. I have never refused an orgasm."

Adriana explained, "Well that's because you have a huge sexual appetite, my love. Come, let me take you to brunch."

Some people crave food, some alcohol, some drugs, and others crave gambling, shopping, or working. I crave sex, love, attention, flirting, romantic relationships, intrigue, and affection. That said, I only crave affection from someone I am in love or in lust with. I adored Adriana and she gave me fabulous orgasms, but I did not desire to be affectionate with her. Kissing, cuddling, and sleeping over were definitely out.

When I did fall in love, AKA infatuation, that person became of paramount importance to me for it was only through them that I got my affection. I was affectionate with my daughter but that was a non-sexual affection and not at all the same kind of experience. My mother was rarely affectionate with us kids and I can barely remember those few times she hugged me or stroked my forehead. I am sure this lack of affection from my primary source was at the seed level of much of my sex/love addiction. My first strong and steady doses of affection came from my first boyfriends and so I had affection completely wired up with sex. And wired indeed was my state of being when I couldn't get this combination just right.

I was having plenty of sex, good friendships, tons of flirting but was deeply missing a good sensual cuddle. My mind and heart would wander back to those long languid mornings curled in Yigal's arms. But no longer would I allow myself to entertain a reprieve. It had been months with no contact from Yigal. He was dead to me now. Most people dreaded Monday mornings but I couldn't wait to get back to the law firm and my flock of flirty fellows. Monday through Friday were definitely the best days for me in the seduction department. But also, Rebecca would come back to me Monday through Friday and her love and affection also filled my soul. It was those dreaded weekends that needed constant attention and maintenance.

Chapter 5

Keeping Peace in the Middle East

Even though I was sleeping with several young guys who were totally inappropriate for marriage, I still managed to keep Elan, Mr. Grey Ponytail, at bay. He had too many qualities that I could easily fall in love with and so I continued to resist. But one night, after weeks of having platonic lunches and walks in Central Park, I was in a drink-and-dial state of mind. Girls-night-out had not produced any new hotties, so I decided to give Elan a call at 2 a.m. God forbid I should spend even one night alone.

"Wake up Elan!" I yelled into the phone.

I heard his deep and groggy Israeli accent, "Shanti? Is this my beautiful Shanti?"

"Elan, where do you live? I'm coming over!"

Drink-and-dial usually entailed revealing hidden feelings of desire or love. However, once I dialed Elan's number I thought, "Why reveal my hidden passions? Why not show him my passions?"

Within fifteen minutes I was in Elan's apartment.

Now, one might guess that I stormed into his apartment and threw myself at him. I actually prefer a guy to pursue me, it's such a turn on. Once I've given someone the green-light signal, through a glance or a slight touch, and my green light was searchlight-bright that night, then it's the guy's move. Alcohol was a big help that night, as usual. It gave me a boost of courage. I liked alcohol but if getting a buzz did not produce sex, then it was a waste of dead brain cells.

Lying sensuously across Elan's bed, the only piece of furniture in his small studio apartment, I gave him the perfect opportunity to pounce on me. Instead, he gave me a show-and-tell tour of his space. I was drunk, now bored, and getting dangerously close to passing out.

Elan asked, "Would you like some soup?"

Half asleep, this strange offer woke me up for a moment, "Soup?"

"Yeah, would you like some soup? I made some really great soup tonight."

"Aaaaahhh, maybe tomorrow. I have to go to sleep now Elan," and I closed my eyes.

I felt Elan tuck me in with all his blankets and then kiss me on the back of my neck while he spooned me. He was totally adorable. Wow, this was an epic event: I was cuddling and sleeping over without having sex. It freaked me out but I was too drunk and exhausted to think much, until the early morning light sobered me silly. I got up and while sitting on the bowl to pee I tried desperately to construct a good exit strategy. Since I was nearly fully dressed it would be easy to slip out without waking him up. Good plan. But as soon as I walked past his bed I heard his sleepy voice.

"You want some eggs?"

Shit! No, I didn't want any eggs. I wanted to get the hell out of there. But what I said was, "No, Elan, thank you. I have to get home. Rebecca's father is dropping her off within the hour and I need to change clothes and put on my Mommy hat."

I felt horrible lying to Elan, who was the sweetest guy. But I was jumping out of my skin in discomfort. I couldn't stay another moment.

"Okay. You want to come over another night for my soup?"

"Ummm, I'm sure I can but I will have to call you later."

Sitting in the cab on my way home, I felt relieved that I'd escaped a near fatality: being cuddled to death! This was an eye-opening moment when I felt there had to be something seriously wrong with me. I was never like this before my break-up with Yigal. It depressed me terribly but I was too tired and hung over to contemplate it further. Within ten minutes I was in the safety of my own bed and happily slept until noon. There really is no place like home, especially after a close encounter of the cuddling kind.

One of the great effects of having so many lovers spinning at any given time is the lack of time for rumination when a date falls short. If Elan is not The One then there is Joe, Jim, or Jerry waiting in the wings for a try.

That night I had a dinner date with Karim, my Saudi airline pilot. This would be our first face-to-face meeting and I was incredibly nervous. We'd been building toward this night for over a year so I looked especially beautiful for him. We were dining at Balthazar, a trendy restaurant in Soho. Karim had asked where I wanted to go the day before, but I warned him that a reservation at Balthazar could not be made at the last minute.

He was so smooth in his response, "It's okay. I'm sure we won't have a problem."

I arrived at Balthazar promptly at 8 p.m. but could not see Karim anywhere so I sat at the bar. Maybe he did not look much like his photos? Ten minutes passed and I still did not see anyone that resembled his photos. I started worrying that my year-long, long-distance flirtation had been with a fictitious character. I had heard of guys making fake profiles with fake pictures just to chat with pretty ladies. I prayed this was not the case. In high anxiety, I approached the hostess to see if Mr. Haddad had indeed made a reservation for 8 p.m. I watched her go down the list with her finger looking for a Mr. Haddad but there was none. My heart totally sank until I saw a reservation at the very end of the 8 p.m. list for Prince Karim.

"WTF Karim is a prince?" I screamed inside my head.

I thanked the hostess and told her, "Please tell the Prince that I will be in the powder room if he arrives while I am downstairs."

"Powder room?" I questioned myself, "I have never referred to the bathroom as the power room before."

Funny how a bathroom becomes a powder room when communicating about a prince!

I needed to escape the crowd in case Karim, I mean Prince Karim, walked in to see me gasping in shock and delight about his hidden identity. I needed several minutes in the powder room to calm down. I reapplied my lipstick, accepted a perfume spritz from the attendant, and proceeded up the staircase. I was beyond nervous and reminded myself of some old runway modeling mind games to calm my nervousness.

I told myself, "You are exceptionally gorgeous tonight, walk tall and proud. All eyes are on you. You have nothing to prove. Own and enjoy this walk of self-assurance my dear. You can do no wrong."

When I approached the hostess she had a big smile for me as she announced, "Your party has arrived and is seated. Let me show you to your table."

Still nervous I had to keep talking to myself, "Breathe, smile, own and enjoy this walk. All eyes will be on you, especially the prince. The prince?! Enjoy it my dear."

Sure enough, as the hostess escorted me to the table I recognized Karim. His smile of recognition and attraction calmed me down instantly. My prince stood up to greet me with his 6'3" inches of handsomeness. Damn, I was done for.

Karim opened our dialog: "Lovely to finally meet you in person, Shanti."

I found myself uncharacteristically tongue-tied, "Yes, it is."

He took a long, slow look at me for several moments after I sat down, which I found terribly uncomfortable yet exciting. My attraction to him was instantaneous and his gaze made no room for me to hide it.

Karim spoke, "You are quite beautiful in your photos but you are much more radiant and beautiful in person. This is an unexpected surprise indeed."

I giggled nervously, "Oh, thank you. That you are real is an unexpected surprise!"

Cocking his head and squinting his eyes he looked completely baffled by my statement.

I explained, "Some people post fake dating profiles and photos. Then, when it comes time to meet in person, they do not show up."

"Really?" Karim asked.

"Oh yes, really. I actually thought you might have been one of them when you were a few minutes late. I know ten minutes is not terribly late but the thought crossed my mind that you might be a "no show" so I went to..."

My nervous chatter stopped abruptly when he flashed his gorgeous smile.

I continued, "To...I'm, I'm just happy that you are here."

"As well am I."

Though Karim was much heavier than his photos, he still had that handsome face and deep sexy voice. I loved his Saudi accent. I am a total sucker for a foreign accent. Whisper in my ear with your foreign tongue over dinner and you can lather that tongue all over my body for dessert.

When dinner was over, the waiter asked if we wanted dessert.

Grabbing his belly Karim replied, "I think I've had enough desserts this past year. However, my slender lady would most assuredly like one."

He was right. No resistance to French pastries. I remember gaining fifteen pounds the first six months I lived in Paris. Not the best plan for a fashion model. But I gradually cut back once I started appearing on magazine covers. I got that this was a serious career and I had better take it seriously.

When we left the restaurant Karim announced, "I am not wanting to let you go yet. Would you join me at my hotel lobby for a drink?"

I thought, "Dah, you had me at prince!" but what I said was, "I would be delighted."

Karim motioned to a man in a black sedan. Oh I see, Karim has a driver. Of course he has a driver, he is a prince after all. During the car ride he was proper, gentlemanly, and very quiet. He was not a big gabber anyway but at least in the restaurant we had dialog. Maybe he did not want his driver to hear our conversations? I did not know the reason for this silence but I did not want to break it lest I soil royal protocol. Clearly the driver had to be a regular, for he drove us uptown without an address being exchanged.

We stopped at the Ritz Carlton on Central Park South and everyone we passed seemed to know Karim. Maybe that was just their job but he was very friendly in exchange, more animated than I had seen in our short two hours together.

Thinking, "Hmmm, maybe this is his regular New York hideaway? I could definitely get used to this."

Karim guided me towards the lounge area with a gentle hand on my lower back. It was a brief sensual touch but it melted away my lingering anxiety. It had been many years since I lived in such a lavish manner and I felt rusty, not sure what was proper at each turn. But like a good tango partner, I relaxed into the dance and let him lead.

Away from the driver and concierge, I felt safe to break the ice: "It is very beautiful here."

Karim looked around momentarily, as if neglecting a scene that begged for acknowledgement.

"Yes, it is comfortable," he said. "I usually stay here when I'm in town."

Though I never brought up Karim's princely title, nor did he declare it, it was clear that he could not be faking such status. He oozed old-world money. I knew the difference.

Not skipping a beat I asked, "And how often are you in town?"

Karim replied, "Depends on business, sometimes four or five times a year."

Away from the formality of dinner and his private chauffeur, seated side-by-side, I now felt more like my real self, even amidst this lavish lounge. I began shooting from the lip, much more my style.

I said, "Clearly an airline pilot does not stay at the Ritz Carlton."

Karim smiled, "No, I have never been a commercial airline pilot, strictly small private twin engine aircraft, for sport only."

I replied, "Well as long as you're not flying into buildings I'm good with that."

Karim laughed, "I remember I liked that about you when we first spoke on the phone. You say what is on your mind. I find that rare and refreshing."

As Karim placed our drink orders, I looked around and saw flashbacks of my modeling days in such palatial hotels.

Though Karim was only six years my junior I knew culturally that we would never marry and so I entered him on the tryst list.

Karim woke me from my dreamy bubble with his soft deep voice. "If you don't mind I'd like to hear about your lesbian friend. I find that story fascinating."

Laughing loudly in stark contrast, I said, "I bet you do!"

Karim looked over his shoulder and I asked, "What? Are your spies checking out our conversation?"

Quietly he uttered, "I am just reserved and cautious by nature. We Saudis don't discuss sexuality in public. It is not acceptable. I know that you do this here in America but it is not our custom."

I could have asked what topics would be acceptable, but instead I asked, "Well then is there somewhere else you'd like to discuss this subject?"

For a moment, through his reserved presentation, I caught glimpses of a devilish spark dancing in his eyes.

"Perhaps," he paused and then continued, "but for now we can discuss your lesbian situation here. However, I ask that you keep your voice low, if you don't mind."

For the next half-hour we drank, whispered, and laughed quietly as I shared my new and fun experiences with Adriana. When I finished my drink Karim asked if I'd like another.

I replied, "Oh no, between wine at dinner and now this cocktail I am toast."

He then asked, "Would you like to go home now or would you care to join me upstairs?"

Geez, no public display of affection first? Guessing that was not Saudi protocol either.

Tipsy, turned on, and curious what it would be like to have sex with a Saudi prince, I responded, "I would be delighted to join you upstairs. However, I cannot sleep over."

Karim replied, "Of course not."

Did he play the same game? I did not know but my procedure seemed understood and welcomed.

In the elevator we stood side-by-side in silence, looking straight ahead. Even though we were the only ones in the elevator, there was still no display of affection. We stared straight ahead until I glanced up at him with a smile. He returned with his own. Then, in a bold move Karim placed his hand ever so gently on my ass for a few moments. How such a brief non-invasive gesture could get me so excited I still do not know. But I do know that it ignited a wild sexual torrent in my loins and I could barely wait to lie with him.

Karim's suite was absolutely magnificent. It threw me off my lustful game for a few minutes while I took it all in. There was a gorgeous elegantly upholstered Italian-style living room, a super sexy all white bedroom, a walk-in closet, and a huge spa-like bathroom with a Roman shower, deep Jacuzzi bathtub, double sink, and a separate toilet room with a bidet.

"Karim, this is spectacular!" I exclaimed.

"Is it? I don't know. It is comfortable."

I asked, "Comfortable?" and bemoaned, "Would love to see what impresses you!"

Karim finally grabbed me, "You impress me."

He lay me down on his king-sized bed, kissing me ever so sweetly.

Karim was an A-plus kisser, soft and sensual, with lots of lip and minimal tongue. Who ever told guys to shove their tongues down our throats was seriously misinformed. I have never once heard a woman say she liked that, and yet it is the number one technique I usually need to train a man out of. We kissed for the longest time, which was getting me wild with desire. When Karim started to remove the top portion of my dress, my breasts were eager to feel his touch, his tongue, and my nipples erected in anticipation. When he ventured to remove the lower portion of my dress my moans became louder.

"Please dear, not so loud," he begged.

Panting I joked, "You have your secret service men in the closet?"

Karim replied, "Not in the closet but down the hall, yes."

"Oh really? I was just kidding."

That sobered me out of my sensual delirium for a moment.

Karim continued, "But hopefully they will not knock on the door tonight."

"Knock on the door?!" I panicked.

"No, now I'm just kidding. They would call first."

Pulling my dress off completely, I slowed Karim down enough to ask, "Do you have any condoms?"

"No, do you?" he asked.

Disappointed I had to admit, "No, I don't."

I almost always carried condoms but since this was a blind date I had not anticipated it going this far. I should have known myself. It was usually sex on the first or second date.

I then asked, "Can you call the front desk? I'm sure they would have condoms."

Talk about inadvertent buzz-kill. Karim jumped off the bed and covered the phone.

"No, no, we cannot call the front desk."

I was puzzled, "Why not? I am sure they would have condoms."

He stumbled a bit, looking for the words but all I could understand was, "Ahh...mmm...see...no."

I figured it was another Saudi protocol so didn't question it. Yet I was turned on like crazy and wanted to continue.

Karim looked lost and asked, "What are we going to do?"

Without a word, I slowly pulled down my panties and began masturbating myself in front of him, seductively and masterfully. His eyes were locked on my pussy, as though he had never seen such an act before. That notion only got me higher. I teased and tortured Karim in an exhibitionist euphoria, knowing that the voyeur in him was transfixed. He took my lead, removed his pants, and started to masturbate himself, all the while glued to my pussy. It was one of the hottest sexual experiences I had ever enjoyed and I struggled not to cum too soon.

When Karim begged, "Please, please, I want you to cum!"

I moaned to him, "Whenever you are ready. I am so high I could come any time."

I could see Karim's cock about to explode as he begged again, "Yes, please. Please cum. I want to see you cum!"

I tortured my dear Prince Karim for another few minutes and finally released my orgasm. At that precise moment I saw a blast of semen shooting out of his cock and with this simultaneous orgasm I felt like I had the experience of a male orgasm, and I loved it.

Breathless, he looked at me with his gorgeous deep eyes. "Wow...that was...incredibly hot."

Karim pulled me towards him to snuggle. For the first time in a very long time I was melting into a man's arms. I felt the intense urge to cry, it felt like being with a man that I was falling for. But I wouldn't allow that. I quickly talked myself out of crying.

I told myself, "Shanti, you can not fall for this guy. Prince or not he is at the top of the list of inappropriate marriage material - too young, lives too far away, conservative Muslim and royalty to boot. His family would never ever accept you. And even if they did, are you going to live in Riyadh with your daughter?"

We both lay there with our eyes closed and soon I felt the muscle twitches of Karim falling asleep. As I lay there and absorbed the magnificence of his hotel suite I did indeed feel like a princess. I soaked in the sweet chemistry and tender feelings between us and for the first time, wished I had not previously declared my need to leave. But I knew it was for the best. I couldn't fall in love with another inappropriate Middle-Eastern man. I began to dress.

When Karim heard me open the door he jumped out of bed and embraced me.

"This was a wonderful experience. I hope we can do this again when I return to New York," he said.

"It was very special for me too, Karim. We will definitely see one another again. I can barely wait."

I walked down the hallway and inwardly waved to his security team next door. Surely this was not the first time he brought a woman to his room. They probably had my photo from the dating website to know I was a "safe" guest. I passed several bellmen in the lobby and one of them escorted me outside to signal a taxi. I was across the street from Central Park's horse-and-buggy liveries, but even the sweet smell of horse manure could not disturb the sensual fragrance of my prince, still lingering on my skin.

Within ten minutes I was home. I looked about my bohemian apartment with its eclectic decorations, a stark contrast to the Ritz Carlton suite. I sat on my grandmother's stuffed chair and smiled. I had created such a magical night for myself. It was fun to feel like royalty for a few hours but I was equally happy to be home in my funky little one-bedroom apartment. Rebecca was with her father but I was drawn to her room and wandered inside.

Immediately I thought, "I get to be a loving mother and yet a wild woman too. Life is good!"

And with this notion I returned to my bed in the living room and put myself to sleep in profound contentment, as I often did when my sensual fix had been quenched.

Chapter 6

Life with Lover Adriana

The next morning, even before getting out of bed, with my eyes barely opened I groped for the phone amidst my sheets and called Adriana.

"Aaadrii? Are you driving?"

Adri was always cheerful when I called and I visualized her beaming as she replied, "Hey Mamacita how are you? No I am not driving, why honey?"

"Because I need you to sit down."

I could hear the panic in her voice, "Oh my God what is wrong cookie?"

I didn't want her to worry but admittedly I loved how motherly she was with me. It was the kind of mothering I always wanted from my mother.

I replied, "Nothing is wrong but you might be shocked, in a good way though."

"What? What is it? Okay I'm sitting."

And I proceeded to tell her every detail of my magical night with the prince.

Adriana listened to my very long rendition. She gasped and sighed throughout, and finally chimed in.

"Honey I am so happy for you! Do you think you will marry the prince? You will be like the new Princess Grace. Princess Shanti!"

Adriana knew me at this point better than anyone and so I was surprised she even asked such a ridiculous question.

"Adri, you know I cannot marry a guy like this. He is Saudi royal family and security forces would have me beheaded in two seconds once they'd discovered my rap sheet. No, he has to marry a young Muslim virgin. That's just how it is there."

She asked, "Oh okay. Will you see him again?"

"Hell yeah. He is handsome, sexy, worldly, gentlemanly, wealthy, and good in bed. Well, at least good at watching."

We both laughed hysterically, which turned into me crying.

"Mamacita, oh, why are you crying? You know I can't resist you when you cry."

Choked with one of those heaving sobs I confessed, "I just don't understand why I can't fall for a guy who is appropriate husband material. I can't have another Yigal trauma, falling in love only to find the guy's family won't accept me. It will kill me. You know that."

"Oh honey, well, maybe you shouldn't see your Muslim prince again?"

"No, he lives far enough away that I won't see him often enough to fall for him. Besides, I could use a little royal treatment in my life. Fine restaurants, luxury hotels, and gorgeous jewelry, I like that."

Giggling with delight Adriana replied, "Yes, of course. You deserve that. How many men are you seeing right now?"

"I don't know, 12-15, something like that," I told her.

"Oh wow, more than I thought."

I went on to explain, "I know it sounds like a lot but they don't all live here. I only have half a dozen steadies in the New York area and they are constantly rotating. It's a lot of work to keep even six in gear."

Adriana started to laugh, "Yes, I know, three strikes and they are out. You taught me about your dating baseball rules."

"Exactly. If it doesn't look like we can move towards marriage someday, then I am wasting my time and they are out."

My tears escalated again and Adriana comforted me as she always did, "Oh my love, please don't be sad. Everyone wants you honey. Please don't cry. I promise you that you will find your true prince someday even if I have to travel the world and drag him back myself!"

My relationship with Adriana was unlike any I had ever experienced before. She was my lover, my best friend, and at times like a mother, even though she was ten years my junior. Adri was caring, compassionate, loyal, and attentive, just like the mother I always wanted. Yet because of our sensual connection she was also like a lover. However, since we didn't make out it almost didn't seem like we were real lovers. It was a complex relationship for sure, but the most important one to me at the time. We spoke on the phone at least a half-dozen times a day, usually starting the day and often bookending it at night, unless I had a date. Adri, on the other hand, was not dating at all when we met. She told me she was still too vulnerable from her recent break-up to date. But I guessed she was satisfied in many ways just to have me - I was her surrogate girlfriend.

One night, several months into our relationship, I invited Adri for dinner at my apartment.

I announced, "I have something special to discuss with you. Can you please bring a bottle of wine to dinner at my place?"

Adri's voice bounced with delight, "Of course I can my love! To what do I owe the honor of a nighttime visit? This is usually sacred man-hours, no?"

I replied, "Not telling. You'll just have to come."

I made my favorite pasta dish with olive oil, garlic, salt, and hot pepper flakes. It is the simplest sauce but when mixed with fresh sea scallops and broccoli, then topped with freshly grated Parmesan cheese, it becomes a gourmet delight. I filled the space with flowers, incense, candles and soft lounging music. I dressed in a long flowing negligée with matching robe, and my three strands of pearls purchased during my modeling years. This was a set-up for a romantic evening.

When Adri entered my apartment she immediately gasped, "Oh my goddess. I think I just died and went to heaven! Look at you!"

She fondled my breasts until I took her by the hand.

Adri gasped again, "Mamacita, you did all this for me?"

With a knowing smile I replied, "All for you. Let me take your coat."

"Honey, this is magnificent. You are usually the one in tears but I think I'm going to cry now."

Adriana did cry for a brief moment. For once in our relationship I took the helm and I could feel the relief and appreciation pour down her face. I was often very needy with Adri and although she confessed that she loved that about me, I wanted to give back to her in a powerful way.

The pasta was not quite done and so we chatted over the delicious Spanish wine she brought. Adri sold Spanish wines for a living and was well aware that I was a francophone. However, she made it known when we first met that she would convert me to a hispanophone.

"Adri, this wine is as delicious as you, my sweet."

"Ooooh, you are making my Spanish heart blush. Are you trying to make me fall even more in love with you than I already am?"

This was the perfect segue for the discussion I wanted to have. However, it was far too early in the evening. I wanted her to enjoy her dinner, so I waited until dessert. When the teas were sipped and the fruit tarts nibbled, I revealed the purpose of this special evening.

"Adri, my precious friend, I invited you here tonight to give you a taste of what you deserve and more. You are the most special person in the world to me, next to my daughter, and you deserve to be treated like this every night."

She cooed in her timid manner when feeling her love and attraction for me.

I continued, "However, as much as I love and adore you, and you know that I do, my romantic attraction is for men. Clearly I can be sexual with you but I guess romance with women is not in my tool kit. If there were one woman on the planet that I could fall in love with, it would be you. But, honey, I don't feel romance towards you."

She dropped her chin, "I know that, my love."

52

An uncomfortable silence followed. I let it be while she took this in. After a while I continued, hoping she would understand. "There is a man smell that just turns me on. Guessing it is testosterone. With you, all I ever smell is perfume."

I heard her moan of disapproval but I continued, "Then there is the sensation of rough stubble above soft lips..."

With that Adri interrupted, "Oooh yuck never mind. You are a hopeless heterosexual."

"Adri, I knew you would be sad but I no longer want you waiting in the wings for me. It is not fair to you. I want you to find a true lesbian who will totally adore you and lavish you like I did tonight. Honey, I am not going to wake up someday and suddenly realize that I am a lesbian. I am a bisexual at best, and more like a heteroflexible who likes pussy sometimes."

Adri repeating, softly, "I know. I know my love."

I could feel her pain and started to tear up.

She asked tenderly, "Does this mean our friendship has to break up too?"

"God, I really pray not. You are my very best friend and I would be totally lost without you. Clearly I can date while we are friends."

Which prompted a genuine laugh from both of us as she highlighted the statement, "Oh, and you can date!"

After our much needed comic break I reminded Adriana, "You, my friend, you haven't dated anyone for months. So, we can experiment. If after a few weeks you are still not dating or putting forth an effort, then we have our answer, I will have to bow out of your life, even though it would completely destroy me."

She asked, "Do I have to put a ring on her finger to prove I'm dating?"

"Wise-ass! No, just show me her U-Haul truck."

"Double wise-ass. One more question. Can we give each other orgasms until I find her?"

"What a silly question," I replied.

With that I took Adriana's hand and led her to my bed where I took her over the edge of ecstasy.

As we spoke several times daily, I heard all of Adriana's many actions around finding a girlfriend. She joined lesbian dating web sites, went to lesbian social events, and occasionally stepped out to lesbian bars. Adriana was a woman on a mission. I was not sure if it was a mission to find a girlfriend or simply a mission not to lose me. However, determined she surely was. Adri would tell me all about her romantic email exchanges on the dating sites, their coffee and wine date follow-ups, their personalities, and their pros and cons.

I would invariably ask, "Was she hot?"

"Yes she was hot. But it's not all about being hot Mr. Hot Pants. I swear you date just like a man!"

"So I've been told," I confirmed.

Adriana, unlike me, could not have sex just for the sake of sex. She needed to be in love.

I teased her, "You are indeed the U-Haul operator Rachel said you were."

"Okay stop! What is wrong with wanting to love someone that you sleep with?"

"Nothing is wrong with it Adri. It is the most beautiful way that brings about the best fulfillment. I wish I could be like that again. I'm just teasing you."

There was nothing at all wrong with Adriana's desire for a deep intimate relationship before having sex. I wished desperately to have that again. I used to hold sexuality that way but it felt like lifetimes ago. It really got bad after Yigal and I broke up after two years of monogamy and I became polyamorous. The past two years had been a revolving door of lovers. In some ways I knew my promiscuity was connected to my intense pain at not being able to marry Yigal. However, I was too terrified to contemplate my promiscuous path lest this Band-Aid be taken away from me. That's how I kept my booty train running.

If I was an alcoholic you could compare my sexual acting-out to an alcoholic who starts drinking as soon as she gets up in the morning. Pain starts with the morning light and needs an immediate quench. I would be on the phone or the Internet with at least two or three people who adored and/or flirted with me, to kick-start me out of bed. Then my office compadres would carry me through nine-to-five. If I had my daughter Rebecca that night

I'd be on the Internet cruising for guys as soon as she hit the pillow. Then, for nights when she was not with me, I'd have my dates all lined up.

As I look back today, it was a lot of work to keep my pain at bay. But at the time, it was a necessity that I never questioned. I was happy from the moment I entered the office until I fell asleep at night, because of all the sensual attention I was getting. I was only miserable for a few hours in the morning, and during most of the daylight weekend hours. Nothing a good run by the river or retail therapy couldn't cure.

I remember taking Rebecca to the playground one Saturday afternoon, before there were smart phones with Internet connections, when I was experiencing intense pain. I was in desperate need of my fix, with no men in sight, only children, moms and nannies. All I could think about was when I would next feel a man adoring my body. And that made me want to go shopping for some new hot lingerie.

Twenty minutes into our stay at the playground I called Rebecca, "Honey, can you come here please? We have to go."

"Oh Mom, no, we just got here," Rebecca whined.

"We are going to a really fun place called Bloomingdales. I need to buy some new pajamas and I will buy something special for you too."

Rebecca was not happy and I felt really bad that I did this to her. However, I could not stay in the park another moment with my pain.

As soon as we entered the threshold of Bloomingdales I got my retail fix and calmed down instantly. I took care of Rebecca's needs first, still feeling bad that I had yanked her from the playground. She wanted a new dress, so off we went to the children's department. Her beaming smile, holding her new purchase, took away some of my guilt but that somehow made me start questioning how out of control my sensual life had become. I was questioning, but not yet digging too deep. My daughter, now happy, escorted me to the lingerie department, all excited to help me find the prettiest "pajamas." Of course, if Rebecca showed me an outfit that was not sexy enough I could merely say, "That's not my style." Funny enough, Rebecca found me the sexiest negligées of all.

Chapter 7

Sensual Training for Lourdes

Less than a month passed from the time I pushed Adriana to start dating until she announced that the hot Spanish girl she met at Henrietta Hudson, a lesbian bar, was now her girlfriend. Finally, Adri found someone hot! And true to her U-Haul leanings they soon moved in together. Lourdes was beautiful, sweet, caring, and charismatic. They made an adorable Spanish couple. But within a few weeks, Adri met me for lunch wearing a very disturbed face.

"Adri, what's up cutie? You look terrible."

She reluctantly divulged, "I don't know honey. I'm enjoying Lourdes, most of the time, but…"

"Yeeees, but…" I interjected.

"But, well, uhm…"

"Spit it out girl. What's up?" I asked.

With a heavy heart she announced, "She is not giving me orgasms like you do."

I burst out laughing, "Damn girl I thought someone in the family died! Okay, Okay, I know orgasms are important, crucial in fact, so I get it. This is no laughing matter. But seriously, can I laugh a minute more?"

Adri started to laugh softly.

Turns out Adriana had been faking orgasms with Lourdes from the beginning. Yes guys, women can fake orgasms with other women too. No one is immune. This is a rough problem though, because the only way the clitoris turns around is to admit the lie or to at least stop lying. However, when the partner just stops lying the lover can't understand why all the routes to orgasm stopped working. They never understood that their methods weren't working in the first place. So coming clean is the best way but it can be confronting. It is a thick soup that I myself sunk into a couple of times, and it is not fun.

A compassionate lover will understand the predicament that caused their partner to create the lies, and will be open to finding whatever techniques work for them, physical or emotional. However, a lover with a delicate ego might blame the partner for all the inadequacies, rather than questioning their own sensual abilities. No two human bodies are alike, even lovers of the same gender, and it takes time to know one another's erotic systems.

It is also possible that a delicate lover could lose trust in their partner after being lied to, and dissolution of the relationship could result. Adriana tried the less risky method first and stopped faking the orgasms. However, she still was not able to orgasm. Lourdes then became frustrated and perplexed.

Adri called me in the middle of the night after Lourdes was asleep.

"She doesn't know what is wrong, why she can't get me to cum any more. What do I do?"

Groggy I replied, "You're calling me in the middle of the night. Is this a frustrated phone-sex call?"

"Stop making me laugh. This is serious, Shanti. I need help and you are so good at giving direction. I think I have to tell her the truth."

"Sounds good," I replied. "See, that was easy. Can I go back to sleep now?" I begged with a groan.

"I hate you."

"Love you too Adri."

A couple of days later Adriana shared the results of her truth-telling.

"Lourdes took it well at the beginning but now she is starting to feel inadequate because I am still not cumming," she said.

"Did you tell her that you had orgasms with me?" I asked.

"Yes, I did." Adri replied.

"Ugh, that didn't help I'm sure."

Adriana responded sharply, "Stop with making me laugh. I really don't know what to do. You spoiled me sexually and now you have to fix this."

"I have to fix this?"

Adri started to laugh and I continued to massage her funny bone by saying, "Hey, this orgasm stuff is serious business, not a laughing matter, remember?"

Adriana then asked, "Honey, would you be open to showing Lourdes how you get me to orgasm?"

"Are you completely insane?" I asked.

"Yes, I am completely insanely and frustrated and I need your help."

Still dumbfounded by Adriana's request I replied, "If you have the balls to present this proposition to Lourdes and she accepts, then I accept."

"Yes!" Adriana rejoiced.

"The things we do for love," I reminded her.

"And I do love you," Adri exclaimed.

Then I told her, "Go practice your proposal. You're gonna need it. You're totally crazy."

Adriana was an amazing saleswoman - she sold Spanish wines to the French of all people. I was not surprised that she convinced Lourdes to try her crazy sensual scheme. At this point, Adriana and I had stopped being sensual when they moved in together. Monogamy was a must for them and I honored that. I wasn't sure how Lourdes felt about my friendship with Adri, though she always seemed genuinely happy to see me. However, with latex gloves and lube at the ready, this would not exactly be a casual night on the town.

I welcomed the new couple into my home without candles, flowers or incense. I did not want to confuse this "procedure" with a ménage-a-trois. I was merely showing Lourdes my sensual techniques so that she could make Adri cum. We were not all going to get naked together. In fact, Adri was the only one who got naked and this happened only at the very end of the evening.

I spent the first half-hour talking with the ladies about what they wanted in their relationship, emotionally and sensually. Once that was clear, I explained to Lourdes my experience of Adriana as a whole being and then specifically as a sexual being.

"Adriana likes to run the show. If you haven't already noticed."

They looked at one another and laughed.

"Adriana has no problem giving you orgasms Lourdes," I asked. "Am I right?"

"Oh yes, you are very right about that," Lourdes replied.

They both faced one another in flirty recognition.

"Great. Adriana, however, needs to surrender in order to have an orgasm but as you have experienced, she doesn't surrender easily."

Lourdes chimed in, "Yes, she is so bad to surrender."

Lourdes' English was not as developed as Adriana's but I understood what she meant here.

"So, Lourdes, what I found was that I had to dominate Adriana in the bed, or she would not orgasm."

"What is dominate?"

Amused, I shot commands to Adriana: "Stand up Adri. No, not there, over here."

Adri started laughing.

"You see Lourdes, she laughs because she likes to be dominated in bed. It is fun for her because she is usually in control at work and in relationships."

Then I told Adri, "Stop laughing."

But Adriana could not stop laughing so I raised my hand as if to strike her but I did not. She immediately stopped laughing.

"You see what I mean Lourdes?"

Her eyes bugged out of her head as she asked, "You want me to hit Adriana?"

"No," I laughed, "don't hit her! But do take control and make her do what you want her to do. Adriana often says she doesn't need an orgasm and I can stop touching her. I know it's bullshit so

I just push her back down on the bed and tell her we'll stay here all night until you cum so get comfortable."

Lourdes looked confidently at Adriana and nodded. She was starting to get it.

Once Lourdes started taking the reins of power, Adriana began to reveal her shy side to Lourdes with blushes and giggles, the start of her surrender.

As I saw that both girls were on my program, I announced, "Okay ladies, it is time to start the procedure. Adriana, go into the bathroom, take off your clothes and put on the robe that is hanging on the back of the door."

"Yes, sir!" Adriana replied.

While Adri was disrobing I explained to Lourdes how to fuck someone in the head before fucking their body.

"Adriana is stubborn," I said, "so you have to be strong with her. She will resist every time but she likes you to be forceful. Sometimes I tell her that I will stop touching her since she doesn't seem to like it. Then she begs me to continue. She is a real head case."

Lourdes seemed puzzled by "head case" so I told her, "In bed Adri is stuck in her mental thoughts, always thinking, thinking, thinking. Our job is to mess with her mind by controlling and dominating her so her body can relax."

"Ah, okay," Lourdes replied softly.

I wasn't sure she fully understood but I knew she would get it once she watched me messing with Adriana's head.

Adriana emerged from the bathroom with her submissive shy eyes shining.

"See, she is half-way to surrendering. You see how shy she is right now?"

Lourdes nodded.

"I suggest you never touch Adriana sexually until she is at least in this space. When she is in her business head," I pointed to her head, "you may as well kiss the night good-bye. She will never cum and you both will be frustrated."

Adriana protested, "No!"

Lourdes and I both laughed.

I said, "Wonderful, we want her begging."

Then I directed Adriana, "Okay head case on the bed."

I had Adriana keep the robe closed while lying on her back. I asked her to open her legs and bend them so that the soles of her feet were touching one another in a frog-like position. I placed a pillow under each knee.

"Lourdes, can you come onto the bed and lay beside Adri? Perfect. Now, you are in charge from the waist on up."

She looked puzzled so I showed her where Adri's waist was, and directed her from there to the top of her head. I continued to mime my commands as I spoke.

"You can stroke her tummy, her breasts, her face or kiss her on the mouth, as you feel inclined."

Adriana interjected, "This is a lot of attention for me to have. I feel kind of uncomfortable and…"

I cut her off: "Good, feel uncomfortable, you need to get used to being adored. Right Lourdes?"

"What is adored?" Lourdes asked.

Adri and I giggled, then I mimed the motions of adoration with my hands in prayer, gazing softly towards Adriana.

Lourdes replied, "Ooooh yes, I understand!"

Then we all began giggling together.

I returned to my command post. "Okay, the fun is over ladies, time to get to work, we need to get this girl to cum!"

I gestured Lourdes to open the top of Adri's robe and begin touching her upper body and breasts while looking into her eyes. This was about their connection and not mine, and I wanted Lourdes to feel that.

After I felt their connection deepen I said, "I am going to put my gloves on then open the robe below her waist. I'm gonna touch her inner thighs and her outer lips. It's her warm-up, gets her ready for more intense touch.

I was not sure Lourdes understood but she was watching my every move and that was more important. When I felt Adri's pelvis gyrate I knew she was ready for more so I took out the lube. I used vaseline when there were no condoms involved. Vaseline can break down latex condoms but is fine to use with latex gloves that are thicker and no chance of semen escaping.

Adri, a germophobe, insisted on all her partners using latex gloves on her pussy. Yet I discovered a wonderful effect from the gloves. They felt really sensual. More importantly, there is no fear of a jagged nail cutting the sensitive clitoris. This is a real fear of many women so guys and gals who don't wear latex gloves, keep your nails well filed. It is very difficult to surrender while worrying about having our clitoris cut!

As I took out the lube I saw Adriana's body stiffen.

I asked Lourdes, "Did you notice how Adri's body got tight?"

Lourdes' look begged for translation so I mimed a stiff body.

"Yes, oh yes I see this," she said.

"Here is where Adriana likes to get into her head," and I pointed to Adri's head. "So now, we can tease her a bit."

Lourdes looked lost again. Yikes, it's hard enough to train someone sensually never mind language translation on top of it. I took a deep, slow, breath and continued.

"Lourdes, teasing is like joking. Watch what I will say to Adri now. 'Adri, this really is a lot of attention to have put on you, you are right. I think I'll stop now and we can continue another time.'"

Adriana sat up straight up and protested, "No, please, I'll be a good girl. I'll take all this attention I swear."

Lourdes' eyes widened in wonder as I gently pushed Adri back onto her back.

"Okay Adri, I'll get started again but if you tighten up I will have to stop."

"Yes Ma'am," Adri beamed.

I thought it interesting that between me and Adri she always addressed me as Mamacita. However, when Lourdes was with us I was Ma'am. Mamacita was too intimate a term of endearment I guessed. I wanted to tell her that we were in an extremely intimate spot with my fingers on her pussy while her girlfriend watched. But I kept the thought to myself and just smiled.

Back at my bedroom-operating table, I jumped in with both hands. I spread Adriana's outer lips with my left thumb and middle finger then lubed her inner lips with my right fingers.

I asked Adriana, "Are you ready for a fun ride?"

"Yes I am ready!"

"Are you ready Lourdes?"

Lourdes nodded, smiled, and looked at Adriana with adoration then bent over to kiss her. I slowed them down by stroking Adriana's inner labia for a few more minutes.

Then I told Lourdes, "Now I'll lube the hood of her clitoris and stroke her there. She will begin to surrender more, or she might tighten up. Let's see where this stubborn bitch wants to go."

They both began to laugh until I put the lube on Adri's clitoral hood and began stroking, ever so slowly. The room became silent - except for Adri's soft moans. She closed her eyes.

Lourdes came around to my side to see what I was doing.

I said, "Most women are extremely sensitive to direct clitoral stimulation until they are nearer to their peak. So right now I am stroking her clit through her hood. You see?"

She looked closely and smiled, "Yes, I see that."

Adriana's moaning became more intense. "Okay, you hear how her moaning got louder?" I asked Lourdes.

"Moaning louder?"

I mimicked Adriana's moaning sounds.

Lourdes responded, "Oh yes, yes, okay moaning. I understand."

"Now that she is moaning loader, she is ready for more direct clitoral touch. So I will lube and touch her clit with just the lube only, no finger pressure yet. You see?"

Lourdes watched me as Adriana's head began to sway side to side.

"She likes that!" Lourdes exclaimed.

"Yes, she likes that. She is being a very good girl tonight and taking all this attention. Let's take her even higher. I will use my index and middle finger and press down a little and stroke her clit very gently, see, she's getting erect."

Adriana let out a gasp but her body did not tighten up so I knew it was not pain but a gasp of ecstasy. This was too tough to translate so I let it go for now. Lourdes was transfixed on my fingers.

I told Lourdes, "Sometimes I stroke her up and down and other times in circles. Sometimes I go very slowly, other times faster. I like to mix it up, same way I do myself."

"Yes, you make changes so she does not get boring?" Lourdes asked.

"Yes, you got it. We do not want our princess to get bored."

Adriana was no longer responding to our banter, only the strokes on her clitoris. I knew she would be ready to go over the edge soon so I teased her a moment.

"Adri, is it okay if I stop now?"

"No, no, please, don't stop!"

"Okay Lourdes, we have her just where we want her. Adriana is ready to rock and roll."

"Yes, I am ready too!" Lourdes declared enthusiastically.

I showed her how to take Adri even higher by peaking her up and down with slower and faster motions. When I felt like Adri was about to go over the edge I'd slow down until she calmed down a bit.

"Alright Lourdes, I'm going to take Adriana over the edge by using faster steady strokes. Are you ready?"

Whether she understood me or not she responded, "Yes!"

I started to increase my stroking speed on Adriana's clit. Her swaying head now flailed rapidly.

I told Lourdes, "Keep the speed of the strokes steady so she can ride her own wave. Watch, any minute now she is going to cum. Her thighs are quivering. Can you feel it?"

"Yes, I think I am have orgasm too!"

"Great! That is how it works, when you feel the orgasm in your own body while you stroke her, it means she is feeling it in hers. That is a very good sign."

And with that came a loud gasp of ecstasy as our dear Adriana allowed herself to surrender to her blissful orgasm.

I disappeared into the bathroom to get Adriana her clothes and then reentered the bathroom to clean up. But really I just wanted to give them this intimate time to kiss and cuddle. When I came out, Adri was dressed and they were sitting close, talking softly.

"How do you both feel?" I asked.

In unison they announced, "Great!"

"Good. Let's let it wash over you and in a few days, if you have any questions, give me a call. Okay Lourdes?"

"Yes, I think I will have many questions still about how you ... make her not to be strong. You know what I mean?"

I replied, "Yes, I know exactly what you mean."

Adriana laughed softly.

"You see how she knows that she is a head case? She loves making us work hard to please her. She is such a bitch. But what can we do? We love her anyway. Okay ladies, it is time for me to say goodnight. Enjoy the rest of this beautiful evening."

I heard not a peep from either of them for almost a week, until Adriana left me a voicemail message one morning on her way to work.

"Honey, I really need to talk to you but I can only talk when I am out of the house. Lourdes is frustrated and ... well, I guess I am too. Please call me."

I called her immediately to take her out of her misery. She could barely wait to spit it out.

Adriana confessed, "Oh God honey, I hope I didn't make a mistake having Lourdes move in with me so quickly."

"Ah, having U-Haul remorse are you?"

"Oh shut up already I am in serious pain right now. Stop with the U-Haul jokes!"

Adri had never been so aggressive with me. I knew she was in deep trouble.

"Adri, I'm really sorry. No more jokes. What can I do for you honey?"

Adri told me, "I don't know what you can do for me. I am still not having orgasm with Lourdes and now she is angry and telling me that I should move in with you since you are so good at it."

I cringed. "Oh boy. I was wondering how she took the sensual training."

Adri clarified, "No, at first she was very happy about your demo but when her techniques didn't work on me she got frustrated, then angry, and now she is very jealous of you and our friendship."

"My dear Adri, I was afraid that might happen but you insisted."

"I know, I know, I was wrong. But I don't know what to do now."

Having no solution at the ready and running late for work we scheduled a chat for lunchtime.

In the breakfast lounge at the office, I shared my friend's dilemma with my close co-workers. The guys offered their services to help those poor struggling lesbians. Yet everyone was stumped. However, in our banter I came up with an idea. Adriana had an appointment near my office so we met in person for lunch.

I started in immediately, "Adriana, I have the solution to your problem but you're not going to like it."

Adriana asked, "What is it my love? I don't care how difficult, I need to work through this."

I began, "Lourdes feels that she is an incompetent lover so of course she is feeling horrible. But really honey, it is you that is the problem. I know because I had to strong-arm you many times to get you out of your head and into surrender. Orgasms don't happen without surrender."

"Well, okay, so what do I do?" she asked.

I continued, "You first of all need to apologize to Lourdes for making her wrong. I am sure you have been making her wrong or she would not be so upset."

"Okay, I can do that. Then what?"

I launched into to my idea, "This is the part you will not like. You are going to have to train her to your specifications. You want her to magically be the perfect lover for you but it doesn't usually

66

happen that way. You remember what I told you I went through with Yigal?"

"You made him take sensuality training courses with you. Lourdes is not going to do that. Look what happened after your demo."

I jumped in, "First of all, you don't know that she won't take a course. Second of all, It's not necessarily that SHE needs to learn but that YOU need to learn how to train her."

"Ugh, you're right. I do hate this solution. I really hate to train lovers. You know that. Why can't they all just know exactly what to do?"

Adriana started to laugh for the first time that day and it filled my heart. How I loved this girl.

Part II: **Intrigue**

Shanti continues to add men to her harem until she is accused of being a sex addict. If thirty is too many then is eight enough? She tries desperately to control her unmanageable sex life. The roller-coaster is exciting at times but it's making her nauseous.

Chapter 8

My Multi-Colorful Life

In the months to come, Adriana was cumming more and more and her relationship with Lourdes was deepening and growing. This also meant that we no longer spoke on the phone five to ten times a day. This left a huge hole in my heart and as I was averse to feeling sad, I medicated my pain the way I knew best: with sex. As Adri got cozy in her new relationship bubble, I got wild with my sexual exploits. Within a few months, my lovers tally doubled. Before Adriana started her new relationship with Lourdes I had been juggling ten to fifteen lover at a time. But when Adri and Lourdes entered blissful monogamy, my lovers tally quickly doubled to thirty.

I actually had to create lists to keep my lovers straight. Next to each name I also kept pertinent details like email addresses, phone numbers, where we met, and something unique about them. I had guys call me that I couldn't remember and managed to keep them yapping until I got to the lists to figure out who they were. I had an A list, B list, and C list. Depending on the infraction, like canceling a date at the last minute, an A lister could end up at the bottom of the C list in a nano-second.

Of course Yigal was at the top of the A list as he was my primary partner and love of my life. When I had enough men to keep me busy, I pulled Yigal back into my fold. I couldn't live without him. Everyone else's position would fluctuate daily. It was rare if I completely erased someone from the lists. I never knew if there might be a last-minute cancellation and needed everyone at the ready. Those available at a moment's notice usually made it to the A list. I even kept guys who were non-marriage material in my C list safety net, for a rainy day.

The three-strike rule prevailed for all those marriageable men in close proximity. Since they lived close, our first dates and any successive dates were closer together and therefore they were out quicker. I was brutal, but I still kept some of the non-marriageable men past the three-strike rule if they were excellent lovers. Guys like my prince always got top billing because he was super exciting, super rich, and super hot, even if he was not marriage material. He was on the A list for sure. The lists would boggle my friends' minds and even my mind at times. However, I preferred to busy myself with their management and upkeep rather than tumble down my terrible tube of tears.

One day, a friend of my co-worker's visited the office and heard of my male harem. She asked me, "Did you ever consider that you might have a sex addiction?"

I immediately felt defensive but covered it with my flirty reply, "No my dear, this is merely my sensual swan song. I will soon tame my tangled flocks and clip my wings once more. For now, I have no fear of flying."

I do not remember her name or her face but I will never forget what she was implying. The idea that I might have a sex addiction struck a fearful chord within me. It was as if an inner wisdom came alive with her suggestion and it terrified me.

I went online as soon as I got home that night to see what qualities sex addicts had that I might have. I stumbled onto one of the 12-Step sex-addict websites and read, "...many of us never knew that our problem had a name. All we knew was that we couldn't control our sexual behavior. For us, sex was a consuming way of life. Although the details of our stories were different, our problem was the same. We were addicted to sexual behaviors that we returned to over and over, despite the consequences." If this didn't ring a bell! I took their self-assessment test and identified with over half of the behaviors and thought processes of sex addicts. What I learned made me extremely uncomfortable. But I searched no further and reassured myself that this was only a temporary phase.

That upcoming Friday, in the deep freeze of February 2004, something shook me violently out of my frozen denial. Rebecca went with her Dad that Thursday night instead of Friday night and I took advantage of the opening. I had a Thursday night lover sleep over, which was rare but it was my FBI guy and I often made exceptions for him as he was as commitment-phobic as I was. No chance he would get attached. We had sex before going to sleep and sex on Friday morning when we got up. Then I came home for lunch to entertain an out-of-town lover who only had lunch available before his flight.

"Screw lunch, I want to get screwed!"

After work I came home to change my clothes and change the sheets, again, to prepare for lover number three that evening. After I booted lover number three out of my bed that Friday night and locked the front door, I began to cry.

This was highly unusual behavior for me as I was always glowing at night, high from sex. It was the morning light that usually prompted my tears, hung over from the night before. At that moment I saw that I was spinning out of control and no amount of sex was helping.

I cried for an hour, missing Yigal and hating him at the same time for creating this mess. Yes, I was not above blaming others, even with all the transformational work I had done. I believed none of this would have happening if Yigal had agreed to marry me. It was hard not to blame him. I wanted desperately to speak with Adriana but it was after 2 a.m. on a Friday night and she would be asleep with Lourdes. I continued to cry.

Then, what my co-worker's friend had said came back to me, "Did you ever consider that you might have a sex addiction?"

I thought to myself, "Shit, I can't have such an embarrassing addiction. How shameful!"

My brain went into fix-it mode. I was such a guy in this way. I continued talking to myself, "Wait, I know what I can do. I am just going to stop all this sexual nonsense and the problem will go away. That's it. I am cutting the lists down to only one list with six or eight guys maximum. I will keep Yigal, of course, then the prince, my FBI guy for a quick booty call, he lives only four blocks away, and only four or five men of marriage material. When they strike out, that's it. They go completely off the list for good."

I felt better instantly, assuming I conquered what might have been a possible sex addiction. Ah, if I only knew what lay ahead. Though I felt better, I still wished I could call Adriana. I wanted to call her when I was happy, sad, mad, scared, excited - we were totally co-dependent on one another. But I didn't care. I saw no downside to our relationship, only positive love and support.

In the morning, as soon as I opened my eyes, I called Adriana. For once she was the one who did not sound good in the morning.

"Hey," Adri replied in a solemn tone.

"Adri my love, what's wrong?"

"I don't know. I'm just..."

I felt her pause as if she was looking to see where Lourdes was. Lourdes did not like Adriana to make phone calls when she was around.

Adriana whispered, "Just not happy with Lourdes no matter how hard I try."

Sex always paramount in my mind I asked, "Are you having orgasms?"

Adri responded, "Yes I am cumming now and then, but it's beyond that. We have been fighting a lot. Can I come over and take you to brunch? I could really use your wisdom right now."

"Of course my precious angel. I'm ready in ten minutes, you know me," I told her.

I got her to laugh a little.

She replied, "I know. I love that about you. Always ready for action!"

Since I had already solved my problem, or so I thought, I was happy to listen to Adriana's wounded heart.

She confided in me, "Mamacita, I don't know how much longer I can do this dance with Lourdes. You know how possessive, controlling, and jealous she is, right?"

"Yes," I replied.

"Well, on top of this she is still not a great lover. But...there are also some other things about her that I have not shared with you."

"Really? Keeping secrets from me? I can't believe you've withheld things from me. Why?"

"Well, I don't know. I guess I didn't want to hear you talk about that U-Haul thing again."

I was holding back a laugh because I could see Adri was in deep pain. So when she started to laugh I let it rip. We both laughed for what seemed like ten minutes.

"Thank you Mamacita. I needed a laugh. So, here is what I have not told you. The woman that Lourdes was in a relationship with for two years before me was her sugar mommy."

"No way!"

"Yes and I have moved into the same position without really knowing it."

Totally perplexed I asked, "How exactly?"

"Well, she lives with me rent free, which is no big deal. I would pay the rent and utilities anyway. But I also buy all the food, her new clothes, her toiletries, and anything else that she needs. When we go on a trip I pay for the plane tickets, hotels, rent-a-car, and you know, everything."

I replied, "Oh wow, I wondered how she was able to live here on translation jobs alone as her English is not so great."

"I know, her English is terrible and on top of this she does not have a green card."

We sat quietly for a while looking down. I needed to digest this bomb and did not want to react.

Adriana broke the silence, "You must be mad at me."

"What? Oh hell no, not at all. Your story just threw me back to my relationship with Guillaume, the French guy I told you about that I kept for a couple of years when I was a model."

Adriana replied, "Oh yes, I forgot. You told me about him a long time ago. But you were very young at the time. Too young to know any better."

I explained, "In love, naive, and a sugar mommy. I totally get it honey. Please don't feel ashamed. I have been there too. It starts gradually, paying for a few things here and there, justifying why they don't need to pay rent and before we know it we are sugar mommies."

"Thank you my love. But you could blame it on youth. What can I blame it on?" Adriana asked.

"Blame it on that damn U-Haul."

Snorting with laughter she said, "Shanti stop, you are killing me!"

Our stomachs hurt from laughing. When the giggle fest subsided I could address Adriana in a more serious way.

"So, what do you want to do with her now?" I asked.

Adri replied, "If we were living apart I would just see her less and less and then gradually phase her out."

"You sure you want to phase her out?"

"Yeah, I'm pretty sure."

I thought long and hard. "Once you are certain you want her to move out, have the break-up talk and then give her a month to find a place."

She argued, "But you know how hard it is to find a place in New York. Can take many months."

"That's not your problem," I insisted. "Lourdes found you to crash with after her break-up, she can find someone else to crash with now. Your problem is coping while she is still living there. I suggest you fill your dance card quickly and not come home much after work."

Adriana took my coaching to heart and was out gallivanting nearly every night. She began to hang out with a tribe of polyamorous bisexuals, doing all sorts of group sex experiments. I was surprised how out-there she went, but happy she was moving away from Lourdes.

"Shanti, you should join us some night, we are having so much fun!"

"Adriana, you are too out-there even for me. I just cut my lover's list down to eight from thirty and do not want to rack it all up again with your group-sex tribe. Adri, your dance card is more than full. It has exploded!"

She laughed in wild abandon. As for Lourdes, she was out of Adriana's apartment within three weeks. Guess she couldn't take Adri coming home at 4 a.m. any longer. She got the message. We did not know if she found herself another sugar mommy or not. We didn't care. We were simply happy she packed her U-Haul and left.

Now that Lourdes had moved out, Adri and I went back to being lovers, or as she called it, "sensual research partners." I had missed all the sweet attention she put on me so it was lovely to have it back again. However, her new incarnation was a bit too wild for where I wanted to go so we didn't socialize much. I did not want to fill my dance card in fact, I was hoping to soon find The One and hang up my dancing shoes.

Adriana invited me everywhere and one afternoon she invited me to a polyamorous meeting. There was to be a quest speaker who had authored a book on polyamory. Not that I wanted any more pointers on exploring the lifestyle I had been leading for the past two years, but I was curious to see how she herself managed it. I was living this lifestyle blindly and inventing the rules as I went along. So I was open to learning new tips on how better to manage my balancing act until I found The One.

"Yes, Adri, I will come to this polyamorous meeting with you."

"I surely hope you will cum multiple times!"

Adriana was back to being her wild-child self and seemed very happy. At the meeting, Adriana was fawning over me in a corner, fitting in quite nicely with this openly sexual group. A few minutes before the speaker began, a super hot guy with a caramel complexion and long dark hair walked into the room. Our eyes locked in a lustful embrace.

Adriana chimed in, "Ahhhh, you like that guy!"

"What guy?"

"The one who is undressing you with his eyes."

I played dumb, annoyed that she could read me so well. "He's okay," I replied.

"No way, I know you too well and I know your type. He looks like Yigal. You like this guy."

I avoided the conversation, "Shhhh, the speaker is starting!"

Through-out the lecture we were on good behavior until the question-and-answer session. I thought these people were supposed to be experienced in the polyamorous lifestyle yet they were asking, in my opinion, really lame questions.

One man asked, "How do I persuade this new woman I like to be polyamorous with me and my wife? She got very angry when she found out that I was married."

The speaker was calm and rational, giving him pointers on ways to make the new woman feel safe. I didn't like her answer so I whispered to Adri what I would tell him.

"First of all, you lied to this woman by withholding the truth about your marital status. Second of all, you don't persuade someone into a lifestyle. Go find a woman who likes this lifestyle already!"

The entire Q+A session proceeded like this, with me quietly, and sometimes not so quietly, critiquing the speaker's answers or the guest's questions - or both. We were obnoxious giggling loons, Adri and me, shooting out comments from the peanut gallery. At times I would pipe up and share my righteous opinion to the group. I was any speaker's worst nightmare. Attention-seeking is a strong branch of the sex/love addiction tree and I was an attention-seeking tree-hugger for sure.

After the Q+A session, there were refreshments, wine, horrible wine as Adriana was quick to point out, and lots of mingling. Adriana managed to get us to Mr. Hottie, who was with a very pretty lady he introduced as his girlfriend. Adri did all the talking since I was quiet, which often happened when I was attracted to someone. She also managed to get Mr. Hottie's card for me, something about contacting him regarding wine sales. I peeked at his card.

"Leonard Hernandez? What kind of name is Leonard for a hottie?!" I thought to myself.

This conundrum inspired me to bust through my shy shell, "Where are you from, Leonard?"

"I was born in Costa Rica but I grew up here in the Bronx." Leonard replied.

"Is Leonard a typical name from Costa Rica?" I asked.

"I don't know what my mother was thinking. I think she wanted to give me an American name. She had her heart set on moving to America someday and we did a few years later. You can call me Lenny if you prefer."

I wanted to say, "I'll call you tomorrow Mr. Hottie," but what I said was, "okay Lenny, you can call me Shanti."

"That's a beautiful name. Where are you from?"

"I adopted this name while living in India but I am American."

Lenny paused a moment then asked, "You have a slight accent though."

Embarrassed I replied, "Ugh, I know, lots of people tell me that. I have mostly foreign friends, lots of French, Israeli, and South American friends."

Adriana piped in, "Spanish too!"

I clarified, "Yes, and Spanish, so I pick up on their broken English I think. I know it's weird."

Lenny proceeded to ask for my business card, right in front of his girlfriend. Well, we were at a polyamorous meeting after all but still. I felt really uncomfortable while handing it to him, though I did indeed hand it over.

Now that we both knew how to reach one another, I needed to leave Mr. Hottie's presence because it was too difficult to hide my attraction for him. I sensed that his girlfriend might have felt it and I did not want to disrespect her.

I announced, "Good-night you two. Nice meeting you both. Adriana and I have a dinner date."

I grabbed Adriana's arm and walked away.

She asked, "Who are we having dinner with?"

"Shhhh, can we get out of here now?"

"Of course Mamacita whatever you want."

In the upcoming weeks, Leonard emailed me often and I was happy to respond. I asked him many questions about his interest in polyamory because it was a lifestyle I wanted to leave. I was hoping that would be his story too. Sadly, he was just embarking upon this lifestyle and wanted to explore it. Damn, he does not make my list for a marriageable man. At least he was not too much younger than me. Is nine years younger too young? I knew the answer. Too young, too commitment-phobic, too polyamorous, too not right for me. But he was so hot damn it! Little did I know the impact this man would have on my life.

Chapter 9

The Push and Pull of Didier Bellamy

Falling for Mr. Costa Rica Hot Stuff reminded me that I should focus on men my age or older, which always brought Didier Bellamy back to my thoughts. Didier, my guinea-pig boyfriend experiment after my first break-up with Yigal spring 2001, was handsome, creative, successful, and smart. If only his narcissistic monologues didn't bore the crap out of me. The Didier Bellamy show was interesting for sure, the first time. However, there were times when I found his egocentric orations unbearable.

The beauty of dating a slew of different people made it easier to tolerate people's intolerable behaviors. If I'd had enough of someone's idiosyncrasies I'd put them on ice for a while until they thawed out, in which case I'd usually forget why I put them on ice...until the next encounter.

Didier broke up with me because I would not be monogamous with him. I wanted to continue on with my polyamorous path and he would not accept this.

I was shocked by his conservative stance and asked, "But Didier you French are the inventors of sexual liaisons, no?"

"Yes, well, this is true but I am a monogamist French guy. This is just who I am."

At that juncture I was unwilling to be monogamous because that meant no longer seeing Yigal. So Didier stopped seeing me. I was sad to lose him, but had to accept his decision. I continued on with my promiscuous train. However, Didier contacted me on a trip to New York about a year later and asked if I'd like to have lunch with him to catch up.

I replied, "Ah yes, lunch, that would be safe now wouldn't it?"

Nothing about my suppressed grief, rage, and fear-fueled promiscuous train was safe. If I wanted a man there was little chance he could escape my clutches and I wanted Didier.

He laughed nervously at my bold lunch declaration. "Okay, well, yes, lunch is much safer, you are right, ha, ha, ha! I forget how smart you are."

We met for lunch at a lovely Italian place near my law firm. Of course I looked particularly hot that day.

"*Salut Didier. Ca va?*" I asked.

"Oh my God, yes, *ca va bien*! Wow, you look very beautiful. Yes, lunch is safer, you were right my darling," Didier declared.

The last time we dated I had just broken up with Yigal for the nth time, finished four years of college, and was working part-time in real estate. I was very unsettled. By the time we met for lunch I had been in my high-paying legal secretary position for nine months, and was more secure in my mind and my wallet. My heart, however, was a constant mess, covered over by my endless string of lovers. Didier, uncharacteristically, opened by asking several questions about me. The conversation usually revolved around him.

"My God, you really look amazing. I mean you have always been beautiful since your modeling days. We first met in 1979, you remember that?"

I smiled, reveling in his attention.

He continued, "But you look especially beautiful now. Are you in love, *ma cherie*?" he asked.

I had stopped seeing Yigal for a time after he broke off our engagement and I followed through with the abortion. But I did not want to go into details about that with Didier. Didn't want Didier to know I had returned to Yigal after Didier said goodbye, only to leave him again.

I simply replied, "No, not in love with anyone in particular. I am in love with many."

"Yes, Miss Polyamory, I remember. Are you still seeing your young Israeli lover in this polyamory soup?"

Didier was fishing. He knew that Yigal was his only big competition.

I was happy to announce, "No, we are completely finished."

"Okay, I see. Then we have a lot to talk about."

We had a lovely lunch that led to dinner the following night and of course, Didier came home with me, as I had hoped. We had a very sexy night together and it inspired a post-orgasm cuddle and chat. He was one of the rare guys that I cuddled with.

"Didier, honestly, you travel far too extensively and work far too much to keep any woman happy."

He replied, "I know baby. This has been the sad story of my life."

So I asked, "Then why can't you accept to see me and enjoy me, when you are in New York and stop getting all possessive? Isn't it nice to be with me now?"

"Well, yes, it is very nice. But my ego has a hard time with this polyamory stuff."

My response came instantly and naturally, without any manipulation. "Okay, so don't keep in touch with me when we are apart. This way you won't know what I am up to. Then we make plans right before you arrive, we see one another when you are here, and you go to your next destination. We will only communicate when we are together and don't ask me about my harem because it upsets you. We can live in our own bubble of a relationship when you are here. Can that work for you, *cheri*?"

"Hmmm, yeah, I guess so. It is very nice to be with you in bed this way. I have to say."

And that is how I lured Didier into being polyamorous with me. I just took away the polyamorous label and packaged our relationship into its own unique special bubble. I adored our times together, a few days every few months. In fact, when he took the pressure off me to be monogamous, I started wanting him more.

On one of his trips to New York we had such a fabulous time together that he asked, "Would you like to come visit me in Paris sometime?"

"Oui, oui cheri, I thought you would never ask!"

Paris had been my second home so to be there with a guy I adored was heavenly. To make this trip truly heavenly, I decided to bring Rebecca with me. She would be on vacation in April and

Didier would be in Paris at that same time. It would work out perfectly. This way Rebecca could enjoy Paris too. She was now eight and had not been there for three years. Now she would understand much more about the beauty and culture of this incredible city.

However, I did want to see Didier alone at night so I also invited my friend Debbie along to share our hotel room and I paid for her plane ticket. Debbie was one of several women that camped-out in my apartment while we were under attack on 9/11. Rebecca knew Debbie well and felt comfortable with her. We were all excited to go and spent weeks in preparation. I, of course, bought a few new killer outfits, lingerie, suitcase, and polished my travel kits. I had a feeling that since I was finally free of Yigal, I might open myself completely to Didier and the prospect was very exciting.

Rebecca had a condition for going to Paris though. She wanted to go to Venice for a few days first. I reached out to Didier to meet us there for a couple of days. At first he said yes and later he reneged, citing work overload. But how much work can a screenwriter do? It would have been a quick and easy trip for him. I was surprised. But I figured I had best satisfy Rebecca's request; lest she rebel against Paris and so we went. We had the most magical time. Venice truly is the romantic city of all cities. I was so happy that I got to share it with my daughter.

I joined Didier for dinner on our first night in Paris. Debbie met us at our hotel that same day, flying in from New York. It was all a perfectly coordinated and seamless canvas. I wore my very best new hot outfit from Pookie and Sebastian, revealing my new lace camisole in the cleavage. I also lathered myself in Calypso Mimosa fragrance, knowing Didier was an absolute sucker for scents. On a secretary's budget I could not afford a pair of Manolo Blahniks but I bought a perfectly great knock-off to strut my Parisian stuff. Giving Rebecca a good-bye kiss on both cheeks, à la française, Debbie walked me to the door.

She noted quietly as I left, "I see you are pulling out all the stops here for Didier. I have never seen you this decked out at home."

I replied, "Paris, my dear Debbie, is not New York. Paris demands the ultimate in beauty and romance and I will never disappoint her."

Dressed to kill, I met Didier at Chez Andre, one of his favorite restaurants. I was ready for action. However, to my shock and surprise, there were eight other people sitting at the table.

Didier whispered in my ear, *"Cherie,* I hope you don't mind, I have a little more business to discuss with them and then we'll be alone."

They were all discussing a new movie project and though I looked like a knock-out, there was only an occasional remark back and forth to me. I was nearly invisible.

"Wow," I thought to myself, "I could really take a tumble here with this slap in the face."

Instead, I decided to make the most of it. Though I sat next to Didier I might as well have sat across the street and that's what I decided to do. The thought put a huge smile on my face, so I followed it into action. After finishing my main course I excused myself for the toilet and instead went to a bar nearby. I returned nearly an hour later. Didier stood up the moment I arrived and approached me.

"Cherie, what happened to you? I had the manager go the ladies room to find you but you were not there. Where did you go? You had me worried."

"Oh really, I was not aware that you even noticed me. That's nice to know," I replied.

"Oh mais no ma cherie, come on. Of course I noticed you, and you are looking so extremely beautiful tonight and you smell absolutely divine."

I began to smile for the first time with Didier. The two glasses of wine at the bar also helped. Didier then asked, "So where did you go?"

"I went to the bar at the Plaza Athénée. I love it there."

I started to walk back to our table but Didier stopped me. He pulled money out of his wallet. *"Voila cherie,* let me give you money for that. It is expensive at the Plaza Athénée. You always did have good taste."

"No worries. I did not have to pay," I replied with a grand smile.

Didier flashed me a devilish look and said, "Oh my God, you really are something like I have never met before."

"And never will meet ever again," I replied. I walked back to our table with my smile of conquest.

Didier's movie tribe never did leave. They stayed right through to dessert and coffee. So I lavished my drunken pallet with *crème brûlée*, knowing that soon they would all have to go and finally leave us alone! Outside the restaurant Didier apologized profusely for the borage of business.

"Oh *ma cherie*, I am really sorry. I did not expect them to hang out with us all night. Now I am completely exhausted. Would you mind if I put you in a cab to your hotel and make it up to you tomorrow night?"

I thought, "He has to be kidding, right? He's not going to fuck me after all this bullshit with his business partners?"

I was dumbfounded. I wanted to slap Didier in the face. Instead I slapped him with my icy words.

"You have a lot of nerve canceling on me Didier Bellamy after dragging me to this boring work dinner on my first night with you in Paris."

Didier replied, "I know, I know, I really am sorry but I would not be any good to you tonight *cherie*. I would only pass out as soon as I hit the pillow. I have been up since 5 a.m. and I am totally exhausted. I would hate to disappoint you."

He gave me a long kiss on the neck as he got drunk on my perfume and said, "Mmmmm you smell delicious. What is this divine fragrance?"

"You don't deserve to know," I replied.

"You better go before I wake up. Tomorrow will be just you and me. I promise *ma cherie*."

And with that promise I returned to the hotel, slightly tipsy and sexually very frustrated. Thank Goddess for the Parisian bathtub shower hose. I washed off my make-up and my foul mood as I sprayed my pussy to orgasm.

By 6 p.m. the next day, after a fun time touring the city and shopping with the girls, I received a note to call Didier. I expected him to ask where I would prefer to dine that night.

I returned his call, *"Oui Didier, Ca va?"*

"Salute ma cherie. You are not going to believe this but I have to work with this film crew again tonight and we will also be up very late."

I was shocked and enraged but I kept silent, for fear of massacring him with my tongue.

"Cherie, are you there?" He asked.

Barely audible, I replied, "I am here."

"Yeah, okay, so this is what I'm going to do for you. Do you have money on you?" he asked in an upbeat fashion.

"Yes," I replied.

"Take your daughter and your babysitter out for a very nice dinner tonight and tomorrow I will reimburse you with cash. Okay *ma cherie?"*

"Didier, I paid for my friend to come to Paris specifically to watch Rebecca so you and I could spend the nights together. Do you want to reimburse me for her plane ticket as well?"

Didier explained, "No, listen, this is completely unusual what is happening right now with this project but it has to get done. Well, welcome to my crazy world, I know, I know. Tomorrow I promise you we will be alone. I told my team that."

Though I was having a good time sightseeing, shopping, and eating delicious French food with the girls' club, my mind was mostly on Didier. I was starting to question whether it was a good idea to pursue him. As a lover in New York, I was on my own turf and in control. If I had a bad night with anyone there were a half-dozen standing by. I was starting to experience emotional and physical pain from being abandonment. I had depression, insomnia, intense headaches and nausea at various times throughout those two days. Years later, when I got sober from my sex/love addiction, I discovered these were common symptoms of withdrawal, similar to the withdrawal from drugs and alcohol. I did not want to spoil the trip for the girls so I tried my best to put on a happy façade but I was dying inside. After dinner, and after Rebecca went to bed, I had a heart-to-heart talk with Debbie.

"Deb, I think this trip to see Didier was a mistake."

We were good friends and I didn't mind her telling me things that might hurt for I trusted her with my heart. I was ready and expected a blow him off speech.

"Well Shantz, you have always known he is a work-a-holic. Some wealthy men are like that. That's how they became wealthy in the first place, hard work and long hours. There is a cost for everything. Poor guys have plenty of time but no money to wine and dine you. What I don't like and I don't understand is why you didn't ask him to pay for your travel expenses. Three plane tickets are mighty expensive on a secretary's salary. That was kind of dumb of you."

"Yeah, I know. But he did pay for the eight-night hotel stay in Paris."

"Yeah but this is no four-star hotel honey, if it is even a two-star hotel. Shantz, this guy has millions. You are a struggling single mom and a secretary. His cheapness bothers me more than his work-a-holism."

I knew in my heart that Debbie was right. It did bother me that Didier never offered to pay for our plane tickets. But the truth was, I never dated wealthy men, not even during my modeling days. I did not know how to ask for monetary perks if they did not offer. I either bought my own needs and wants or did without. The idea that anyone would want to give me lavish gifts was alien.

I confessed, "I know Deb, extracting money from men is something I definitely need to learn. But what about seeing him tomorrow and the rest of the week? Should I see him or blow him off? He's being such a devil."

"Well, you don't want to blow him off now because he is paying for the hotel. What if he gets mad and decides not to pay the hotel bill?" she reminded me.

"Oh yeah right. See that's why I don't like depending on a guy financially. I hate this!"

Deb continued, "Anyway, you might have a totally fabulous time with him tomorrow night and you will forget all about these past few days."

I reminded her, "Three days in Venice and two nights in Paris. That's nearly a week in my book!"

"Okay but take a chill pill tonight. Why don't you get dressed up and stroll around Saint Germain. Have yourself a fabulous dinner at a quaint restaurant and drink at a sexy bar and enjoy Paris. I'll stay here with Rebecca. It's why I came after all."

The idea of enjoying my time at night without a man was foreign to me in New York and even more foreign to me here. But Debbie was right. Seeing the festive fashions, lights, and romantic sights of Paris did lift my spirits. It brought me right back to the days when I roamed these streets as a young fashion model. Ah, such magical memories. What's amazing about Paris is that the gorgeous architecture rarely changes since it is staunchly protected. It's a time warp. Most of the stores and restaurants stay in the same locations. It was comforting.

During my Parisian night promenade, I landed at the world-renowned Café de Flore where famous artists, writers, and philosophers held court since its opening in the 1880s. I watched the people parade go by after I ordered my *Croque Madame* sandwich, a grilled ham-and-cheese with a fried egg on top. While waiting I sipped on my favorite bistro drink, *un panaché bien blanc*. *Un panaché* is a combination of beer and lemonade. Sounds gross but French lemonade, spelled and pronounced limonade, is like Sprite or 7-Up. *Un panaché bien blanc* translates to a *panaché* very white, meaning there is more limonade than beer. Since I was never a great beer fan, this was the perfect solution.

With my *panaché bien blanc* I enjoyed my favorite accompaniment, a Marlboro Light cigarette. Since Rebecca was out of sight I was safe. No child wants her parent to smoke and perhaps die of lung cancer. That's why I kept this nasty little habit a secret from her, one of many secrets. She was too young to be made aware and anyway, I was too unconscious to understand. My harem of men, and occasionally women, were definitely not habits I was willing to share with my daughter at age eight. I took care to protect her from finding out.

That night in Paris was so sweet, reminiscent of my modeling days two decades before. It was a magical time in my life: I was young, beautiful, famous, and full of life. I traveled the world and hob-nobbed with the rich and famous. I never imagined in college that modeling could bring such fulfillment to my life, and it was Paris that opened these gates.

The next day, after a lovely time visiting museums and shopping with my girls, Parisian night number three was fast approaching. My heart began to race by 6 p.m., with no news from Didier. But I showered anyway and hoped for the best, still expecting the worse. I pulled out new outfit #2 and began to make my preparations, not knowing where or when. It was nearly 7 p.m. when the phone rang in our room.

"*Salut ma cherie! Comment tu va?*" Didier asked how I was doing. Didier always spoke to me in French when he wanted to charm me so I felt our night together would be safe.

"*Tres, tres bien mon cher,*" I replied.

Didier continued, "So listen, I have a reservation at Brasserie Lipp, not far from your hotel. Do you know it?"

"It is directly across from Cafe de Flore," I replied.

"Yes, you know Paris so well my dear."

"I was sitting at Cafe de Flore last night and looking right at it," I confessed.

Didier seemed surprised, "Oh really? Is that where you took your friend and your daughter for dinner? It is cute but not the best food. It is merely a coffee shop my dear."

"I went there last night by myself."

Didier remarked, "You are the only woman I know who goes out at night by herself."

"Well, when you abandon me I have little choice. Better than staying in the hotel room," I replied.

"*Oh mais no cherie.* Let's forget about that now. Tonight we will have a wonderful night. This restaurant is where the film crowd of Paris meets. It is not easy to get a reservation at the last minute but I know people there. I will meet you at eight, okay?"

When I hung up the phone Debbie noticed my disappointment and asked, "He canceled again? What's wrong?"

"No, he did not cancel but he might as well have."

"Huh?" she asked.

"We are dining at a restaurant full of his film buddies. What makes you think we will be alone?"

"What the fuck?" Debbie exclaimed.

Rebecca giggled.

Deb continued, "Oh sorry Rebecca. Shantz, this guy is something else. Maybe he's just insecure and needs to impress you or something by taking you to a celeb hang out?"

I replied, "Whatever it is, tonight I get to the bottom of it."

Though my outfit looked sexy and bright on the outside, my hopes for night number three in Paris were dim. The glow on my face had to be dim as well. I have a terrible poker face. Women spend enormous amounts of time and money to make their faces beautiful - facials, scrubs, creams, make-up, Botox, and surgery. However, the most beautiful part of a woman's face is her glow, her *joie de vivre* and I felt that my joy had died. I am a notoriously bad liar. It took all my acting abilities to find my smile again. After talking it out with Debbie, we decided I should pretend I was a great American movie star about to meet a French friend for dinner, not a lover. This way I would not be expecting anything from him and therefore, would not be disappointed.

Though our table was for two, several of Didier's buddies did indeed come over to us throughout the evening. He also pardoned himself several times to visit their tables. La la la la la...it was a mild version of night number one in Paris. So when the conversation turned to marriage at the end of dinner I was beyond shocked.

"Excuse me? You want to marry me? Where is this coming from? Are we on Candid Camera?" I asked.

"No, I have been thinking about this for a few months now."

"Well you have an extremely strange way of showing it."

"I know I am not easy to live with. Why do you think I have not remarried for over twenty years? I work too hard, I am always late, and I cancel at the last minute. But I would make you a good husband. I would be loyal to you and your daughter and give you a good life. You love Paris and speak French so you could be happy here a few months out of the year, no?"

Didier's proposal took me completely by surprise. I felt no romance or joy in it, especially after feeling jilted for nearly a week. I had already decided to flush him. Maybe he sensed that and gave it his last best shot? But he sounded sincere and so I started poking at his proposition.

"How exactly do you see this working, on a practical level?" I asked.

"I would get a bigger apartment in Paris for both you and Rebecca to be more comfortable. My house in Los Angeles is already very big and you will love it, I am sure."

I was nearly paralyzed with confusion. "Thank you for asking me to marry you, really. I am very flattered yet totally shocked. But I really can't see how this would work."

Didier began to laugh. "You have to be kidding. I am offering you the life of a queen and you cannot see how it would work?"

I replied, "No, seriously, I don't see how this would work. First off, Rebecca's father lives in New York and our divorce agreement says we will not live more than 50 miles apart. Paris and LA are both more than 5,000 miles from New York, never mind 50 miles."

"Mais ma cherie. I can find you a lawyer to get you out of the agreement when you can prove that the new life you are offering your child is better than what she now has. I will send her to the best private schools in the world."

"Okay, that is great. Then what about my job?" I asked.

"What about your job?"

I told Didier, "I happen to really like my job. I know I am not making millions, traveling around the world, but I spent four years in college for this and I really don't want to let it go. I love my boss and all the people I work with, they are family to me."

Didier took a long pause and put his arm around me. "Patty baby, I know you are not used to a man taking care of you. This I do know. But I want to be that man for you if you will allow me."

I felt Didier's sincerity and it was very touching so I took a pause to think about his offer. I watched as Didier stared at me with a grand smile.

When I came out of my contemplation I proposed, "If you want me to quit my job, marry you, and follow you around the world, you will have to buy me out."

"Excuse me?" Didier asked, completely shocked by my proposal.

I continued, "If after a few years this marriage does not work out, then I am screwed. Most divorces are not friendly and with your millions you will hire the best attorney and I will end up with nothing. It will be much harder to get a job once I am off the work grid for several years. That is the reality."

"Oh my God I cannot believe how you are thinking," Didier exclaimed. "Where is this coming from *cherie*? You do not trust me?"

"It is not you personally Didier. I don't trust the institute of marriage any more, even though the romantic in me loves it. It cost me over twenty thousand to divorce my husband, that was cheap, but I am still paying for it."

"Okay, so how much money would make you feel comfortable in a prenuptial agreement?"

Thinking quickly on my feet, "I would want you to pay me a hundred thousand per year for life, plus the cost of inflation, in addition to our joint living expenses and travel and schooling. Then, if we divorce, you give me two hundred thousand for divorce and relocation fees to move and find a job. Then you keep all your inherited properties and your millions. It's a great deal for you and a secure deal for me."

I wished I could have photographed Didier's face but one of his colleagues passed by and mirrored it for him.

"*Salut Didier. Ce qui et faux?*" which means, "What is wrong?"

If Didier was shocked by my counter to his proposal, I was shocked that he shared my proposition with his colleague. Though they spoke in French I understood most of what was said. Didier did most of the talking, as he always did. He basically recounted everything I proposed to him with an air of the incredulous.

When his friend had heard enough he simply walked away and said, "*Les filles...*" which means, "Women..."

We spent the next hour in heated discussion. Didier was appalled.

"How can you come up with such a money scheme? I am completely shocked. You have never been this kind of girl. What happened to you?"

Trying to get Didier to see my point of view, I replied, "It is not a scheme, Didier. It is a perfectly healthy reply to your marriage proposal. I would be the only one suffering if we divorced because we would be living your lifestyle completely - nothing would change for you. However, I would have to reinvent myself, again."

"*Mais no,*" Didier replied in a soft tone.

"*Mais si* Didier! Listen, I spent seven years, after my divorce, reinventing myself, one year trying this and that, then four years of college and now I finally have this great job that I love. It was extremely difficult and costly both emotionally and financially to divorce so I know what I'm talking about."

Didier replied, "But you are expecting to divorce from the beginning."

"No, I am not expecting or wishing for divorce but only being rational, for once in my life, in case it does happen to me again."

Didier actually took a pause to take in what I said.

"*Mais, mais, no cherie,*" he responded, "I could not start a marriage in such a way. I am sorry. I am a gentleman and a romantic. I cannot operate love like a business deal. No, really not."

Neither of us had any appetite for dessert. We parted without a mention of spending the night together.

Didier kissed both my cheeks and told me, "I will call you tomorrow."

But I knew very well that was merely a formality. When Didier was hurt he would disappear. And so the next few days I did not hear from him. I reached out to him the morning of our last night in Paris and practically begged him to see me. He agreed to meet for drinks, not dinner. I knew that meant he was not happy to spend too much time with me. But I accepted the crumbs.

At first there was an uncomfortable silence between us, until the wine kicked in.

I broke the silence. "Didier, I understand why you are hurt. I wish I could marry you and forget about security. But the pain of the past seven years is too fresh for me."

"I know my baby."

"Didier, I really do wish I could accept your proposal. I think we would make a great couple. But..."

I lost my words.

"It's okay baby. I understand you too but... it is still a crazy idea you have."

"Oh come on now!" and I proceeded to tickle him.

We both laughed and continued to get drunk. As Didier had an editing session early in the morning with his team, he had to excuse himself. He was about to leave without kissing me so I grabbed him.

I made it clear, "Hey, just because we are not getting married does not mean we cannot see one another, okay?"

Didier looked at me tenderly without words. Then I poked him under the arm to make him laugh and he did.

"Yes, alright, okay," he replied.

But that was the last time that Didier and I connected as lovers. Even though we enjoyed no physical lovemaking that trip, it was in the air and in my hopes. His damn marriage proposal ruined everything, even though it warmed my heart to know he wanted me in that way. I still fantasize what my life would have been like if I had married Didier Bellamy, my life as the wife of a famous screenwriter.

Chapter 10

Don't Ooops Where You Eat

Since I cut Stuart off sexually, due to his being married already, I needed more office intrigue. I began to entertain myself with the clients. I did not have to see them every day in case the tryst went cold, which they always did at some point. Most of my boss's clients lived in other countries and flew in only a few times a year. The clients appreciated my dedicated service, both in and out of the office. Sometimes the after-office meetings were merely dinners, drinks, and diabolical flirting. But at other times we hit the sheets. Of course my boss, Mr. Tanner, was never consciously aware of these private meetings. Although I did suspect he caught wind of them as our after-office flirting bled into our inner-office meetings.

"Good morning Señor! Wonderful to have you back in town. Can I get your cappuccino this morning? Extra foam, yes?"

"Oh yes, you remembered just how I like it!"

Such an offering was classic, a perfect moment to make the client feel appreciated. Some of the secretaries abhorred serving coffee, believing it degrading. It was my favorite activity because I got a chance to flirt in an acceptable way. Mind you, as most of the clients were not from the U.S. the flirting protocols were nearly non-existent, especially for those south of the border.

I was certain Mr. Tanner delighted in the personal attention I gave to all his clients. Adriana often teased me that Francisco Maldonado da Costa, my boss's biggest client from Argentina and worth billions, was my Big Fish Sugar Daddy.

She once told me, "You weren't even fishing but this huge fish jumped into your boat."

Adri was quite right about that. I was never very interested in Señor da Costa as a lover. He was Mr. Tanner's biggest client and off-limits. He was too old, and he was not my physical type. However, one day I was busy on the phone with another client when he waltzed by my desk. He tried to catch my attention a couple of times but I was focused on my call. Then he came over to me and placed a huge wad of cash in my hand. It appeared to be all $100 bills. I put the other client on hold.

"Señor da Costa? What is this?"

"Shshshsh!" he whispered. "Take one of your hot young boyfriends to Le Cirque and have a great time. Merry Christmas Shanti!"

As quickly as he came he left. But before returning to my previous call I counted the bills in my hand. Ten crisp 100 dollar bills. That's a thousand dollars. I was completely high. For the first time in my life I understood why being with wealthy men turns women on. Señor da Costa had just become extremely interesting to me.

Upon his return to New York the following month, he invited me to dinner and I accepted with glee. I met him at Plaza Athénée, one of the most expensive hotels in the city. He told me to meet him in the lobby.

However, when I arrived and announced to the desk clerk that I was waiting for Mr. da Costa he replied, "Oh yes, Mr. da Costa is expecting you. Please go upstairs, Miss Owen."

"Hmmm..." I thought to myself, "this does not feel comfortable."

Yet, true to my sex/love addiction, with minimal to no boundaries, I went up to his suite and knocked on the door. He opened the door a crack but all I could see was part of his face. How odd.

"Come in, come in," he said.

As I entered his suite I saw that he was completely naked. I was shocked. Clearly I knew what was next. But Señor da Costa's naked body was not unattractive; he was in fairly decent shape for a 68-year-old guy, and nicely tanned. But I needed a little more seduction and foreplay to get turned on. Within moments he had pulled off my dress, opened a condom, and in five minutes he came.

Then he slapped me on the ass and announced with a smile, "Let's go! We have a reservation at Jean-Georges in five minutes."

That was the fastest Wham Bam Thank You Ma'am I had ever experienced, with no orgasm for me. But it all seemed worthwhile as we had an exquisite dining experience and the most interesting conversation and laughs. Señor da Costa was a fascinating man, albeit a rabbit-fast lover.

In the following months he became my first sugar daddy. He would pay me $1,000 when we had sex and $500 when he visited the office with no sex, just office flirtation. I didn't understand why he paid me the $500 when we didn't have sex, but one day it all became clear.

We were having difficulty at the Brazilian consulate for several weeks. They were refusing to pass any new business transactions because they were angry with the U.S. Government. Washington had recently created a new policy requiring Brazilians to get a visa to enter this country. In return the Brazilians were making it difficult to set-up new companies. Señor da Costa needed to have documents passed through immediately or his merger would fail and it was worth hundreds of millions. I organized all the documents and contacted Raul from the mailroom for a rush delivery. Raul was not only a hot office flirt, but he was also a fast runner. If I told him I needed a rush job it always got done on time. However, Raul was out that day so I contacted the next in line, Goran, the savvy Croatian.

An hour later, Goran returned from the Brazilian consulate with a somber look on his face as he handed back the envelope.

"Shanti, they would not approve these documents."

"Shit Goran this is bad."

"I am sorry Shanti" and he started back to the mailroom.

Just then I had a genius idea.

"Wait," I asked, "was the person you dealt with at the Brazilian consulate a man?"

"Yes," he replied.

"Did he seem straight?"

Goran looked totally lost, "What?"

I figured we got lost in translation. "Did he seem like he might be gay?"

"Gay? No. Why?"

"Perfect"

I dug into my personal folder on the computer's desktop and printed a racy photo of a girlfriend and me. We were dressed for a "pimp and ho party." In the photo my girlfriend wore low-cut tight jeans and was topless. She painted her breasts with two huge flowers and wore a cowboy hat. I was wearing the tiniest black G-string and a completely see-through black halter-top with a China-doll pink wig. We both looked very cozy with grand smiles of seduction. I presented the photo to Goran.

"Oh my God, Shanti, is this you?"

"Yes, shshshsh, that's me on the left. Now, I want you to go back to the Brazilian consulate…"

He cut me off before I could finish, "Shanti, I told you the guy said no they would not pass these documents."

"Goran, you did not let me finish. We're going to do business girl-style, okay?"

He looked so confused that I burst out laughing.

When I finally settled I told him, "Look, I'm putting this hot photo into this four-page document. You are going to return to the consulate and present the documents to the same guy and right before you hand them over, pretend to trip and drop the documents on the floor, like it was an accident. When you pick them up, be sure to make the photo visible for a minute then pull it back like you are embarrassed. The guy is going to want to see the photo again. Show him. Then tell him you don't know how that got into the pile. Tell him it is a photo of Mr. Tanner's secretary and you must have grabbed it by mistake when you picked up the papers at my desk. Then apologize for the lack of professionalism and beg him not to say anything or I might lose my job. Then let him keep the photo."

Goran looked incredulously at me, "Shanti, this is crazy."

"I know. But I'll give you a copy of the photo when you come back. Go!"

Meanwhile, Señor da Costa called me twice to see if the documents were back yet. I had never heard him so anxious and aggressive before and no amount of flirting would curtail his fury. I decided to speak with Mr. Tanner about it.

But he said only, "What can we do Shanti? The Brazilians have the control now."

I told him I had sent Goran back, though without giving him the details.

Mr. Tanner replied, "Well, that's a good effort Shanti but I don't have very high hopes. Tell Señor da Costa, if he calls again soon, that I am going into an outside meeting and will call him when I return."

I busied myself with filing, and I thought about what might happen if this deal fell through. Señor da Costa would be livid and I feared that might affect me financially; no more office gifts from my Mr. Big Bucks. At the end of this tense hour I spied Goran rounding the corner but he was not smiling. My heart sank.

With a serious face Goran said, "Shanti, I did my best and ... I got it!"

"What? You got the documents signed?"

Goran beamed, "Yes, the documents are signed."

I was so excited I made him recount his every step.

"You know Shanti, it happened exactly how you said it would. How did you know?"

"Because I know men, I've slept with enough of them. Plus the guy was Brazilian, he had no chance to say no to me."

Goran continued, "When I told him that this nearly naked girl with the pink wig was Mr. Tanner's secretary, you should have seen his face. He looked like he saw God!"

I went to my wallet, and pulled out a fifty-dollar bill, and handed it to Goran.

"No Shanti no, I cannot take this from you. It is my job to deliver the correspondences."

"Goran, you went far beyond your job description. Take this and have a few grappas on me. Oh and wait, let me print out another copy of this photo for you. But don't show it to anyone here."

I printed two copies of the photo, one for Goran and one for me. I was so excited that my scheme had worked that I wanted to flash the star photo to Mr. Tanner. I truly didn't care that I was nearly naked. It got us the deal!

As soon as Mr. Tanner returned from his meeting, I showed the signed papers to him.

Mr. Tanner stared at the documents, dumbfounded, and asked, "Shanti, how did this happen?"

I flashed my sexy photo and recounted the entire scenario to Mr. Tanner.

Chuckling, Mr. Tanner said, "Oh Shanti, you know how to handle these Brazilians. Good public relations. Brava!"

"Do you want to call Señor da Costa now? He called several times quite concerned about this merger."

"No, no," Mr. Tanner replied, "I think I'll let you do that. You sealed the deal after all."

When I contacted Señor da Costa I immediately took him out of his misery, "You got it, the documents are signed."

I then went into all the sexy details. Laughing he replied, "Oh Shanti, you did business Brazilian style. You are a very good girl, my darling. I shall take you to a wonderful dinner when I get back to New York."

After we hung up I smiled and stared at the winning photo, proud of my ingenuity and happy that my wallet would be expanding again soon. So that is why Señor da Costa paid me even when we didn't have sex. He is a smart businessman. He knew I'd work much harder for him if I had extra perks. He was absolutely right.

I had never been a girl who could be bought before. Never understood the appeal until now. But I was having so much sex with so many partners that this financial bonus got me high, really high. I wanted more of it. My sex addiction was kicking into another level.

Chapter 11

Sexing with the Boss's Son

If it wasn't bad enough that I was sleeping with my boss's biggest client, and getting paid handsomely for it, I also took to sleeping with the boss's son, Eliot Tanner. Eliot was an adequate attorney but he surely didn't warrant a corner partner's office. There was lots of gossip about how nepotism was his only ally.

Eliot traveled more than most of the attorneys and was frequently away for months at a time, mainly in South America. We often joked that he was making drug deals, likely the only way he could afford to keep his corner space. Eliot just didn't fit in at the firm. He never socialized after work or joked or flirted in the lunchroom. In fact always ate at his desk. He was like an alien so E.T., his office nickname, suited him. Eliot was a bit of an odd duck who, unlike most of the office males, was cold to me, which suited me just fine. Besides being the boss's son, he was married and therefore off limits.

However, on one Friday night I was in the office late doing "personal" correspondences since Mr. Tanner was out of the country, which happened often. I wandered down the hallway to make copies of my discount tickets to the Copacabana that night, I planned to meet Cassy, Ms. Flower Tits from the sexy photo. We were both dance-alcoholics. She was a lot of fun, a "tell it like it is" kind of girl who kept me in stitches with her boldness.

As I was walking down the hall to the copy machine and anticipating my fun night out with Cassy, I passed E.T. sitting in his office. He was just staring at the wall, like an alien, looking sad. I knocked on his window, not wanting to intrude if he preferred to be alone.

"Can I come in?" I asked.

"Sure," he replied.

"Hey buddy, you don't look so good. Anything I can do for you?"

Eliot confided, "My son is having trouble in school and the counselor blames my separation from his mother."

I was surprised that he opened up to me. "Are you and your wife living apart?" I asked.

"Yes. I feel terrible. I think I'm ruining my son's life." Eliot had tears in his eyes. He was so open and vulnerable, it threw me off completely.

I shared, "Divorce is tough, I know. I divorced my daughter's father a few years ago. But she was too young to really know what was going on."

He asked, "How old was she?"

"She was three," I replied.

"My son is twelve and my daughter is eight. They know exactly what is going on."

"Eliot, do you really want a divorce?"

"Yes, but I don't want to hurt my children."

I looked at Eliot with compassion, "You will hurt your children more if you stay together in an unhappy marriage. They will be forced to endure horrendous fighting or heart-numbing coldness between you two."

Eliot stared at me intently without speaking. I continued, "I remember the moment I decided to leave my ex-husband. I felt it would be better for my daughter to at least see me being affectionate with boyfriends than for her to experience no affection between her Dad and me. I wanted her to know that affection is important."

Poor E.T. looked like a broken man, just like the dying alien in the movie. I felt sorry for him. But it was his devotion to his children that changed my feelings for him and for the first time in over a year I felt attracted to him. He was a man about to divorce so he fit in with my criteria, and he loved his children immensely so he was a good guy. Without asking Cassy if it would be okay, I invited him out dancing with us.

"It will be good for you, will help you change your mind for a little while. Besides, my friend Cassy is a hoot. She'll make you laugh."

When we arrived at Cassy's door she looked at Eliot with daggers in her eyes, "Who the hell is this?"

"He's an office stowaway that needs some lovin'," I told her.

"You and all your office creeps. He's not getting any lovin' from me. I hate men tonight."

"Oh, just tonight?" I asked.

"Shut up," she barked.

We entered her fabulous apartment and she opened a nice bottle of wine. While dressing, she recounted her current difficulties with her soon to be, but not soon enough, ex-husband, Viggo. She asked, "Can you believe this mini-dick mother-fucker wants me to pay him alimony?"

Cassy was a successful and highly paid stockbroker. Viggo was a waiter, very handsome. They met sailing in Europe, and she dragged this live souvenir back with her. They were blissfully married for a year and stuck it out another two, until he got his immigration green card.

Hoping Cassy might warm up to Eliot I shared, "Eliot is going through a divorce too."

She shot back quickly and got right up in his face, "You better not ask your wife for alimony or you can just leave here right now."

Eliot started to laugh for the first time that night. Cassy was in rare form.

When we got to the club I jumped onto the dance floor with total abandon. Next to sex, dancing was always my drug of choice. I had never known Eliot to be attracted to me before but while I was dancing I noticed him wearing a perpetual smile. I pulled him over to join me.

"Shanti, you are such an amazing dancer. I never would have guessed."

"Why not? Because I'm a white woman?"

I gave him a strong shove into the nearest chair and uncorked a lap dance. He was toast. Within moments we were making out.

True to protocol I had sex with Eliot that night, I even dragged him back to my place. My sanctuary was usually sacred to Yigal and my FBI guy. But Eliot was staying with a friend since separating from his wife, not a great place to make yummy hot noises. Also not protocol was allowing him to sleep over, but we cuddled all night. I felt lost in this new emotional space, there was great danger afoot: my primary lover, Yigal, might lose his number one spot.

Eliot spent many a nights with me in the next month. I was totally falling for him. But there were problems in paradise. Eliot was newly separated and looking to join my polyamorous lifestyle. He had been married for 15 years and wanted to bust out. I was willing to let him explore for a while.

We continued to see one another and I coached Eliot on how to be a responsible poly-player. He was a terrible student though. We'd be at a party or club together and he'd be hitting on every chick he fancied.

I pulled him aside, "Dude, no. You find your bitches when you go out by yourself. I don't want to see you hitting on girls while I'm with you."

"Shanti, are you jealous?"

"Hell yeah!"

"But I don't understand. You've been polyamorous with Yigal for years."

I explained, "But Yigal never, ever, spoke to or even looked at another woman when we were together."

"Really?"

"Yes, really. And I expect the same respect from you."

One night I got a frantic call from Eliot. "Shanti, I am scared. My mother discovered that you and I are sleeping together. My brother must have told her."

"Okay, so what?" I asked.

"She wants to have you fired and she's pressuring my father."

I found this enormously funny and burst out laughing.

"Shanti, this is not funny. You have to look at it through my mother's eyes. To her, I am still married. This is really bad, Shanti. I don't want you to get fired."

I replied, "You should tell your mother that she is damn lucky that I have not been screwing her husband."

That got Eliot to chuckle and chill for a moment. For some reason I was not worried about his mother, not at all. I knew how valuable I was to the firm. I was the social director, the welcoming committee, and I was actually a damn good secretary, precise, neat, organized, and responsible. Who would have thought?

Eliot was not in the office the next day so I called him. "Hey bro, what up?"

"Listen, I convinced my mother not to have you fired. But the condition is that I have to move to the Buenos Aires office."

"What?" I exclaimed.

"Shanti, that was the only alternative. I'm packing and heading out in two days."

I couldn't speak. I was losing my almost number one guy and I started to cry.

"Oh Shanti, don't cry. You have so many guys. You will be fine."

"Yes, but you are my almost favorite."

"That's the sweetest thing any woman has ever said to me my dearest Shanti."

Within a few weeks I received a lovely email from Eliot about how much better his children were doing since he moved to Buenos Aires. He was surprised, delighted, and puzzled.

I suggested, "It is easier for them to digest the marriage separation when you are living in another country. That explains why you are not with them. When you were in New York and not seeing them every night it was too real and painful. You made a great decision without even knowing why."

One Monday morning I answered the phone to hear Señor da Costa's voice. "*Hola* Señor da Costa? Mr. Tanner is in Paris this week. Can I get a message to him?"

"No, but I have a message for Shanti," he said.

"Yeees..."

"I spent a very nice weekend here in Buenos Aires with Eliot."

My heart nearly stopped. I felt the gig was up.

"He told me all about what a wonderful time he spent with you in New York."

I was caught red-handed and didn't know how to cover it up as I laughed nervously.

"You are a very bad girl," Señor de Costa said.

"Yes, you are right. I am a very bad girl."

"But you are so bad that you are good," he replied with glee.

Then Eliot got on the phone.

"Shanti, you never told me you were boning da Costa."

"Well I don't kiss and tell, like you do!" We both laughed out loud.

"Damn," I thought to myself while catching my breath, "got away with it again. There must be some slutty angels up there protecting me somehow. Thank you!"

When Eliot returned to New York for a visit, he told me that he was going to try and patch it up with his wife. Then, in the next breath, he asked when we could have a sleep-over.

"E.T. you really are an alien. I am not going to sleep with you if you are trying for a reunion with your wife."

"Why not?" he asked.

I replied, "Because you have to give it a full chance and I don't want to be in the way"

"But I miss my Shanti."

"We will stay friends so you don't have to miss me. But no sex."

We did indeed remain great friends and we are great friends to this day. When Eliot finally left his wife for good, we never resumed our romance, the spell had been broken. He was too much of a dog for me anyway. I wanted to find a monogamous guy and Eliot wanted to piss on every fire hydrant. My heart never wanted to live a polyamorous lifestyle. I've always been a monogamist. But, I accepted polyamory for it was the only way to hold onto Yigal. Most of the time it felt more like "polyagony" and the pain pushed me to medicate myself with sex. So my promiscuous train kept rolling.

Chapter 12

Agony and Ecstasy

With Eliot no longer available, I did what I always did to lick my wounds: I called Yigal.

His voice got me in an instant, "Hey, where have you been my cutie pie stranger? Find yourself a good man? You forgot all about your Yigal?"

Unable to hold back my tears, "I could never forget about you Yigal. No matter how hard I try, it is always you that I love, you that I miss, you that I long for."

"Oh no, no, please Shanti, please don't cry. I can't take it. You know that. What can I do cutie?"

"You can come over and see me, spend the night. I need my Yigal fix."

"Of course Shanti you know I will always come when you need me, always."

This was the power of our primary relationship. If one of us was in dire straights, we dropped everything and everyone to be by the other's side. Tonight was that kind of a night.

My blindly destructive sexual life was all about me hoping to find someone to replace the love that only Yigal could fill in my heart. What would have truly mended my shattered heart would have been to stop seeing Yigal completely. This would have been excruciatingly painful in the short run. However, in the long run, complete disassociation could have brought about a deep healing. What I did instead was avoid and bury this pain in promiscuity, with my incessant need to find someone to replace him. My girlfriends meant well, but they only prolonged this pain by pushing me to date several men. I take full responsibility here. They suggested, but I accepted.

God, if Yigal himself wasn't enough of a drug, he brought the drug ecstasy with him that night. Neither of us was into drugs and I was surprised.

"Did one of your girlfriends give this to you?" I asked.

"Shanti come on now, stop that. No, my friend Richard gave it to me. You met him a couple of times. He said it would make us closer."

"Closer? Yigal, I don't need help in getting closer to you. I need help getting rid of you. You are the most addictive drug on the planet."

"Shhhh now stop and listen to me. This is the first time either of us has tried ecstasy so it will be special. We will take it tonight and never take it again, okay?"

I had zero willpower with Yigal. Hell, I had practically zero willpower will any man, truth be told. I was a love addict at my core but I branched out into sex addiction when I could not find that love or keep that love. Finding love in all the wrong places.

I told Yigal, "It's Friday and you will sleep over and cuddle me all night, so okay, I'll do it. But Yigal, I'm scared. You know I'm not big on drugs."

"What's to be scared Shanti? You'll be with me. Richard says it is the most amazing sexual drug. You're going to love it. I brought this beautiful old romantic movie with me and we'll order in and cuddle and make love all night."

I hate to advocate something that's detrimental to health and brain cells, but that night, taking ecstasy with Yigal, was the most magical night I had ever experienced. His friend Richard was right, it brought us even closer together. We must have spent all night long in awe of one another, expounding upon how much we loved, cherished, and absolutely adored one another.

Yigal kept telling me, "Shanti, look at yourself in the mirror. Please."

He wouldn't continue until I looked. "Can you see how beautiful you are? You are the most beautiful women I have ever met. Your face is so beautiful but your eyes, the spirit inside your eyes, is even more beautiful. I think you are an angel. That is why I can never leave you."

If ecstasy is supposed to be a sexual drug, that part of it did not work for us. We were normally very sexual but the drug dropped us deeply into our hearts and we bathed in love without actually making love. We were angels making love in our hearts instead of our bodies. It was blissful, beautiful, and completely other-worldly. When we awoke we were both still high from the drug and we vowed that we would never, ever, leave one another, no matter what. Whether it was the drug or our hearts talking or both, it felt deliciously warm and secure and it gave me the strength to keep going.

We became inseparable for weeks after that ecstasy trip. Normally we tried to limit our trysts to once or twice a month so as not to get too reattached. After that ecstasy trip, we started seeing one another at least once a week and sometimes more. Who knew a drug could have such a powerful effect?

Yet a dark event occurred that August 2003 that would pull me down from the ecstasy high I had been riding. I was at my desk when the lights went out and my screen went dark. We were experiencing a citywide blackout.

A blackout? I didn't recall a blackout without thunder and lightning, it was sunny and hot. Turned out that our overworked air conditioning units had overwhelmed the power grids, affecting the entire Northeastern and Midwestern sections of the United States and as far North as Ontario in Canada. Still, I didn't get the magnitude until everyone in the firm was called to the conference room.

The office manager announced, "We will be closing the firm as soon as this meeting is over. The elevators are not working and there are no lights in the stairwell. However, The security guards will be on each floor with flashlights."

I got an immediate flashback to 9/11 and my heart started racing. Is this blackout a terrorist attack? Rebecca was with her Dad on vacation, thank goodness, so I knew they were safe in the countryside. But Yigal, Yigal was supposed to meet me outside the office that evening. I had a bottle of wine and snacks in my bag. We were going to the movies. Cell phones were not working so I could not reach him. Too much like 9/11 and emotionally I was back there all over again.

I decided to go to Yigal's office, eight blocks away. I left a note with the doorman at my building in case Yigal came by looking for me. But when I got to Yigal's building, I learned that Yigal left and went straight to his garage to get his car. So I walked back to my office to see if perhaps he drove there. Saddened, my doorman said he had not been by. I hoped maybe he drove to my apartment so I walked home. Since no trains were running there were thousands of people walking. It was surreal to see so many thousands of people walking up and down Park Avenue.

All of a sudden I heard the cell phone ring in my purse. It was the first time in over an hour that my phone worked. My heart leaped, hoping it was Yigal. But the caller ID revealed that it was my sister. Janet Owen flashed on the screen. I was stunned. I had not spoken to my sister in almost a year. I nearly let her go to voicemail but since this was the only call coming through I felt it must be divine intervention.

"Hello?" I asked, pretending not to know who was calling.

"Hey girl, you okay?"

Janet sounded sweet and concerned, not like the angry bitch that had ripped me a new asshole the previous August, during my traumatic engagement break up and abortion.

I replied, "Yeah, I'm fine. Why? Is there something going on that I should know about? Was there a terrorist attack?"

September 11, 2001 was only two years ago. Was still fresh for us New Yorkers. Janet was completely traumatized by the events of 9/11, so much so that within six months she sold her co-op apartment, closed her business, and dragged her husband out to the suburbs of New Jersey. Living and working downtown, she had suffered intense lung problems, nightmares, and PTSD. Hearing her concerned voice instantly melted all my resentments.

Janet replied, "No, not a terrorist attack. I thought the same thing too. The radio says it's an overload with the electrical grid, too much A.C. use in this heat wave. Where are you right now?"

"I'm walking up Park Avenue on my way home, with about 10,000 other people."

"Well, you should get home as soon as possible and eat the food in your refrigerator, otherwise it will all spoil. And stay in for the night."

"Why stay in for the night?" I asked.

"Well, during the last big blackout there was a lot of looting so very likely it could be unsafe hon."

"Oooh okay. Hadn't thought of that."

"I'm going to hang up now," Janet said, "we need to save cell batteries. The radio says power is off until tomorrow."

I didn't want to hang up and during the awkward pause that ensued, I replayed the nasty voicemails and emails she sent me a year ago. But I shoved them aside, thinking back to 9/11 and how lucky we were to be alive.

Out of my heart and mouth came, "I love you girl."

Janet replied, "I love you too."

Though our declarations felt awkward, they began our healing process. Indeed there was still deep love between us. As I trudged up Park Avenue, I dropped a big piece of armor that had been blocking my heart to my sister. I felt a hundred pounds lighter and happier.

Meanwhile, there was no sign of Yigal nor any note from him. He was driving and surely would have made it to my place before me. There was no call from Yigal either. Other than that magical window of communication with my long-lost sister, my cell phone lay dormant for the night. It became all too clear to me that Yigal had driven back to his home in New Jersey without a single concern for my welfare. As I locked myself into my apartment for the night, preparing for 90-degree temperatures with no A.C., my temper began to boil. Yigal, once again, had proved that he could not be counted on in a crisis. It was 9/11 all over again, when he went MIA for twelve hours and here today, Yigal was nowhere to be found. The emotional high from our night of ecstasy, weeks ago, finally crashed. The summer spell was broken. I would put Yigal on ice for months. Oooh how I wished I could have bathed in a bucket of ice that dark, lonely, sweltering night...

Chapter 13

Red Sox Burlesque

Born near Boston to a family of sports fanatics, I was a staunch fan of all teams from Beantown. Living in New York during baseball season, was especially rough for the Yankees/Red Sox rivalry was in constant play.

The Red Sox faced the Yankees that fall 2003 for the American League Championship. My beloved Red Sox were playing strong and each game they won sent me skipping through the office waving my red knee socks, gloating. Tom Flannery was our office controller and a die-hard Yankees fan.

Tom bemoaned, "If you are so sure your loser Red Sox will beat the Yankees tonight, then let's make a bet."

"Oh they are winning tonight. No question about that Tom," I declared.

"Great. If you are so damn confident, come into the office tomorrow morning wearing nothing but those damn red socks when they lose."

"Huh, you're on Tom because there is no way the Sox will lose tonight."

That night I stayed home to watch the game alone. It was too important a game to have a crowd of Yankees fans screaming in my ear. I prepped by cooking myself a hearty hotdog dinner with baked beans, and even drank beer, which I don't even like. I wanted to get in the baseball mood. I even wore my red knee socks for good luck.

I was tucked in tight for the night, watching every pitch, swing, hit, strike, fly ball, run, and catch. By the top of the eighth the Red Sox were leading 5-2 and I could finally breath easy. I almost called

Tom to gloat. But then the Curse of the Bambino reared its ugly head at the bottom of the eighth: the Red Sox gave up three runs. Sweating in mid-October and not from the weather, I did not move from my chair. Ninth inning no score, tenth inning, no score, top of the eleventh inning, no score. Then in the bottom of the eleventh inning my hopes were lost as the Yankees scored a home run to defeat my beloved Red Sox 6-5. For the first time I understood why men weep when they lose a game for I too was wiping tears from my face.

Devastated, I decided I would call in sick the next morning to avoid the taunting jibes. But then I remembered the bet I had made with Tom. It was such a silly bet. Clearly I could not come to work totally naked but for my red knee socks. Yet the image continued to intrigue me.

I thought to myself, "I know how to turn this loss around. I will show up naked at the office with only my red knee socks. I'll wear my long black trench coat over my birthday suit until I get to my desk. That will take the focus off my loss!

When I arrived at the office I called the always on-time Tom and my conservative buddy, Iris, to my desk. Iris got there immediately but she was not a baseball fan so I kept my coat on as we killed time talking about Mr. Tanner's whereabouts. We always ordered in when Mr. Tanner was away so we could chill in his office at lunchtime, a gorgeous corner office overlooking all of Manhattan.

I heard Tom's maniacal laughter as he rounded the corner with his shit-eating grin. I allowed him to have it for a few moments for I knew in the end I would win the surprise prize.

He asked, "How about those damn loser Red Sox huh Shanti?"

"Yes Tom, you're right. What can I say? We suffered a terrible defeat." Then I got up and opened Mr. Tanner's office door, beckoned them inside, leaving the door open. I paced Mr. Tanner's office, "But you know Tom, I am not a sore loser, as I suspect you would be, if the cleats were on the other foot. However, a bet is a bet..."

I opened my trench coat. God I wish I could have photographed the shock on their faces! It was beyond priceless. Right there I had fun with my revenge.

Tom and Iris squealed like stuck pigs and looked over their shoulders to see if anyone was nearby. But I didn't care. My nakedness fed a strong exhibitionist need in me. The danger was exciting, an incredible turn on.

I thought to myself, "This is truly great fun! Let's see who else I can call." I spent much of the morning entertaining the troops by flashing my birthday suit.

Around 11 a.m. I got a call from Joyce in Human Resources. Joyce and me, well, we were not the best of friends, even though it was Joyce who recommended me for this position. She soon found out that the sweet temp secretary she had hired turned into a desk diva. Joyce would often criticize my sexy office attire as inappropriate. I knew it was not coming from her but from one of the female partners.

I often told Joyce, "If Mr. Tanner and his clients have no problem with my outfits then she shouldn't either."

When Joyce called me to her office that day I knew one of the office piggies must have squealed. "There's a rumor that you are prancing around the office flashing your red bra and panties."

I got up and flashed Joyce my birthday suit. She was visibly shocked but also smiled. "You see the rumor was false, I am not wearing a red bra and panties at all."

What inspired me to flash Joyce? I have no idea. I could have been fired. Perhaps my sex addiction was so ingrained in me by then that I saw nothing wrong with my sexploits.

I told Joyce about the bet with Tom. She and Tom were tight buddies. I guess that's why she was so cool about it. Joyce clearly could have fired me, but for some reason she covered my naked ass instead and not a word was spoken about it again.

Before leaving her office, Joyce asked, "Have you brought anything else to wear today?" She was trying her best to suppress her laughter.

"I have a bag of boring gear, yes," I replied.

"Great. Let's put it on, shall we?"

I later heard from Iris that Joyce was once a wild child herself before she had children. I'm guessing that this over-the-top antic of mine quenched some thirst of hers. From that moment on, we became great friends.

Chapter 14

Winter of My Damn Discontent

The winter of 2004 grew long and extremely cold. So too did my trail of marriageable men. I had pruned my list to prove to myself that I was not a sex addict, and now the pickings grew slim. Occasionally I just wanted sex, without looking for Mr. Right, and so I would dip into the no-no list of off-limits men. Yes, I kept my hidden list deep in a drawer for emergencies.

As the snow finally thawed in April, so too did my sex drive. I had just spent a week in South Beach with my daughter Rebecca on her school vacation. It was her wish, not mine. It was going to be extremely frustrating to be in party central and not able to join in. But Rebecca wanted to go to the beach and that was where she chose. Needless to say I was returning to New York in great need of an orgasm. I thought about the men on my list.

Young guys are so simple. Their hormones run really high so when they know they are going to get some, they are easy to enlist. Older men like Didier have considerations like, "Is she using me for my money? Is she a good partner for me? Will she cheat on me? Will she love me?"

I guess their hearts and brains start working when the testosterone wears off. Whatever, I found their "considerations" to be boring so it was back to the no-no list for me, I needed my fix.

Rebecca's Dad picked us up at the airport, dropped me off, and took Rebecca for the weekend.

My loins leapt. "Yes, Momma's gonna get her some tonight!"

As soon as I dropped my bags I called the hottest dude on my short list, and left him a voicemail message.

"Dude, I'm back. Let's go dancing at this cool new spot, then come back to my place. Call me."

I'd been away for a while, I had to check the sex suitcase under my bed. Most people keep their sex paraphernalia in a drawer by the bed but with a young child, that is too risky. So I used this really cool small plaid suitcase with a lock. It was out of sight under my bed and out of child-curious reach.

Opening the suitcase, I made sure there were enough condoms and lube to carry us through the night. I also made sure that my porn stash was tidy and my toys were clean. Dildos, vibrators, ticklers, and of course my butt plug. That was my secret weapon. Oh I liked it on me, sure enough, but I also used it on the guys. I always covered it with a condom for ease of cleaning, especially if we both used it. Most of the guys protested when I said I wanted to use a butt plug on them. However, once they got a blow job with the butt plug in place, they never went back.

Yigal often protested, "You are turning me into a gay guy!"

He loved it though. Yet he felt ashamed that he loved it. I explained to Yigal many times, and to the other guys as well, "The anus is not only for gay men to enjoy. It feels good to women and straight guys too. There are tons of nerve endings that get a delicious massage with a butt plug. Plus, a guy also gets his buried cock stroked at the same time. Added bonus!"

I truly loved using the butt plug on men, for they went wild with ecstasy. For us women, there are actually more nerve ending in the anus than in the vagina. So the taboo anus has all kinds of joys. A few men adamantly refused my butt-plug invitation but then I would explain that they were raining on my parade.

I laughed so hard when one guy continued to refuse, saying, "I never liked parades anyway."

An hour passed without a call back so I pulled out my lists to see who else might be around. I was seriously looking for sex, not a relationship this night, so I cruised the no-no list. I placed a few "Hi, just checking in" calls, discovering that two of my young hotties were out of town and the others weren't answering. I started to panic, and then I got angry.

"Fuck, I'm here this weekend without Rebecca and horny as hell damn it! This is why I need to keep a longer list of men."

I went online to cruise for a last-minute hook-up. By now it was nearly 7 p.m. Completely flipped out, I called Adriana for solace.

Adriana answered, "Hey Mamacita you are back!"

"Adriana, I am not well."

"Did you get sick in Florida?" she asked.

"No, I got sick as soon as I got home."

"Yeah, it's still pretty cold here."

"No, not physically sick from the cold but mentally sick from the cold trail leading to no one," I explained.

I finally broke down and cried.

Adri tried to understand, "Honey, oh dear. But, I really don't know what you are talking about my love. Can you try to explain it a little better for my Spanish brain to comprehend?"

"Adri, I am sick. I am. I have a problem and I don't even know what to call it."

I sobbed harder as Adriana interjected, "Honey, is Rebecca there?"

"No, thank God, I would hate for Rebecca to see me like this. How would I even explain this to her?"

"Well, do you think you could try to explain this pain to me?" Adri asked.

Still sobbing I began, "What is wrong with me Adri? I spend all of my free time searching for guys, spending time with them, and then having sex with them. The next day I get completely depressed because they are not The One and I start all over again. Whenever I have free time and I don't spend it with a guy, I feel like I'm going to die. The pain is unbearable. That is completely crazy! What is wrong with me?"

Adri agreed. "It is crazy to want a guy that bad. But you are asking a lesbian, remember?"

Laughing and crying at the same time I told her, "Adri, I hate you. You always get me to laugh when I don't want to."

"Okay, I can be serious."

"Adri... I have an intense emotional problem that I can't figure out. Maybe I need to see a psychiatrist. How devastated I get when I am without a man or without sex is just not normal."

"I cannot help you with the man part but I can definitely help you with the sex part. You want me to come over tonight?"

Though I had been wanting sex that night, when no guy responded, I sank into loneliness. I realized then that what I really wanted was love. It terrified me. I finally looked my sexual monster in the face, if only for a brief moment.

Through the torrent of tears, I thought, "Could all this desire for sex be covering my real need for love?"

I contemplated Adriana's offer. Though sex with her would definitely take the edge off, what I really wanted was to fall in love with a man, so I could forget about Yigal. Therefore, I countered to Adriana.

"Sweetie, I would so love to see you tonight. However, what I really need to do is dance. There's this great new club I've been hearing about. Would you please come with me?"

Adri replied, "Ugh Mamacita. I am in my pajamas already. If you just wanted me to come to your place I would throw on a coat and drive down. But a club?"

"Please Adri. I don't beg you very often but I am in a terrible way. I'm scared. Dancing helps me get grounded."

Of course I did not mention that I also was in desperate need of my fix, to find a new guy. My list was dangerously short.

Adriana became curt: "I really do not want to go out dancing. It is the last thing on earth I want to do tonight."

My heart sank and I started to cry again.

She asked, "Honey, what is going on with you?"

"I told you Adri, I do not know! I am fucked up! Please I beg you to come out with me, for just a half-hour, then you can leave."

"A half-hour, you would be okay with that?"

"Yes, I promise you. I just don't want to go by myself. I know it sounds crazy but this would really help me so much."

"If this is one of those afterhours clubs then I will not go." Adri made clear.

"No, no, it is more like a lounge, you can be home early."

"Okay," she agreed.

"I love you Adri!"

Adriana was the first person I had ever let into my terrifying addiction turmoil. Even though we were best friends, I was afraid to show her the extent of my desperation.

In the high of knowing I might get my fix that night, I frolicked through my closets for a fun outfit to wear. Feeling whimsical, I chose my new orange and black bomber jacket, an orange halter-top, black bell-bottoms, a pair of black platform sandals and my new over-sized blonde Afro wig. I was ready to disco down. The wig was over the top, but I remembered my commitment to myself when I bought it:

"This is totally adorable but you can't buy it unless you commit to wearing it."

It was sitting in my closet with the tags on and screaming at me, "I want to come out and play!"

Chapter 15

One Wig Too Many

Outrageous outfits became my norm both in and out of the law firm. At work I pushed the envelope of corporate conservative with short, tight skirts and plunging necklines. Outside the office, the world was mine. I lived in New York, wild-child capital of the world, so who would care? I often went to clubs in my lingerie, accessorized with high boots and long jackets. I was a living, breathing, Victoria's Secret Barbie and no one ever complained. When I was hunting, I pulled out my most deadly weapons.

My costuming craze began in my early twenties when I returned from Paris to New York. Punk rock was still the rage and my short spiky hair-do fit in nicely. Though punk-rock music was not my favorite, I preferred the more danceable beats of our material girl, Madonna, I did so love the rebellious outfits. My rubber barf bracelet was a favorite accessory along with the blue raccoon tail I attached to my hair. My torn cropped sweatshirts matched nicely with my size 48 khaki pants, sucked in with a belt. They complemented my combat boots.

For some reason I left my femininity in Paris, the most feminine of cities. Every cathedral, cobblestone, and bridge pulled it out of me. But New York was rough, dirty, and aggressive, just like punk rock, and I played to it in both fashion and attitude. Captivated by CATS on Broadway, I added tiger stripes and spots to my nights on the town. My costuming needs were creative, but also quenched my constant thirst for attention that many sex/love addicts crave. Notice me! Love me! Need me! Halloween was once my favorite holiday but after nearly every night became Halloween I grew jaded and bored by the organized holiday.

"Why would I want to be one in a sea of many?" was my battle cry.

And wigs. During my modeling days I got tired of short hair and started complaining to my agents. They discouraged all attempts to grow it out: in the era of David Bowie, it was my signature look.

Yet still longing for longer hair, I bought a couple of long auburn wigs. I adored the new attention I was convinced I got with the longer locks. Then I tried changing wig colors, lengths, and textures. I would get very different reactions from men as I went from blonde to black to red, blue, green and my favorite, baby pink. Caucasian men seemed to look at me more when I was blonde, while dark-skinned men loved the black hair. All guys, and many women, would stop me on the street when I wore my long curly auburn wig. I guess it looked best on me because it was closest to my original brunette color, so it went better with my skin tone. But when I went clubbing I preferred my rainbow assortment. Soon I became a self-professed hair-behavioralist and once I got started, I could not stop. I was a wig-a-holic and felt no need to detox.

In the immortal words of my former gay roommate Joseph, "You have one wig too many."

In later years my costuming craze would escalate to far greater heights, just like my sex/love addiction, including boots so high they were like stilts.

"Can you see me? Can you see me?" I begged to be noticed.

Outrageous costuming brought me enormous attention. It was no longer a desire. It had become a necessity. Starting with sports as a girl, then modeling, acting, and now my new corporate career and social life, getting attention was always my goal. Many sex/love addicts have attention-getting as one of their mainstays. It surely was mine. I equated attention with love and could not get enough of it.

I returned from the heat of Miami's South Beach to a cool Saturday night in early spring of 2004. I much preferred the cooler temps of our New York spring. Being so pale I never tan well, which had me avoid the beach whenever possible. Plus there are fewer costuming options in hot weather. Just too darn hot to heap on all that velvet, sequins, and feathers with my wigs! So on this cool night, my over-sized blonde Afro was a comfortable accessory.

Part III: **Monogamy**

Her heart wanted monogamy, but with Mike, Shanti picked a bird more broken than she. Make up to break up, that's all they did. Shanti's love addiction was in full flight. Therapy to the rescue as Shanti starts untangling this complex web of sex/love addiction.

Chapter 16

Spring Blooms in My Heart Again!

On that cool Saturday evening, Adriana picked me up at nine with a sour face, so sour my huge Afro couldn't melt her.

"Oh Adri, come on. I promise you we will have fun tonight."

"What's to have fun at a heterosexual lounge? I'm doing this for you."

"Awwwweeee, I love you for this. But Adri, where is your conviction? Heterosexuality never stopped you before. You sucked me right in."

Finally I saw a sweet crack in her seriously sour face. She barked with a smile, "I hate you!"

"I hate you too!!"

At the lounge I headed straight for the bar, Adriana following. Leaning over the bar I asked the bartender if he had any Spanish wines. Adriana sold Spanish wines, one would think she would tire of drinking them. But she was always checking out the competition.

I declared, "I am buying drinks tonight babe."

She giggled and nuzzled up to me, "My Mamacita. I'm going to put my hands all over you so no guy will come near."

I burst out laughing, "Really now? You think men won't notice a tall hottie with a blonde Afro, being pawed by a cute little brunette?"

She joined in on my laughter to create more of a stir. Just then I noticed a tall, dark, and extremely handsome guy staring at me. He was super hot! Adri had lasar radar for my attraction to men.

She told me, "Aaaah I see who you are looking at. Ugh, another Yigal. Don't you get tired of the same kind of guy?"

"Nope, and this one is super hot!"

Raising my margarita, I invited Adriana to raise her Spanish wine, "Honey, thank you a million times for coming out with me tonight. I was seriously in a bad place and you rescued me. I love you!"

We drank and spoke more about my crash that afternoon when Mr. Super Hot came walking over.

"Hello ladies. Am I intruding?"

Adriana snapped back, "Yes you are but you are Shanti's type so what can I do?"

He looked at me as I smiled and shrugged, embarrassed. He extended his hand to me, "Hi, my name is Mike. I'm sorry, I didn't catch your friend's pronunciation of your name."

Adriana barged in again, "Her name is Shanti. Don't you speak English?"

I laughed at Adri's man-hating responses.

Mike addressed Adriana, "Yes, I am American and speak English, in fact I have a degree in English. Where are you from my dear?"

"My name, though I am sure you could care less, is Adriana. I am from Spain and I speak perfect English."

I could not stop laughing. Her rudeness was so over-the-top it was comical.

Mike turned back to me, "Do you speak or just giggle?" which made me giggle even more.

I replied, "Yes, I speak and I speak English as well."

"Where are you from? You have a slight accent."

I rolled my eyes and sighed for I often got this line of questioning and felt embarrassed by it.

I explained, "I'm from Massachusetts, but I spent many years in Paris, traveled a lot, lived in India off and on, and most of my friends are from elsewhere. I guess that's why I have this weird accent sometimes. I don't know how to fix it."

Mike smiled that smile a guy gives when he wants a woman. "Well, I don't think you need to fix it. It is almost as charming as your Afro."

Adriana piped in, "If you like the Afro, wait until you see her real hair!"

Mike, while looking at me, addressed Adri, "I can see her real hair hanging out both sides of the wig, interesting way to wear a wig, like a hat."

Adriana piped in again, "Well, Shanti is the most interesting woman on the planet."

It was funny to watch two people, before my eyes, vying for my attention. My attention addict was in heaven. I reached towards the bar for my margarita, needing a buzz for their verbal brawl. Little did I know I would jump onto their bandwagon.

Mike asked Adriana, "Is she really that interesting? How would you know?"

Adriana began her speech, "First of all, we are lovers and she is the best lover I have ever had and believe me, I have had many, maybe not as many as Shanti, but I have been around."

My eyes bulged out of my head as Adri called out my promiscuousness. Yet she was too busy talking to notice my glare so I pinched her arm.

"Ouch! Stop!" Adri exclaimed.

"No you stop Adri."

I turned to Mike: "I am very sorry for my friend's rudeness. We are best friends and yes, occasional lovers. But I am heterosexual, she is the lesbian."

Mike replied, "And you don't think you are bisexual, having sex with men and with your girlfriend?"

"I know it sounds weird. Well, I don't know, maybe I am bisexual but I am not bi-romantic."

He looked puzzled, "Meaning..."

"Meaning I have never fallen in love with a woman romantically."

Adri interjected, "Not yet."

Mike looked at me and said, "Well, I will leave you two ladies to your time alone. By the way, where did you get that name, Shanti? It's Sanskrit and you don't look Indian my dear."

Mike's arrogance was starting to show more, I didn't like it. I replied, "I adopted it while living in India."

"Ah, you did mention living in India. What was your given name?"

"Patty Owen, well, Patricia Owen. But those name combos weren't available when I joined the Screen Actors Guild. So on one of my trips to India I heard the name Shanti, liked it, and adopted it as much for the sound vibration as for the meaning."

Mike nodded, "Means peace, right?"

"You know your yoga."

Mike replied, "Yes I do. I have been doing yoga, chanting, and meditating for many years now."

"Cool," I replied.

Mike took a long, slow look at me, "Actress, yeah, you look like you need a lot of attention. Most actresses do."

Adri jumped in, "And she deserves all the attention she gets, asshole! Shanti is a goddess."

Mike replied, "My oh my, you have yourself a bulldog bodyguard and built-in audience. Enjoy your night ladies."

Mike walked away but not without shooting me that I want you look, even as Adriana blurted out, "What a total asshole!"

"Yeah, whatever. That's too bad. He's super handsome but he knows it. The arrogance is ugly."

Adriana asked wearily, "Mamacita, how long do I need to stay at this heterofest?"

I looked at Adri lovingly then kissed the top of her head. Barefoot I'm a good six inches taller but on my platform shoes I towered over her. I told Adri, "Honey, you can go at anytime. I am so grateful you walked me through the doors."

Adri replied, "But you don't know anyone here."

"That's okay. The music is great so I will get lost in dancing. I need to dance."

My dearest Adriana, oh how I adored her.

After she left I ordered another margarita and moved to the dance section of the lounge to find barely a soul. It was only the D.J., me and one other person. But as soon as I arrived he played my current favorite, *In Da Club* by 50 Cent. I jumped, screamed, and nearly spilled my drink. Aaahhhh this was exactly what I needed! Dancing made everything all right.

As the room began to fill I inhaled the remainder of my margarita and danced in complete delirium. It never bothered me to dance alone. In fact, I preferred dancing alone to dancing with a guy who had no rhythm, or with some creep who wanted to rub his johnson up against me. This night was no exception. Somewhere around song five or six I noticed our arrogant bastard watching me from a corner.

I considered taking a rest but then I thought, "I'll torture him with my erotic dance moves, show him what he can never touch!" How I delighted in my sensual games of mischief. They made me feel powerful.

Arrogant Mike finally made his way over to me as I took a cigarette break by the window. We could still smoke in bars and lounges back then. I did my best to look out the window and not look his way.

He asked, "Hey, where's your girlfriend?"

Still looking out the window I replied, "She left. She hates hetero clubs."

"So, why are you alone?"

Wanting to cut his balls off, I finally looked at him and sniped, "So, why are you so arrogant?"

He looked shocked, "Am I?"

I let the silence answer and returned to looking out the window and smoking.

Mike replied, "Awwee, I'm not such a bad guy. I'm a big puppy really."

I choked on my smoke. Mike interjected between hacks, "Maybe you...should...stop smoking?"

When my coughing subsided I responded, "Maybe you should jump off of your cruise ship on Da Nile and see how arrogant you are?"

Mike actually appeared to digest my reaction and replied, "Listen, I am very sorry if I insinuated you are an attention-monger. That was rude of me. I'm sorry. I am also an actor and I get it. Yes there is a need for attention but also a great desire to create, to give."

Mike seemed genuinely sincere and that allowed me to desire him once again. I dragged him to the dance floor for an I forgive you dance. Words are often overrated. As we exchanged flirty smiles, two guys came up beside Mike and spoke in his ear. Mike pulled me over to a quiet area.

"Hey, I'm traveling with these guys and they want to leave. Can I get your phone number? I'd love to see you again."

After giving Mike my number we stood for the longest hug I'd ever experienced with a stranger. It was the kind of hug you exchange with a long-lost lover. It was sweet, passionate, and full of deep longing and love. I didn't want to let go of him.

As soon as Mike was out of sight I decided to leave as well. I got what I came for, a new romantic possibility, a fix. Crossing the street for a cab I saw Mike with his crew in the distance and began crying.

I thought, "Why didn't I take his phone number? What if he loses my number? What if he doesn't call me? God, why am I so stubborn about not taking a guy's number?"

I hated the idea of chasing men yet that's what I did all day long. I cried all the way home.

Chapter 17

Dating Mike

Two, three, then five days passed with no news from Mike. I assumed he wrote my number down wrong because that hug could not possibly lie. Vowing on day six of no news to take a guy's number in the future, the phone rang.

"Hi is this Shanti?"

"Yes, who is this?"

"It's Mike from the lounge last weekend."

I should have been ecstatic but I was miffed.

"Hey, what happened to you? I thought you wrote my number down wrong." There was a long silence. "Hello?" I asked.

"Yes, I'm here." Mike sounded perturbed.

"So, what happened to you? Are you trying to play it cool or something?"

I figured he would get playful with me but instead he played it off. Told me he was busy with x, y, and z plans.

"Whatever dude. I don't care. I am just so happy that you called me!"

We met for dinner the next night at Caravan of Dreams, organic vegan restaurant in the East Village. Mike was half an hour late, not a good sign. When he came bustling up on his bike I was a bit shocked. I had never before dated a guy who rode a pedal bike. Took me by surprise. But he looked athletic on it and that was sexy. I liked that.

Dinner was pleasant though uneventful until the tab came. Mike tallied it up, included the tip, and split it in half.

"It's okay if we go dutch isn't it?" he asked.

It was definitely not okay with me and I was speechless.

I said, "Yes."

But what I wanted to say was, "Yes, going dutch is totally okay if you want this to be our last date!"

No surprise that I couldn't wait to leave the restaurant for I was completely turned off. There was no good-bye kiss outside nor was there a repeat of that heart-melting hug. Yet Mike left me with a bright twinkle in his eye, a huge sexy smile, and a promise to call me the next day.

All I could think was, "Next! Take your dutch ass, peddle-bike-riding self home!!"

True to his word, Mike called me the next day. In fact he called in the morning. So not a morning person.

His greeting was full of joy, "Good morning sunshine. Hey, what are you doing tonight?"

Since Mike woke me up I had no time to adjust my attitude.

I replied, "I am going to dinner with a man who will pay for my meal. That's what I'm doing tonight."

"Wow, do I detect some hostility there Missy?" Mike asked.

"No, you detect a lot of hostility. But it's not your fault. I said Yes to something when I should have said No. So I'm mad at myself."

Mike replied, "Could have fooled me. I do detect some anger towards me."

"Yeah, well, fair enough. Felt you should have warned me before we met that you wanted to go dutch. Anyway, I don't do dutch so I gave you a false response when you asked."

Mike asked, "Wait, are you saying you never go dutch?"

"Correct," I replied, thinking back to my recent Didier disaster when I bought three airfares to Paris myself.

I continued, "We get paid far less than men to start with. Then having kids and staying at home with them cuts us out of the race and sets us back, and we never recover. Yeah, I have a lot of charge on women paying for dates."

Mike then asked, "So what if the woman makes a lot more money? Does he still pay for the dinner?"

"Yes," I replied.

"What? That makes absolutely no sense."

I explained, "I cannot speak for every woman. However, for me it is not sexy to go dutch. If all you can afford is a hotdog, then take me out for a hotdog."

"This makes no sense!"

"It doesn't need to make sense," I replied. "It's about romance. I go dutch with my girlfriends. I don't want to go dutch with a lover."

"So the guy has to pay for everything all the time?"

I replied, "Well, maybe after dating for a while and it looks like it might be getting monogamous, then I could pay sometimes too. However, I will never go dutch. Some nights I pay, some nights you pay. You pay for what you can afford. I pay for what I can afford."

Mike took a pause. "Okay, how about I make dinner for us tonight at my place, get a nice bottle of red wine, and we watch a movie here? Would that be acceptable?"

"Oh yum, dinner and a movie at a private resort, absolutely!"

We both laughed and confirmed our meeting time.

Williamsburg, Brooklyn, was now the cool capital of New York. It was home to hipsters on one side of the Williamsburg Bridge and the Hassidic Jewish community on the other. The contrast was striking, much like my budding relationship with Mike. When I exited the Bedford stop of the L train I walked through a sea of bikes, unlike anything I had seen in Manhattan. I felt overdressed in my sexy chiffon dress, as every other woman seemed to be wearing worn-out plaid shirts and cut-off jeans with combat boots. The style was grunge with a mild preppy twist. Reminded me somewhat of my punk-rock days hanging out in the East Village.

Mike lived in a huge artist's loft, easily ten times bigger than my apartment, shared with two or three roommates. But since Mike had created the space from scratch, he made his room half the size of the entire space. I later learned that this was a grand source of mutiny within his roommate community.

Mike's response? "Hey, they don't like it, they don't have to live here."

My initial read was accurate: Mike was arrogant. Yet he also had a super sweet caring side. Mmmmm, that magical first hug...

While cooking in Mike's grungy yet grandiose kitchen, his roommates, and guests of the roommates, would weave in and out grabbing food from the fridge or passing through to the bathroom. Mike got a kick out of informing them of my No-Dutch rule. This was a first for me, to be with a man who had multiple roommates. Though Mike was only six years my junior, his collegiate style of living made him seem much younger. It was charming at first. Many things are charming at first.

Though Mike's arrogant demeanor was questionable, there was no doubt about his cooking abilities. He began by opening a bottle of organic merlot that he poured into a decanter to air. We sipped our goblets throughout the preparation of Mike's superbly tender, well-seasoned steak with roasted vegetables. Later he served hot homemade brownies topped with vanilla ice cream. Yum! He earned delicious brownie points for the entire spread. When we left the dining room table, Mike grabbed the remaining wine as we entered his private space. Wow, no wonder his roommates were jealous. His space was humungous, easily more than 1500 square feet.

Giving me the grand tour, Mike showed me some of his paintings and photographs. He had taken some really lovely landscape shots but he also took head shots for actors. Knowing that photography can pull in a decent salary, I relaxed a tad about him paying for dinners. We settled on his couch and watched Fellini's *Satyricon*. Strange flick for a romantic night but with that scrumptious dinner I forgave his entertainment choice. However, we actually sat through the entire movie, one I could have easily done without. I don't think I've ever sat through even a good movie with a guy before we started making out. Though I loved Fellini's work and the man himself (I had met him in Rome on a fashion shoot), I was not a fan of *Satyricon*. Not a hug, a kiss, or a hand was held throughout this Fellini ordeal. It was odd, just like the movie.

As the movie finished I stretched, yawned, and excused myself for the bathroom. Planning my exit strategy, I figured I'd tell Mike that I had an early day the next morning and needed to go. But when I returned to his room there were candles blazing and samba music raging.

Finding it impossible to hide my delight I asked with glee, "Ah, is this the final curtain call?"

Mike came up to me and held my waist, "Final? No my dear, we are just getting started."

Mike kissed me passionately, which was very nice although I felt as though he was eating a sandwich while he devoured my lips. But hey, he was a great chef, clearly eating was a thing for him. I surely felt like his kisses were eating my face off!

Somehow Mike's face-eating kisses became more sensual and soft as we disrobed and entered the lover's dance.

"Aaah, this is muuuuch better..." I thought as I sank into our sexing. But I kept wondering what happened to the guy that hugged me so tenderly that first night. I longed to make love with that guy. Little did I know then that this had been my life-long pursuit. I wanted desperately to make love but always resorted to making sex. Sex I understood and could control. Making love was completely unpredictable. It was deep, intense, out of control, and happened only rarely. It was everything I wanted and feared the most.

Like so many men, Mike rolled over after his orgasm, game over. He never even asked if I had cum. Bad bed manners. If Mike were merely a one-night stand I would have made sure I came. Otherwise, what would be the point? But feeling that there was a possible relationship here, I didn't feel the need to be so self-centered and could let my orgasm slide.

"No big deal," I milled about in my head and heart. "I'll get it from someone else tomorrow...or do it myself."

Then I rolled over to sleep. Yet within a few minutes I felt Mike climbing over me. I expected he needed to pee. But when I did not hear footsteps I became curious and opened my eyes. Mike was standing next to me, facing me, with his legs spread wide and bent. He was taking long, deep breaths with a huge smile on his face.

I had to ask, "What are you doing?"

"I'm circulating my sexual energy," he replied.

Thinking I found the weirdo of all weirdos I said, "I'm going to roll over and pretend I didn't see that."

Mike woke me with an invite to stay for breakfast. Yikes, I hesitated but I was beyond hungry so I accepted, praying he wouldn't want sex too. Wasn't sure if I'd be up for another round with him, it was not the greatest sex and it ended on such a weird note. However, all those tense thoughts left my mind while Mike prepared an absolutely scrumptious breakfast of fried eggs, bacon, and blueberry pancakes with real maple syrup. He even curled a slice of orange in the center of the plate. The coffee was fresh-brewed, and so too was my sass.

I then told Mike, "I'm going to be pretty busy in the next week launching my Dynamic Dating Parties so not sure if I'll be able to see you."

"Dynamic Dating Parties. What are they? I thought you said you were a legal secretary."

One fall-out from serial dating: it was tough to remember who I told about what.

"I am a legal secretary, yes. But I also work part-time as a dating coach. Dynamic Dating Parties are like speed dating parties combined with coaching."

Mike laughed, "Yeah, you tell all dem bitches what they're doing wrong!"

I had to laugh too, "Sure I wake up the women but I also wake up the men. You'll learn a lot if you stick with me."

"Yeah, bring it on sister," Mike said.

"Okay Mike, here is your first bit of coaching. Ladies first. Men don't cum until the ladies cum. No questions asked."

Mike's reply, "But you came last night, right?"

"No sir I did not."

"But I heard you." Mike insisted.

"Hey, remember how Meg Ryan faked it at the deli in *When Harry Met Sally*? Sure, I was having a good time with you last night and I made lots of ecstatic noises. However, I did not climax."

Mike looked perplexed.

I continued, "If you want to know if a woman came, ask her. She may lie and fake it but that's not your issue."

"Damn, you don't pull any punches do you?"

I gathered my things and headed for Mike's door to return home. Then I came up with a brilliant idea and turned around.

"Hey Mike, like I said, I'll be busy launching my new business. The website is nearly done but I still need a few more photos of dating couples. Would you be interested in posing with me?"

"Yeah, I don't see why not," he replied.

"Great! And I will get to see you again this week." I said.

Mike smiled softly. Poor guy, I must have bruised his ego with that orgasm-lashing. But hey, bad manners should be weeded out before they grow. Mike moved to embrace me. This time his kiss had less of a sandwich-eating quality. He was tender and felt more meaningful, like his spectacular hug the night we first met.

When our sweet sensual kiss was over I looked into Mike's eyes and told him, "I had such a wonderful time with you last night and this morning. You cook like a master chef and I really enjoyed being intimate with you too... except for that circulating energy thing you did."

"Oh come on now, that is high-level Tantra," Mike defended.

I broke out laughing, "Please, don't do that again. It hits my weirdo button."

Mike gave me a playful smack on the bum.

When I returned to Mike's loft to pick him up for the photo shoot his hair was soaking wet and he was only partially dressed.

I moved in to kiss him on the lips but he gave me his cheek. He seemed very down.

"You okay there?" I asked.

"Ah...just got a case of the blues. Rain can do this to me, lower atmospheric pressure and all."

"Do you want to cancel?"

"No," Mike replied, "I'll be fine. Just slow and not as sunny as you, Tinker Bell."

Mike smiled briefly and gave me a hug. It felt sweet.

He said, "It is important for me to plow through these depressions or I end up in bed for the day."

This was the first time Mike revealed his emotional struggles to me. I thought nothing of it until later, when it became a progressive problem. Note to self: People tell you who they are right up front. Pay attention!

During the shoot, when Mike left for a bathroom break, my old friend Rachel, who was the photographer, told me, "Shantz, this guy is really hot and I think he's nuts about you."

I thought about it and responded, "Weeell, I do like him. But I have the feeling he won't go for me dating my entourage if I stay with him. He is the monogamous kind of guy."

"But Shanti, you want that. You can't keep Yigal forever. You know that girl."

Upon Mike's return I gazed at him more purposefully, more intimately. I didn't know much about him but I did know that he was tall, dark, handsome, sensitive, sweet, arrogant, creative, and a great cook. Mike was only six years my junior so that was not too bad. Yigal was 16 years my junior. He was too young to know what he wanted and my baby clock would be broken by the time he figured it out.

Finished with the photo shoot, Mike and I helped Rachel load her car with gear and then we continued to eat and drink in the restaurant. Mike was laughing and smiling a lot so I guessed his depression lifted. The bill came and I paid for it. Without a word, Mike put his hand over his heart and nodded his head. It was a sweet way of expressing thanks. I was letting myself fall for Mike.

Later, we returned to his loft and made love. It was not sex. It was love and it was something I had only done in the past five years with Yigal. It scared me. I wasn't ready to let go of Yigal.

"Did you cum yet?" Mike asked.

Awweee, he remembered to ask me. But I was far from being near an orgasm. I needed sex to orgasm. I needed to do or fantasize about kinky situations to climax. Yigal was the only one that held the key to the making love orgasm, but I couldn't tell that to Mike.

"I did not cum yet sweetness but it is okay. Thanks for asking. I don't always cum when I make love, especially when I am just getting to know someone. You go. You have one, honey."

Within minutes he released his orgasm and we cuddled in that sweet lover's embrace for a very long time.

After an extended nap we both awoke to hungry tummies. Mike went for groceries and cooked up another amazing dinner. I paid close attention to Mike's recipes for I wanted to replicate them for Yigal. I know, learning from Mike to give to Yigal, bad. But that was how it was back then. I gave the best of everything to Yigal, he was my total love addiction.

After dinner we talked. We talked a lot, and I felt it was time to tell Mike about my other lovers.

"Mike, are you seeing anyone else?"

"Why do you ask?"

"I ask because I am seeing a few people. I just want you to know that."

I gave him a polite "few." What was I supposed to say, I'm dating eight or ten people?

Mike took a brief pause, "I'm seeing a couple of ladies myself."

I wasn't sure if it was true but I felt relieved.

"Okay good," I said.

Then he asked, "Is it good?"

This prompted a discussion about monogamy and polyamory.

I explained to Mike, "I became a reluctant polyamorist after dating a very young Israeli guy whose family would not accept me because I was not Jewish."

"I'm half Jewish."

Feeling the adrenaline surge throughout my body I asked tentatively, "Which half?"

"My father. He's a Russian Jew, second generation in this country. You didn't get Russian all over me with the last name Chukovsky?"

"I figured you were Russian, yes. You look Russian. But I did not think about you being Jewish. There were no Jewish symbols in your place and so I did not think to ask."

"My mother is Irish. How's that for an intense combination?"

"Did she convert?" I asked.

"Hell no. My mother? You don't know my mother."

I was beyond relieved to hear that his mother was not Jewish. Technically, Mike was then not considered Jewish. I felt a ray of hope that his family would not reject me.

I asked, "Does your family have a religious preference for who you date or marry?"

"They'd prefer I date someone who loves me."

"Awweee, that is so sweet!"

I wished desperately that this had been the case with Yigal's family. But after four years of trying I had given up. They would never change their stance against me.

The polyamory discussion went on for quite a while. At times I defended the lifestyle choice, other times I rejected it.

Mike probed further. "So what is your end-game? You just want to keep a wheel of men spinning?"

Feeling attacked I defended myself by giving Mike the short version of my relationship with Yigal, how we stayed together but dated other people in hopes of finding partners that might someday take our places.

I said, "So, this is how I got into polyamory."

Mike took some time, then asked, "Are you still seeing this Israeli guy?"

"Yes, not often but on occasion," I told him.

"And... have you tried monogamy with anyone else?

"I was monogamous with someone soon after 9/11 but it only lasted for a few months."

Mike asked, "Why was that?"

"He wanted children. He figured I would be too old to have more children when he'd be ready for them. So he broke up with me."

Mike said, "That's a breeder for you."

"Why? You don't want kids?"

"No, I can barely take care of myself," he replied.

"But you know I have a daughter."

"Yes, but she is your responsibility, not mine."

Though I was enjoying Mike's vulnerability and depth, I was often repelled by his gruff manners and condescending attitudes. Mike was like two different people in one body. At times so sweet and caring and other times cold and aloof, even cruel. But since I was not dating him exclusively I could let go of his bad qualities and focus on the qualities that I liked. However, one day his Mr. Hyde came out in full force, not to be ignored.

Chapter 18

Meeting Mike's Medea

Mike asked me to join his improve group for a special event. He wanted me to perform and also give my input during rehearsals. Besides photography, Mike also did construction and painting for income. Yet at heart, he wanted to be an actor. With my scars from sexual abuse in Hollywood, I was less than thrilled about his career choice. But without much thought, I accepted Mike's request.

As the event drew nearer and rehearsals were being scheduled, I felt this green glob in my gut, I was revolted by the idea of acting again. With an email message I retracted my offer to support his improv event. I cited my old acting scars and gave my deepest apologies.

Good thing this communication was via email for I could not have handled Mike's reaction in person. He wrote me a set of scathing emails that basically ripped me a new asshole about how irresponsible, inconsiderate, and selfish I was.

I tried to explain to Mike how I left acting due to constant sexual harassment and the idea of acting again was bringing it all up. He could have cared less. I had not kept my word and given him what he wanted. That was all that mattered to Mike.

Three weeks into meeting Mike, this was how he presented himself? I have since learned that people usually show who they are fairly early on and not much changes from there. At the time, I had not yet learned this. Also I was not aware that the dance of anger and narcissism was a complex pattern engraved deeply within me. My mother was rarely concerned about my needs because she was drowning in a sea of her own. Anger was my mother's go-to emotion and I was now embroiled with a man who was just like her.

Days passed without a word from Mike and so I entertained myself with other men and, of course, Yigal. Yigal made everything better. He was almost never angry, always fun, funny, interesting, sexy, loving, and he adored the ground I walked on. Finally, I sensed Mr. Hyde calming down as Dr. Jekyll appeared to be accepting my apology. Mike emailed me wanting to get together to discuss our head-banging.

"Ugh," I thought. "More beating this dead horse? He's reincarnated twice already!"

But still, I found Mike compelling and so I agreed to meet. Mike pleaded his case once more, and as before, it was all about Mike, no compassion for my needs, as I would eventually learn. Even his contributions to me were all about making me happy to keep Mike happy. But it was a couple years down the line before I finally got that about Mike, a narcissist incarnate. At this juncture, I did my best psych 101 performance: listen and empathize if you want them eventually to hear you. It worked and Mike was grateful.

Later he asked me, "Have you ever done any healing work about acting?"

I replied, "I have been meditating for over twenty years. Does that count?"

"I guess not because you are still clearly affected by this."

I hated Mike's poignant response yet I found myself speechless. In between his arrogance and narcissism was great wisdom. I did so appreciate that about Mike and so I put up with this handsome bulldog. No other man that I was dating challenged me. The others all accepted me unconditionally. But Mike, he made me question everything, something I had not done for many years. Until now, I was only interested in staying happy, avoiding pain, staying sexually high, and keeping Yigal.

Chapter 19

Connecting with Costa Rican Hottie

Occasionally I'd keep in touch with Leonard Hernandez, the Costa Rican hottie I met at the polyamorous meeting with Adriana. I kept hoping he might lose his interest in polyamory so I'd go fishing. I sent him an email.

"So... how's the polyamory going?" I asked.

He replied, "Not good. I recently met a really nice polyamorous woman from Mexico. I was so happy to finally meet a bisexual woman who wanted to be polyamorous and not have to convince her. But after a few weeks with her she tells me she wants to go back to monogamy with a man, maybe get married and have children. She wants to be monogamous with me. My luck!"

"Maybe you should try it for a little while? Might not be so bad," I suggested.

"That would mean you and I won't be able to connect then," he teased.

Leonard finally admitted it. He was interested in me. My loins leapt and pulsated.

I replied, "Well, I would absolutely accept your offer handsome if you would be open to being monogamous with me. Of course not right away but ultimately, that is what I'd be looking for. Guess you'd be having the same issue with me."

In addition to being super handsome and hot with his long dark mane and caramel colored skin, Lenny was calm and even-tempered. He was a great sounding board for me when things got tense with Mike. I told Lenny about the abusive emails Mike had spewed.

Lenny told me, "You want him to be your rock and not crumble when you shake the earth."

I didn't know exactly what he meant. Yet deep in my gut it felt right.

He continued, "You need to feel free in your feminine essence, which is wild and unpredictable by nature. Whether you scream at him, throw things, or cancel your plans at the last minute, you want him to remain un-fazed, like a brave soldier."

"Exactly!"

"See, if he cannot be your rock then you can not allow your full feminine nature to crash safely against him. This is the dance of the masculine and feminine."

I asked, "Where could I find such a man?"

"Some men are more inclined this way but most of us need to be trained. I've been taking workshops with David Deida, the man who brought this awareness to light."

"Mike is quite the hot head, he is more molten lava than a rock."

Lenny laughed, "And what about your Israeli man? You never complain about him. He is your primary relationship, right?"

"Yes, he is totally my rock. Well, most of the time. But how can he be my rock if he refuses to marry me?"

Lenny suggested, "Maybe deep down you really don't want monogamy and this polyamorous lifestyle is working for you."

"No, no, my polyamory was born out of pain. I wouldn't do it if Yigal had agreed to marry me. I'd be totally happy just being with him. We were monogamous for the first two years and I was in heaven before we started this crazy polyamorous path. It's only because his parents refused to accept me that we created this insanity."

"Were you monogamous before him?" Lenny asked.

"Yes, well, I only started being completely monogamous when I met my husband in 1989."

"What do you mean by completely?"

I explained, "I was technically in monogamous relationships in the 80s but I always cheated on my boyfriends."

Lenny said, "So, maybe deep down you really are a polyamorous person."

The idea totally terrified me. I wanted desperately to find normalcy in my life.

"Dear God I hope not!"

Lenny ended the email but requesting my home address, he wanted to send me something.

I was imagining roses but what I received was a CD of talks by David Deida. There was no fragrance of flowers yet the gift left an everlasting perfume in my soul. It was in these talks that I heard once more about the concept of men being the rock in a woman's life.

It rang true for me completely. Yigal was the only one that could stand strong during my storms. But then again, Yigal was not giving me what I wanted. Yet maybe, Yigal was in fact giving me exactly what I wanted. Was that possible? I listened to this CD over and over again, soaking in the newfound wisdom. I grew to like Lenny more and more, even with his polyamorous tendencies.

Chapter 20

Managing Mike's Moodiness

The Improv Disaster became our ultimate crash test: we both agreed never to email one another with emotional charge. That said, I was never quite sure what would set Mike off, but I did my best. According to David Deida's theory, I was the rock with Mike crashing his tantrums upon me. Yet for all his emotional drama, Mike was very insightful. I really enjoyed our psychological and philosophical discussions.

Mike stumbled upon my aloneness phobia one day and inquired, "What do you mean you are never alone?"

"I hate being alone so I am almost never alone," I replied.

"That can't be."

I pondered, "Why is that so strange? I live with my daughter, I work in an office, I go to the gym, I date, I have tons of friends and I live in New York for God's sake. It's nearly impossible to be alone here and that's the way I like it. If I wanted to be alone I'd live in the woods."

Mike replied, "But everyone needs to be alone to download and reflect."

"No, not me," I replied.

Mike would not let this go.

He continued, "What do you feel when you are alone?"

"Sad."

"Ah, now we are getting somewhere," he replied with a smile of conquest. "This sadness is looking to be examined and released but you are never giving it an outlet."

I replied, "Yes and I prefer not to give it an outlet."

"Okay Tinker Bell. You can keep flitting around all smiley and shiny but at some point you are going to crash."

I reminded Mike, "Tinker Bell was also jealous and had a nasty temper. She is not all smiles and giggles."

"Well that's good to know. Welcome to the human race."

My relationship with Mike had more the quality of a brother/sister rivalry than the play of lovers. Although our lovemaking was reaching extraordinary heights of ecstasy, due in large part to me letting go of my resistance to training him, outside the bedroom our relationship was often tense. Mike often complained that he had to paint apartments and do carpentry to make money. I confronted him about it.

"What is wrong with being a carpenter? Jesus was a carpenter."

"Very funny Sister Shanti. I hate the stigma of manual labor and being dirty all day long," he said.

I replied, "That stigma is all about ego. Why should you care?"

"I care because I know I am much more qualified than just being a carpenter. I am a good actor," he said.

I replied, "In my book, being a carpenter is way more respectable than being an actor."

"Yes but your book is skewed by your own acting wounds," Mike said.

Then he got quiet, which usually meant he was trying to calm his anger. I braced myself.

Then he said, "So I see you won't be very supportive of my new career."

I replied, "Maybe if you were in your twenties, but you are forty. There are a ton of well-seasoned actors at your age already. Hollywood is looking for an ingénue."

Mike walked away, slamming the door to his bedroom.

That's what he always did when he was furious. I learned to stop chasing after him, to let him cool down. Half an hour of me reading a book and still no Mike. I ventured into the common space, but there was no Mike to be found. Fuming, I left the loft too.

Our disastrous dance of anger often went exactly like that. I did or said something, usually unintentional, and it would piss Mike off. Mike got angry and abandoned me, sometimes for a day or two but most often for a week. I would get angry in response, until my abandonment issues kicked in with intense fear and grief, causing me to apologize profusely and beg Mike to return. I would apologize even if I felt I did nothing wrong, my abandoned child needed him back at all costs. While I was still seeing Yigal and the other men, I was better able to manage my reactions. Yes, I would still get angry but then I'd merely contact other men and have fun with them until Mike resurfaced. But my man train was soon to derail, leaving few survivors.

We made up as we always did after a big blowout fight, with delicious lovemaking. We'd forgive and forget easily, at least I did. On one fine summer night in early June of 2004, I met up with Mike at a French restaurant in Williamsburg. There were candles everywhere. Mike was dressed nicer than I'd ever seen him, a button-down shirt and jacket and he even oiled his thick, wavy black hair that I loved so much. He was happy, sporting the biggest grin I'd ever seen. Something was up but I had no idea what. It was my birthday in two weeks, maybe an early birthday present?

After we placed our orders Mike pulled out a single long-stem red rose from his backpack. It was sitting erect in a small Evian water bottle.

I immediately thought, "That's a bohemian for you."

Though I nursed that casual thought I felt anything but casual. My shoulders tensed, my stomach completely turned, and I nearly fainted. I was not weak-kneed because of Mike's funky flower presentation. I was weak-kneed because of its nature: this was clearly an overt romance operation. Mike stared at me for the longest time with a huge grin. I felt ill. He finally spoke.

"My dearest Shanti, I love you very much. Will you be my girlfriend and be monogamous with me?"

Mmmmmmonogamous? The M word scared the crap out of me. I immediately saw Yigal in my mind's eye, then I saw Lenny, my budding romance. The others were inconsequential and replaceable. I felt threatened and wanted to bolt but I didn't want to lose Mike either. He was currently number two in the rankings.

145

God, I wanted to decline Mike's offer desperately but he looked too happy. I didn't want to hurt his feelings and my love addict couldn't lose him.

Mike asked, "Are you okay?"

"Yes, I am okay, just a little frozen," I replied.

"So... what thoughts are you having at this moment?" he asked.

Teetering between telling the truth and fueling an illusion I chose the truth, leaving out some hurtful details.

I replied, "I'm thinking that although I'd love to be in a relationship with you, I have been with Yigal for five years. It will not be easy for me to let go of him."

I began to tear, completely out of my control.

Mike took my hand with great compassion and asked, "May I ask when was the last time you saw him?"

This is where I threw in a lie: "four or five weeks ago."

Truthfully I had seen Yigal less than one week ago.

"And why haven't you seen him since then?" Mike asked.

I told him, "Because I have been trying to wean myself from him."

"And why would you be doing that?" Mike asked.

"Because I wanted to see what it might be like to only see you."

Mike's smile grew larger. Mind you, I did not say anything about the other guys I had seen in the last few weeks. Sex/love addicts usually hide much of our sexual and romantic activities from others, knowing it could cause a stir. Alcoholics, drug addicts, food addicts and compulsive gamblers do the same. Secret and hidden behaviors are one of the markers of addiction.

Mike continued his inquisition, "And what has it been like seeing only me?"

I took a huge breath wanting to be totally honest or at least honest about my feelings if not my deeds. I told Mike, "It has been very sexy, quite mentally stimulating, and at times incredibly tender and sweet. Yet I could do without the emotional terrorist attacks that you spring on me."

Mike gloated, "Welcome to being in a relationship."

After two months of dating, Mike popped the monogamy question and sent my polyamorous world into a tailspin. I felt Mike might be right, it was time for me to commit myself to one man and Yigal would never be that one. Though I was hot for Lenny I didn't really know him well and Lenny still wanted polyamory so my decision seemed clear.

I told him, "Mike, I am honored that you want to be with me, I care so deeply about you. I am absolutely terrified and part of me wants to flee but yes, I will be your girlfriend and be monogamous with you."

"Alright," Mike exclaimed.

Mike got out of his chair, held me tight, and kissed me passionately. There was a bit of that lip-eating in the kiss but I was getting used to it. Mike's kissing had already shifted dramatically in the bedroom: slower, more sensual, and passionate. That is what I cared most about. The main focus of my life was in the bedroom.

Chapter 21

Mike and Monogamy Revisited

I broke up with Yigal on the phone. Five years of an intense love affair was over. Of course Yigal wanted to meet in person to discuss my decision but I knew that would end in our sleeping together, not a great start to monogamy with Mike. My tears poured like a flash flood as I said good-bye to my deepest love, Yigal.

"Shanti, come on now. Please baby, you know I can't take it when you cry. I hate that we are not going to see each other but maybe this is good, maybe this guy will be the right guy for you."

Sobbing more intensely: "Yigal, how will I live without you?"

"Shanti, listen baby, you know I am always here if you need me, always. But I will not call and bother you. You need to give this a chance."

Yigal continued, "But I will always love you Shanti. I have never loved anyone like I have loved you and I probably never will." I heard the sound of muffled sobbing.

"Yigal, I hate this so much. I hate your parents. I hate your culture!"

"Shanti come on please stop. It is life, that is all. We don't always get what we want. There is nothing we can do about it."

That last sentence of Yigal's reminded me of how he never had the balls to stand up to his parents and this made it easier to let him go.

Preparing to hang up I said, "I'm not going to say good-bye, I'm going to say good night my love. Please have the most beautiful dreams of us. I pray that one day we can be together again.

And just like that, we were done.

I lay motionless on my bed, more from shock than grief. I began asking myself, "What have I done?" Since I was in the disconnecting mood I decided to call Lenny as well. We had mainly an email relationship but since I would be cutting off communication with him too, I thought it would be nice to speak first. Maybe see if I was making the right decision?

"*Hola* Lenny."

"*Hola*. Who is this?" he asked.

"It's Shanti."

"Oh, hello sexy Shanti, nice to hear from you! How are you?"

I told him, "Well, I'm not so great. I've decided to give monogamy a try with Mike."

He replied, "You sound thrilled about it!"

Laughing I replied, "I know, right? But I do really care about him, just sad that I will have to let go of Yigal and people like you."

Lenny responded, "Funny, because I kind of got roped into monogamy myself."

"What? You mean with the Mexican girl?"

"Si Señorita."

"Oh wow, we both got our wings clipped!"

In unison we burst out laughing.

Lenny reminded me, "Nothing in life is permanent. Keep in touch Señorita, if you want to, for I would really like that."

Though I had no intention of communicating with Lenny while with Mike, it was crucial for me to have sexy safety nets awaiting should I fall from this new bout of monogamy. Clearly I was entering this new union with great trepidation. I knew the land mines that lurked between Mike and me so I was cautious. Yet I was also hopeful that Mike might feel safer, knowing that I was all his, and this might lead to fewer explosions. Ah, the delusion of hope.

Two weeks passed with very few bumps. Mike lavished me with an exquisite private birthday party - dinner, wine, presents, a massage, and yummy lovemaking. I was feeling soft and warm with him, perhaps even falling in love with him. However, I could not let myself go there quite yet. Then we approached week three of monogamy. Rebecca was now out of school for the summer and with her Dad most of the time. Summer was Mommy's time to play and I celebrated by spending three days and nights with Mike, wrapped around a weekend at his place. However, all I got was a frozen shoulder each time I approached Mike for affection or sex.

Friday night's brush-off was not such a big deal because I was exhausted from an unusually long week, not from office work but from friends and co-workers who treated me to birthday dinners and drinks. So I rather relished a full night's sleep. But the morning did not produce a sexual feast.

I spoke with Mike over breakfast: "Hey, what's up with you? You seem distant?"

"Why, because I won't give you the sex you want?"

Mike's tone was sharp. I felt like saying, "Exactly, asshole!" But what I said was, "No, it's fine not to have sex. But no affection either?"

"You know Shanti, sometimes I just don't feel like being touched. Is that okay with you?"

I replied, "It is okay but why the anger about it?"

"I don't feel like talking about this. But it has nothing to do with you so you can stop worrying."

I decided to pull out my sneakers and go for a run, giving Mike some space to deal with whatever he had going on.

Mike was in a foul mood and I wanted nothing to do with it, so I allowed my post-running promenade to linger a couple of hours. The weather was sunny but not too hot. The street action was fun, upbeat, festive bohemian and I dreaded my return to the loft.

Meeting Mike in the kitchen, he spoke first, "Did you have fun avoiding me?"

"Mike, I was not avoiding you." That was a lie but I didn't want to start a fight. "I wanted to give you space. How are you feeling?"

"Shitty."

"Would you prefer I go back home?" I asked.

Mike shot me a glare from hell, "No, I would prefer you to stop looking down your pretty little Tinker Bell nose at me. Not everyone can be as perky as Patty."

"I am not always perky Mike but that's besides the point. Can we sit down and talk this out?"

Mike softened a bit as we retreated to his room.

"This No-Dutch rule is not working for me any more," he told me. "Now that we are a couple we are seeing each other more and I can't afford to keep paying for you."

His bad mood was making more sense now. I was spending three days and nights with him and that meant nine meals.

"Mike, I told you when we first met that this rule could change if we became a couple and I am making more money than you. We can share the cost of groceries and maybe take turns treating at the restaurant."

Mike remained silent except for some noisy facial expressions of discontent.

"Mike, talk to me."

"You know what? I am not happy with my life. I hate the work I do but I need it to survive and now it's very sparse. I have no money to do anything."

After a long silence I made Mike an offer. "How about I take you out to dinner tonight? We can rent a good movie and bring a bottle of wine back here. My treat for everything."

I thought he might stay sour but he jumped up, hugged and kissed me, and danced me around the room. And we had an absolutely wonderful night together. Mike was having money stress, that is what I thought anyway. But when I tried to kiss Mike after the movie was over, he pushed me away. I knew something else was still up with him, or not up actually.

"Mike, what's going on?"

"Why, just because I don't want to have sex every day, something has to be wrong?"

"Well, it feels like something is wrong. You are not being sweet about declining me. Why be so aggressive with me?"

Mike replied, "Because I feel your neediness pawing at me. You don't want sex for my sake, you want it for your sake."

I thought about what Mike said and there was some truth to it. Of course I wanted sex for my sake. But, no other man had ever refused me sex before. Rebecca's father Jeremy never rejected me. He just never pursued me. It felt horrible to be rejected. What does it mean if he doesn't want sex? I always wanted sex, except years ago when I was married to Jeremy. I was guessing Mike lost his attraction to me, as I had lost it for Jeremy. I was scared and completely lost. Was the relationship over?

I asked Mike, "So, what am I supposed to do, wait for you to approach me?"

"Yes, that would be good."

I didn't like his answer but I backed off and spent the next two days without sex - not a hug, a kiss, or even a peck on the cheek. We slept on opposite sides of the bed. By Monday night I figured I was safely out of purgatory and went to kiss Mike goodbye but he strongly shoved me away. Three days of frustration and rejection finally came spilling out.

"Mike, I am done. Three days of icy coldness is enough. I don't know what your problem is. I have done everything in my power to be compassionate and patient with you but now I'm toast. I'm out of this relationship Mike."

He just stared at me with his dark evil glare. I threw the new set of keys that Mike just made for me on his table and slammed the front door.

Four days passed with no communication from Mike. But without some explanation for his ice wall, we were done. As Friday soon approached I desperately wanted to go out so I called my old friend Basak. He took me to a fabulous restaurant, a sexy movie, then back to my place for crazy all-night sex. God, I needed that.

As my bad luck would have it, Mike called me Saturday morning during my sex fest. My ringer was off but not my libido. When we were done I played Mike's tearful voicemail message.

"Shanti, I am really sorry honey. Can you please call me? I need to see you. I miss you."

Fuck, now he calls me? It's too late, I've gone and fucked someone else. Well, so much for monogamy. With my heart full of emotions, I needed to think about what I really wanted from Mike, if anything, before I called him back. Three days living with Mike's rejection, then another four days of abandonment with no apology, was hellacious. I couldn't live with that again. But his sweet tearful voice pulled me right back in. I decided to just call him and not over-think this.

"Hi Mike."

"Shanti, thank you for calling me back. I've had a very rough week. I saw my therapist yesterday and discovered a bunch of crazy stuff came up for me with you staying at my place all weekend. Can we please meet up honey? I'd love to hold you and apologize."

Thinking to myself, "Now you want to hold me on your terms? Asshole!" Yeah, I was pissed.

I replied, "I don't know Mike. I gave you up for dead. Three days of distance when I was right under you nose and four more days of zero communication from you. Do I have to depend on your therapist to have a relationship with you?"

My angry distance with Mike crumpled quickly as he broke down in tears. "Shanti, I am devastated. I can't tell you how sorry I am. Please, can you give me another chance?"

I felt it would be better to tell Mike about my night of sexual debauchery in person, rather than on the phone. Having no idea what his reaction would be, I set out for Williamsburg.

Mike greeted me at his door with a huge hug and watery eyes. I wanted to soften but I was still angry. As soon as we got to his room he hugged be again but I pushed him away. Now I was the cold fish.

"Shanti, I don't blame you for rejecting me. I was cruel with you and I'm deeply sorry." Mike's tears began to flow.

"Mike, I'm happy that you're sorry but I have no guarantee that you will not do this again. It's not like this rejection went on for a day or even two days. It was over a long week and I will not live with that kind of abandonment."

"I know, I know. But I saw some really crazy shit about myself in therapy yesterday that made total sense about why I treated you that way."

"Okay, do you want to share that with me?" I asked.

Mike started off by explaining the extent of his financial woes and how my staying for three days without a break put it all in his face. He was no longer able to keep up his mask.

I replied, "But I thought we handled that when I told you we could share the grocery bills and swap restaurant checks?"

"I know honey but I still had shame about it. I felt like less of a man. That's why I wasn't feeling very sexy."

Mike asked to hold my hand. "Shanti, this next part is very vulnerable for me. I need you to understand what happened with me last weekend. Your continuous presence brought up an old wound."

As I became more present I lost all of my considerations and judgments and my heart opened to Mike.

"See, I was molested several time when I was in grade school by a male babysitter and mentor. Phew, I said it."

My eyes began to water.

Mike continued, "I could get into all the details but for now, what I want you to know, is that when you approached me sexually, when I was not interested, it brought up this molestation wound."

Mike began to cry. We embraced for a few minutes until Mike fell to the floor in a flood of sorrow. I dropped to the floor with him, cradling him in my arms. He wept on my shoulder for what felt like half an hour. It was scary for I had never had anyone weep so profusely in my arms. But I knew there was a deep healing taking place and so I just held him for as long as he wanted. Mike's sobs subside.

He wiped his face, blew his nose several times and said, "I'm sorry for dumping all this on you."

"No, it's okay. I'm happy that I could be here for you sweetie. I thought you might never stop crying though. That was a tad scary for me at times. How are you feeling now?"

Mike replied, "Vulnerable, embarrassed, relieved, exposed."

"Would you like to take a walk or do you want to stay here?" I asked.

"I'm starving but don't feel like cooking. Let's go grab a bite, get some air, some sun. I must look like shit."

I smiled, "No, you always look handsome."

Walking up Bedford Avenue looking for a quick fix, we bought a couple of burritos, ate them on a nearby stoop, then took a walk to the East River. In our silence I thought about how to confess my infidelity. Technically, we had broken up so it was not an infidelity, but it was indeed a fuck-you gesture to Mike.

We sat on a huge rock in the park by the river and took in the sun. I tried to think of a gentle way to approach my sex fest with another man last night. With my heart racing I just dove in.

"I need to tell you something about myself Mike. You know how you pull away when you get upset?"

"Yeah."

"Well, I merge when I get upset. When I get very upset I feel like I could fuck the entire football team," I said.

Mike chuckled a bit, "Okay but that's only a thought."

I just looked at Mike.

"Shanti, did you sleep with someone else this week?"

"Yes."

"Fuck!"

Mike jumped up and walked away.

I decided to stay on the rock until the emotional storm passed. I basked in the sun, relieved at least that I had exposed my sexual monster. After a while I decided to leave when I spied Mike walking back to me. He looked purposeful.

"Shanti, I'm sorry that I walked away. You just hit me so deep in my gut. Can we talk about this?"

We settled at a shady picnic table and I went on to explain, "When I am hurt I look for sex. It is my Band-Aid of choice. And since you rejected me sexually and made no effort to reconcile when I broke up with you, I thought we were over."

Mike asked, "But only four days apart and you sleep with someone else? How do you find someone that quickly?"

I got quiet, not sure what to say.

Mike got tense, "Not Yigal. Please don't tell me it was Yigal."

"No, not Yigal."

I saw his entire body relax. Still, I was terrified to reveal to Mike the extent of my safety net and how easy it was for me to find sex.

"Who was it?" he asked.

I replied, "It was an ex-boy toy. This guy was a fling at best, never a relationship. I just needed to feel wanted again."

I began to cry and Mike took me in his arms.

"Shanti, I am sorry that you felt abandoned by me. I didn't take your words as a break-up call but merely a fight and a wake-up call. I see now that I will have to take your words at face value and not merely a threat."

He started to chuckle, "I wouldn't want you fucking the entire football team."

Mike then gave me one of his fabulous hugs. I loved Mike so much in that moment. He saw a very shameful aspect of myself and didn't reject me for it. We began to kiss passionately.

Chapter 22

No More Sex with Adriana

Adriana invited me to her place for dinner one night, not long after my first big break-up and make-up with Mike.

I announced to Adri, while she was preparing the meal, "Mike and me, we are officially monogamous now."

"What does that mean?" she asked.

"That means you and me, we cannot be sexual together any more."

"Why? Most guys think it's hot for two women to be sexual together."

"Mike is not like most men. His mother left his father for a woman so there's a deep lesbian scar here."

"Ugh, this guy has too many scars for my taste."

"I know Adri, but I think I'm falling in love with him."

Mike called during dinner. I excused myself to take the call, but Adriana grabbed my phone. "Hi Mike, it's Adriana, the one you met the night you captured the heart of my best friend, Shanti."

I saw her smile so assumed he was pleasant with her. I never knew with Mike. Adri continued, "I want to get something straight. Shanti says that you two are now monogamous. Does this mean I can't do sensual research with her any more?"

Adriana's smile faded abruptly, as I grabbed the phone. "Mike, I'll call you when I get home honey."

He interjected, "Yes and none of this sensual research bullshit. Sex is sex."

Nearly two months passed without much friction, although Mike would rarely let anything slide if it hit him sideways. But my love for him deepened greatly and so too did my tolerance for his moodiness.

Then, one warm summer night in late August I went to Williamsburg after work to see Mike. I stopped at the pizza place for a slice and ran into Lenny.

"Lenny?" I asked.

"Yes?" he replied.

"It's Shanti."

"Oh wow, I didn't recognize you in your corporate robes."

"Yeah, I know. What are you doing here?"

"Oh I live about fifteen blocks away," Lenny replied.

"You're kidding. Mike, my boyfriend, lives only five blocks from here. How are you? How's monogamy going for you?"

Lenny replied, "Ah, I had to stop that. It just wasn't me. But funny thing is, she moved in and she's still there."

"That must be awkward, no?" I asked.

"Nah, she is like my best buddy now. We decided to be roommates."

After finishing our slices, Lenny walked me to Mike's place. We stopped at the corner to chat about the David Deida CD that he sent me months ago, and more about Deida's philosophy. I still found it fascinating the idea of a man being grounded and steady like a rock for the woman to crash upon. This surely was not the situation with Mike and me and I longed for it.

Then I heard Mike's voice booming, "Hey Shanti. What are you doing? Come up!"

I looked towards Mike's front door but no Mike.

"Up here!"

Mike was yelling from one of his fourth-floor windows. He was sporting a stern face.

I smiled and waved, "Coming!"

Lenny said, "So this is your hot-head."

"Yeah, I know. But he is sweet too."

"Whatever serves you best my dear Princess. Always at your service should you ever need me."

I took leave of Lenny but my turn on for him was not as easy to put aside.

When I got to the fourth floor Mike was waiting with an unhappy countenance. He had never waited for me at the door before. I sensed danger so I put on my happiest face, like somehow that would help?

I moved in to kiss him, but Mike pushed me away. Oh boy, here we go again. "Who was that guy?" he asked.

I explained, "Some guy I know. Ran into him in the pizza place."

Mike said, "I told you I would make dinner."

"I know honey but I was starving." I nuzzled up to Mike. But again, he pushed me away.

Mike told me, "I have a bad feeling about this guy."

"You were yards away. How do you know him?"

"And you were a half hour late chatting with Mr. Charming. I've seen him around the neighborhood before. He's a creep."

Throughout the meal preparation Mike was in a foul mood, throwing dishes in the sink with great force, slamming the refrigerator door, and barking to himself.

"Mike, are you upset because I was late? How many times have you been late and you never call to let me know. What's the big deal?"

Mike pierced me with one of his dark looks from hell but did not respond with words so I filled in.

"If you're not going to tell me what's up with you then I'm going home." I announced.

Mike continued to chop zucchini with great gusto. He did not look at me, nor did he speak. After ten minutes of the silent treatment I grabbed my bag and left. I knew full well that my departure would exacerbate Mike's foul mood but I didn't care. Especially after hearing Lenny talk about how women long for men to be their rocks.

I thought to myself, "This guy is not even a grain of sand, never mind a rock!"

A full day passed with no communication from Mike. I finally buckled and emailed him my apology for leaving but there was no response. No response by day two either. By day three I was deep into my abandonment issues. Thank goodness it was a Sunday for I stayed in bed all day while Rebecca was with her father. I left more voicemail messages but still, no reply. I called in sick for work Monday. I was sick, but what was I sick with? Love sick took on an entirely different meaning for me. It was more like love cancer and I was deep into stage four.

Two more days went by with no reply from Mike. I began formulating my carefully worded email. I wrote it, rewrote it, and edited it at nauseam. Initially there was too much anger and blame in the email. But as I got out my upset, I felt compassion for Mike's struggle as I too had suffered with rage issues. When I felt I had taken enough responsibility for my role in our partner dance of anger, I also acknowledged to Mike that I most likely brought out the worst in him and that we'd be better off apart. I was clear that this relationship was not working for me and wished him a teary farewell.

Two more days passed and still, no word from Mike. I decided not to call him, I guessed that he was done with me as well. I felt sad but mostly relieved. So, what did I do with my sadness? I did what I always did. I called a guy to get laid, to feel wanted, to feel loved, to feel alive again. Without a man I felt dead. One week without my fix and I was shaking from withdrawal symptoms. Ten pounds was enough to lose. I had zero appetite. Time to eat again and so I gorged myself on my favorite food, Yigal.

"Shanti, why did you wait so long to call me?" Yigal asked.

"I was trying to make this relationship with Mike work. It has only been two-and-a-half months since we saw each other last."

"That was too long!" Yigal declared.

"Yigal, I need to find a man that I can spend the rest of my life with. Two-and-a-half months is pitiful. But I can't stay with him, he is just too angry. You spoiled me."

We hung out all night Friday and all day Saturday. Then, while getting ready to see a movie Saturday night, I got a call from Mike.

"Shit, it's Mike," I exclaimed while watching the caller ID.

Yigal looked at my phone. "Don't answer it. He is going to tell you some bullshit about how sorry he is and that he wants you back. This guy is bullshit. Why give him the satisfaction of you

160

being always available? Let him sit in his angry bullshit. He didn't contact you for over a week. Fuck him."

I had never heard Yigal swear that much. He was clearly upset. But I knew he had my best interest at heart so I took his advice. I didn't even listen to the message until I got back to my place Sunday afternoon.

Fairly certain that I would receive a vulnerable message of apology from Mike, I needed to prepare my armor. Mike's anger never threatened me, but his vulnerability was a killer. I had no defense against it. I lay on my bed and took several deep breaths before hitting the play button.

"Hello Shanti, it's Mike. I have been a total basket case all week, not knowing what to say so I said nothing. You are right, you won't be able to have a relationship with me without my therapist. It's only after my sessions that I get the healing and clarity on what is going on with me. I understand why you want to break up with me and I don't blame you. But," Mike started to cry, "but... I miss you so badly. I've been crying every day not understanding why I release my rage onto you, I hate myself for it."

His message was so long that it cut off and he called back for round two. "Anyway, precious. I pray that you will give me another chance, even though I don't deserve one."

Damn, I was screwed. How could I say No to a request like that? Mike's vulnerability cut through my thin layer of armor and I called him right away. But I forgot he had called nearly 24 hours before. "Hello sweetheart," I opened.

"Sweetheart? If I was really your sweetheart, then why didn't you call me back last night? Too busy fucking someone else?"

Wow, Mike knew me well. He was clearly well over his vulnerable phase and back to being abusive so I let him have it.

"Oh Mike, you mean why didn't I call you back instantly like you never called me back in over a week? Sucks to be on the receiving end now doesn't it Mike?"

"Touché my dear. You win."

I replied, "We don't need to have this conversation. I said it all in my last email. Have a good life, Mike."

I hung up and felt proud of myself. I had refused Mike's mental and verbal abuse. I was relieved that Mike was not vulnerable with me on the phone. I immediately got on line and sent an email to Lenny before Mike changed his tune. I told Lenny all about my week from hell. He replied attentively.

"You knew this was going to happen," Lenny said. "But you didn't trust your instincts so you played it out. Now you know."

Thinking, but not writing, "Yes, now I know I finally can have sex with you, Mr. Hot Stuff, because I am free!"

My mood elevated to the ceiling. Like a heroin addict who just injected the needle, I was already feeling the effects of my attention fix. I was in bliss. I realized that with Mr. Angry Monogamy Mike out of the picture, I could start dating sweet, sexy Lenny. Though Lenny wanted polyamory and was not a good choice for the long haul, with Lenny I could still see Yigal. This was the perfect dynamic duo for this sex/love addict. From Yigal I got great love and sex but no commitment. From Lenny, I anticipated great sex and the possibility of great love. What else did I need? Maybe monogamy was not right for me after all.

I loved how quickly Lenny responded to me when I emailed him. That was hot. I loved instant gratification when it came to my man-fix. Actually, more than loving it, I had to have it. If I found a guy that was too busy or too slow on the response time, he never made the cut. I am sure most heroin addicts make sure their dealer gives the same lightning-fast delivery. When we are in pain, time is of the essence.

Chapter 23

Give Me Another Break

"Monday, Monday, can't trust that day" - truer lyrics from The Mamas & the Papas could not have been more real for me that Monday. I started Monday morning off with a joyful gait. I bounced all the way to the office, the office that I loved so much with co-workers that I absolutely adored. On top of this I was back with Yigal, the love of my life, and now I had Lenny, my new hot Costa Rican man, entertaining me and flirting with me. Life was very good.

High on my sex/love fix, I flirted shamelessly with everyone in the office, including Stuart. He was an easy target.

Stuart said, "You seem especially happy this morning Shanti. You must have had an exciting weekend with your new boyfriend. What's his name?"

"That's right," I replied. "What's his name is a great name for him because he is no longer with me."

"Oh, I thought you were serious about him," Stuart remarked.

"No, I'm done with him. He has a horrible temper. Better boys await me!"

Stuart's smile grew. I knew he was hoping that this break up could open possibilities for us again. I allowed the hope. I even alluded to it.

"Stuart, you are drooling on my documents darling. Keep your juices for private times. Catch you later."

After a fabulous Monday morning with my co-workers and clients, not to mention a sexy email from Lenny, I pranced out of the office at 1 p.m. to grab lunch. It was a gorgeous summer day. The sun was high in the sky and with it my soaring joy, until I spied

Mike. He was resting against a tree in front of my office. As soon as I left the lobby, there he was, staring at me with a remorseful face. Just when I had it all happily figured out, Mike had to come and ruin it all. Seeing Mike this openly vulnerable told me our dance of anger was not yet over. How I desperately wanted to sit this dance out. But I had no armor for this full attack of vulnerability. God, why can't I dump him?

With that signature hug from Mike I was hopelessly back in the addictive "love" cycle. I often put the word love in quotes when it really means neediness. I wasn't always sure that I loved Mike, sometimes I loathed him. But I was certain that I needed him. We spent my entire lunch hour in a tiny nearby park with the homeless, seniors, and pigeons.

During this tearful reunion Mike asked, "Were you with anyone while we were apart?"

Timidly I responded, "Yes."

"Damn it Shanti!" Mike jumped up and walked away from me.

"Mike, you can continue to walk away from me when you get angry or hurt but that will only perpetuate our cycle. You abandon me and I fuck someone. That's the way it goes. Keep abandoning me and I will keep fucking someone else."

Mike turned back to me, "But Shanti, don't you see how damaging this is to me?"

I replied, "As damaging as your abandonment is to me."

Mike sat down close to me and got quiet. "I'm afraid to ask," he said. "Was it… Yigal? Were you with Yigal?"

I hesitated, contemplating a lie. But I decided to be honest. If Mike couldn't take the truth then I was not meant to be with him. "Yes," I replied.

Mike sprang out of his seat again. "God damn it Shanti. No! Why Yigal?! You have plenty of other men. I am clear about that now. But why, why Yigal? He is the only one that I absolutely cannot take. Can't you see how hurtful this is? You are still in love with him, aren't you?"

I sat for quite some time contemplating my answer. If I merely wanted to smooth things over, make nice nice, then I would have lied. But I wanted a deep healing to take place, not just a temporary Band-Aid. I told Mike the truth. "Yes, I am still in love with Yigal."

Mike did not jump out of his seat this time but instead, buried his head in his hands and bawled. When Mike finally spoke he asked, "Shanti, if you love him so much, why don't you just stay with him?"

Mike's pain was hurting me. My pain was hurting me. I did my best to explain. "I want to get married again and share my life with someone Mike. This can never happen with Yigal. He has made it a thousand percent clear. I've told you that before."

Crying more profusely Mike said, "Shanti, I am in love with you. Of that I am a thousand percent sure. I would love to be that man you spend the rest of your life with."

I then joined in on the crying scene. Mike's tender devotion touched me deeply.

He pulled me close, "Honey, we need help. We can't keep doing this to one another. Would you be willing to see a couple's counselor with me?"

Off to counseling I went with Mike the next week. In the first session we got clear that Mike could not abandon me for more than three days and I was not allowed to sleep with anyone during those three days. Mike then made a request to the therapist. He asked, "In the event I am so upset I do not respond to Shanti in three days, can I make a request that if she does indeed sleep with someone else that she cannot, under any circumstances, sleep with Yigal?"

The therapist looked at me, "Shanti?"

Expressing an extremely long sigh, as if my entire five years with Yigal were in that one exhale, I responded, "Okay."

And with that declaration I finally stopped seeing Yigal, forever.

Chapter 24

Therapy Keeps Mike and Me Together

I hadn't been in therapy since a previous relationship with a hot-head, not long after my divorce. Mike, hot-head number two, found Ala Konopko for me in 2004, a great core energetics therapist. But I was highly triggered by the full spectrum of Mike's rage. In core we use equipment to open up areas of the body that hold emotional blocks. One piece of equipment, a large foam block that we smash with a tennis racket, moves the anger. During one of our joint sessions, I watched Mike smash the block with such force and verbal assaults I became frightened. But Mike was right about one thing, it was not healthy that I was incapable of being alone. I knew that to be true deep down but was afraid to acknowledge it.

After several sessions with Ala she gave me her assessment: "You are a very strong, courageous, intelligent, and capable woman. But you also have this extremely young wounded child inside that you rarely allow out. My guess is that your wounding began before you could speak because when you are in emotional turmoil, you have great difficulty expressing yourself verbally. Your abandonment issues with Mike hit on your childhood abandonment issues but your capable adult is too logical to allow this poorly expressed child to reveal herself. My role with you is to give attention and voice to this abandoned baby, then toddler, then grade-school girl, until your emotional self grows up and feels as powerful as your intellectual self. You will find, over time, that spending time alone will become easier and even desirable."

Ala was right. After only a few months working with her I was able to survive many beak-ups with Mike and not turn to having sex with someone else to ease my loneliness. I kept the three-day abstinence rule. However, I never agreed not to speak with another guy, or visit with another guy. I kept that element to myself. No one asked so I was not telling. Dangerous waters indeed but danger was a big part of my sexual drug.

2005 was a semi-calm year for Mike and me. I say semi because nothing was ever calm with Mike. But one Sunday morning we both exploded and the scene got quite ugly.

Mike asked, "Would you coach me after breakfast with a monologue I have for acting class?"

I really didn't want to. Instead of pretending it was okay with me, as I had done when he asked me to join his improve group, I simply declined his offer. I told Mike, "I appreciate your appetite to have me coach you but, I'm not feeling that would be a good idea."

Mike responded, "Why not? What's the problem?"

"Mike, you want to be an actor. That is your choice. I support you in following your passion. But I am not willing to help you in developing your craft because it is not a profession I admire any more. I have too many scars around it."

"Wow, that speaks volumes. So you don't respect me."

"I didn't say that," I replied.

"Well come on you alluded to it!"

"Mike, this line of conversation is going down a dangerous rabbit hole and I would rather not."

"Why not? It is already in the air. I can't pretend it never happened. Let's go for it."

I threw down my metaphoric gauntlet, "Okay fine. What do you want me to say Mike, that I love acting? That I am excited that you want to join a profession where few earn more than $500 a year and those in the limelight need to screw everyone in power? Is that what you want me to say?"

"Okay, now we are getting somewhere."

I felt the uglies coming out of me and could do nothing to stop them. Mike was pressing hard and the sexual harassment scars from my time in Hollywood were reopening.

"I'm not going to hide my opinions, especially when you ask me. I have been holding my tongue long enough. Follow your acting passion but don't expect me to be excited about it and don't ask me to aid you with it."

Mike stormed out of his room and slammed the door.

Thinking to myself, "Here we go again." I was not in a calm place to handle Mike's anger, I had my own anger to deal with. I got dressed and left Mike's place without saying good-bye. Oh boy, don't give a doctor a taste of his own medicine for he will barf all over you. That is exactly what Mike did. He must have called ten times that morning, leaving nasty messages, and sent a slew of rabid emails. I responded to none. I deleted without reading them. Let Mike see how it felt to be abandoned.

In that vein I did not contact Mike for two days. Then I called and left a voicemail. He did not contact me for three more days. By this time it was Friday morning and I wanted to plan my weekend.

I reviewed the agreed break-up rules in my head, "No sleeping with someone else for three days if Mike abandons me. Under no circumstances will I sleep with Yigal."

I didn't even include the two days I abandoned Mike. Gave him the benefit of the doubt. But it was Friday morning and I heard nothing from Mike. I couldn't wait to email Lenny.

"Hey hot stuff. Just had a blowout fight with my hot-head and must admit I got really hot as well this time. I'm done with him. You know any good dance places where I can kick it out? I am steaming mad!"

Lenny replied, "I do know a great place. I am actually going there tonight. Would you like to join me?"

Lenny offered me exactly what I wanted. But I was also open to canceling on him if Mike contacted me at the last minute. However, by 7 p.m. there was no word from Mike. All systems go for Lenny!

Prancing about my apartment while getting dressed I exclaimed out loud, "I am going dancing with Mr. Costa Rican Hot Stuff!"

We met at a yoga studio and moved through all kinds of improvisational dances and moving meditations. It was not at all what I had in mind. I had imagined a free-style sock hop with house music. We did a lot of twirling, crawling, growling, crying, and prancing. Finally, towards the end of this fairy dance, the instructor had us pair up and sit with our backs leaning against our partner. Lenny ran across the room to me. His appetite for me was hot, guess he didn't want me scooped up by anyone else. Maybe he had a monogamous gene after all?

Feeling Lenny's sweaty t-shirt was a turn off but I moved past it. Felt his back, his strength, felt his ass against mine, and felt my heat for him rising. When the dance was completely over, Lenny pulled out a clean shirt. That was nice. Then several of his lady fans swarmed around him. While he was lost in a swirl of attention, I checked my phone. No message from Mike. Alriiightie then, time to party. I decided that it was finally time for me to sleep with Lenny. Mike knew the rules. He made his choice.

Lenny took us to a Thai place nearby. The food was delicious but the place was noisy, we had to scream to hear one another. But we plowed through the meal as best we could. The waitress came by to ask if we wanted dessert.

Lenny replied, "We might want dessert but not here. We are going deaf and losing our voices." Then he paid for dinner without a dutch request. Good sign. This showed it was not a friendship meal, guessing he meant business tonight. I started getting those nervous sexual jitters I always felt when acquisition was near. Then Lenny grabbed me by the waist and pulled me in close.

He asked, "Would you like to come to my place for dessert? We can pick up some ice cream and cookies."

I laughed shyly. I loved how smooth he was. "I would love that," I replied, "but I have one request."

"Yes, my Princess."

I smiled at the reverent title he assigned me. I enjoyed it. In a million years Mike would never address me that way. It would indicate a level of worship he would never be willing to offer.

"Can we walk down Driggs Avenue instead of Bedford? Don't feel like running into Mike tonight. Too new, too raw."

"Of course my Princess. Happy to oblige."

Giggling I replied, "I like when you call me Princess."

"Yes my Princess."

We did pick up ice cream and cookies and we did indeed go to Lenny's for dessert. He was a great lover. He got me off with his fingers and tongue in record time. By all accounts I should have been happy. But his chubby belly reminded me that he was not Mike, who was very fit and lean, and Lenny's strong sexual energy without Mike's loving energy reminded me too that he was not Mike. I started missing Mike and regretting my decision to be with Lenny. Though I stayed the night and sexed with Lenny again in the morning, I wanted to go home in the worst way. I pulled the Rebecca card.

"Lenny, I have to pick up my daughter soon so I need to go."

"Of course my Princess. Your daughter will always come first. Let me know when you are next available. I would be delighted to see you again."

Huh, Lenny was not in competition with my daughter? Mike was always upset that Rebecca took a front seat in my life. What a nice guy.

I walked cautiously up Driggs Avenue to the L train, careful to avoid Bedford Avenue and the Saturday afternoon onslaught of hipsters. I was terrified to run into Mike or any of his friends. When I reached the safety of my apartment, I got into bed and cried profusely. I knew this sex/love addiction cycle all too well, even though I had no label for it at the time. I would be high with excitement the night before, hoping that Lenny, or whoever, might be The One. But in the clear morning light, I crashed. After a couple of hours of crying I called Adriana but she was not answering.

Well, that was it for the lesbian contingent. Lesbians were like guys for me in that there was always the chance that they might want me sexually. Straight women never wanted me sexually so I could never manipulate them. I felt no power when someone didn't want me sexually. I decided to call Iris anyway, even though she was straight. I was desperate.

"Hi Iris."

"Oh wow, you don't sound good," she said. "You decided to break up with Mike after all, didn't you?"

"You can tell that from two words?" I asked.

"Yes, I felt it instantly. Remember, I'm an intuitive."

I recounted to Iris the fight and the abandonment. She was patient and compassionate. While I was on the phone, Mike called. I excused myself with Iris, men always took precedence.

170

Neither of us had an appetite to meet in person so we had a phone fight. As with all our major fights, this one centered on my infidelities.

"Shanti, I am done with you sleeping with other men when you get angry with me. I will never take you back if you ever do it again. Do whatever you need to do with your therapist to get out your anger but you need to get that this is the last straw. I will never take you back ever again if you sleep with someone else."

I got quiet, understanding the finality of his stance. Though I knew he was right to make such a declaration, I wanted him to know that I was also very unhappy with him. "Fine. Then I declare that I am no longer willing to accept your silent treatments or raging voicemail messages or emails. Do it one more time and I am out."

Mike laughed maniacally, "My dear, these behaviors have not the same degree of impact as cheating."

"First, I beg to differ. These actions are devastating to me. Second, I never cheated on you, Mike. You got the rule. Three days of no contact from you and I have permission to have sex with others as we are technically broken up."

This fight did not end up in a pool of tears and a loving make-up. We were still fuming but agreed to stay together and meet with Mike's therapist for a couple of sessions.

New boundaries came out of our joint sessions. One: I can never have sex with anyone for one month after a break up. Two: Mike cannot abandon me for more that 24 hours. If Mike is still angry with me after 24 hours, he must communicate briefly, three lines or less, that he is still angry, not giving details, and give me the time/day when he will reconnect. Neither of us liked the new boundaries but we both felt they were healthy boundaries to keep.

Chapter 25

Sexual Abuse Revealed

Rather predictably, Mike and I would have a rosy period of about two-weeks, followed by a week or two from hell, then a sweet make-up session, and the cycle would repeat. Yet I was getting more comfortable with being abandoned while Mike learned to cool off. My therapy sessions were diving deeper into issues with Mom and healing these original wounds - the decades of pain and anger due to emotional abandonment and physical abuse as a young child.

Her beatings most often centered on me playing doctor. The more angry Mom got though, the more I wanted to know about these private parts that made her wild with rage. But that last beating, around age six, was so severe that I abandoned my search for the private parts. She won. Though Mom never sexually molested me, she caused major sexual trauma with her beatings surrounding sexual exploration. Hello, totally normal for young children to do this Mom!

After age six, I followed the path of sexual disgust, as Mom had. I didn't masturbate when many young girls did, it never even occurred to me. Heard about masturbation once in sex education class in sixth grade yet thought it a terribly strange practice. Couldn't understand why anyone would want to touch his or her private parts.

However, once I met my second boyfriend in high school at age 17, that disgust turned into intense attraction. I became endlessly fascinated again with what so repulsed Mom. Attraction and repulsion are two sides of a sadly warped coin. Yet I was having more fun with the attraction end and so my life as a lustful lady began. I discovered orgasms and it was the best feeling in the world to me. Of course at the time I never understood that my intense need for sensual touch was due to the fact that my mother rarely cuddled or touched me sweetly. Perhaps as a baby, but I had no recollection. So at age 17, I found affection and sex all rolled up into one. If I wanted love, I had to have sex. It was just that simple.

Chapter 26

Dating Coach: Dream or Nightmare?

The year 2006 was quite magical for Mike and me. His anger was dissipating, my abandonment issues lessening, and our relationship deepening. We were starting to discuss a life-long commitment to one another. Though my daughter Rebecca was opposed to our union, we didn't give her objections much credence.

Mike said, "She is 13 years old. What does she know?"

But it bothered me that she didn't like Mike. Whenever I would ask Rebecca why, she would always respond the same way.

"Mom, I just don't like him. I don't know why. He is sometimes mean to me with his angry looks and he is not usually very nice unless he is cooking. I just don't like him."

2006 was also the year I got deeper into my spiritual studies and charity work. Back in 2005 I began working on a new charity for children in Malawi Africa that Madonna started through the Kabbalah Centre. It was called Raising Malawi. Adriana and I began studying Kabbalah at the Kabbalah Centre NYC in 2005 and we were learning and growing enormously. This was definitely a contributing factor to my healing and growing ease with Mike. The tools they use at the Kabbalah Centre are a combination of spiritual and transformational. It felt like many of the teachings I learned while studying yoga, meditation, and the Landmark Forum all rolled up into one. Adri and I both loved it there, going at least once or twice a week.

So by 2006 I was deep into my studies at the Kabbalah Centre and the Raising Malawi charity. Mike finally jumped on board too and was coming with me to the center a couple of times a month. At the same time I was expanding my Dynamic Dating Parties and Mike was very helpful in inviting folks and handling the logistics of the parties with me. He was very proud of the great contribution I was making to all the lonely singles in New York and encouraged me to move further in this direction. We were really flowing in our relationship and my heart was completely open to him. I never thought anyone could take the place of Yigal but here I was, completely in love with Mike. It felt like a miracle to me.

All my romantic relationships were fraught with anguish. The pain began with my first boyfriend in high school and got progressively more painful over time. My unhappy eight-year marriage to Rebecca's Dad, Jeremy, served to confirm that I had a major issue in the intimacy arena. Back then I had never heard of a sex/love addiction, but I pursued several avenues to overcome my intimacy issues. Besides therapy I took many courses that focused on dating, relationships, sexuality, and intimacy. My three-year relationship with Matthew, hot-head #1, who I began dating soon after separating from Jeremy, served as the guinea pig and test-bed for my new learnings.

I survived angry Matthew and left him before our wedding. After that, Yigal was a pure pleasure, until of course our broken engagement destroyed our fairy story. The new relationship teachings helped me navigate these muddy waters, yet they were still not helping me pick the right kind of guy.

Though my romantic relationships were an utter mess, I did learn how to date successfully. The sheer volume of my harem, after monogamy with Yigal ended, taught me a ton. Hands on, on-the-Bob-training, was my greatest teacher. I found it easy to date, relationships, not so easy. So I focused on what I did best and found that others could benefit from my dating wisdom as well. I found myself sought after for private coaching, in addition to the Dynamic Dating Parties I organized and hosted. The parties were a success and I thought I could make a living as a coach, but my job at the law firm was getting in my way. I wanted to cut loose and pursue my dream, even though I had no parachute or safety net.

In May of 2006, with a heavy heart I announced my plans to leave the law firm. I made sure everyone knew that my exit had nothing to do with any dissatisfaction in the office. Indeed it was my attachment to everyone that made it nearly impossible to leave. But I was committed to pursuing my dream of being a full-time dating coach.

Initially I had asked Mr. Tanner if I could work only three days a week with Iris filling in for the other two. We actually tried it for a month but Mr. Tanner felt that items were falling through the cracks. The secretary is a boss's best gatekeeper, no doubt about it. But was this indeed true that anything was falling through the cracks, or was this Mr. Tanner's way of keep me five days a week? I must admit, even with all my wild sexcapades in the office, I made a damn good legal secretary. I was precise, detail oriented, self sufficient, driven, and completely committed to my boss and his clients. Okay, maybe a little too committed to some of his clients. But it was time for me to move on and follow my dream of being a dating coach.

"If not now, when?" was my thinking. I was already 47 years old. I contemplated delaying my dream until retirement but who would listen to a 65-year-old dating coach, so far from her prime? So with tears and a champagne send-off, I left the legal haven that I loved beyond measure.

With only a few days to withdraw from constant in-house attention at the firm, I had to kick into high gear and focus completely on Mike. He was being evicted from his loft and needed to purge ten years of stuff. From a washer and dryer, to a huge boiler, to beds and bureaus, bathtub and sink, to a fully equipped kitchen. It all had to go.

Though I needed to promote my Dynamic Dating Parties, after all this would be my only income source, I also knew that Mike was flipping out. I spent my first three weeks out of the firm into the grime of schlepping and moving for Mike. Mike was in a complete panic and Lord knows I always handled my men first. Some say this is a woman's way. I later learned that this is a co-dependent's way, also known as a love addict's way. Never mind that I had just quit my steady job with benefits and a boss, co-workers, and clients that I absolutely adored to start my own business. But no, I had to tend to the very unsteady business of handling my boyfriend. After all, if Mike was unhappy, he might leave me. Abandonment Protection Rule #1: Always, at all times, do whatever it takes to please and appease your man lest he leave your sorry ass!

Though I was not conscious at the time that this was the rule I lived by, it took its toll nevertheless. After three weeks of helping Mike sell, chuck, and store his stuff, it was time for me to focus on me again. Mike was now living in the small bedroom of a three-bedroom apartment in Williamsburg, much the size of the minuscule bedrooms he made for his roommates in the loft.

Payback's a bitch Mike. He was not happy in his new space. So Mike spent a lot of time in my apartment, which was not easy for me. We love addicts have great difficulty focusing on ourselves because keeping our loved one happy is of paramount importance.

One day while Mike was hanging out at my place, I asked if he would help me out by picking up some groceries while I wrote up a new flyer for Dynamic Dating Parties. Well, one might have guessed I asked him to kill his first-born for he raged at the top of his lungs.

"No Shanti. I don't want to do that. That is your job and I am a guest here. Did I ever ask you to go to the grocery store for us?"

Mike went from pleasant to abusive in a nano-second. I was tired, hungry, and for the first time in four years, completely broke. I took a brief pause and searched for paper to start the grocery list.

"You know what? Forget it. Forget all of it. Just take yourself back to your tiny little room and get out of my life. I spent three full weeks completely devoted to you and your traumatic move and you can't take half an hour out of your day to help me. In fact, to help us, I would be cooking for us. I have no income coming in and I need to focus on making money! You are such a self-centered narcissistic bastard. Get out of here!"

Within a few seconds, Mike was out the door. Initially it always felt great to break up with Mike when he was being a bastard. "I'll show him" was always playing in the background. But within the hour the abandonment would sink in and with it, paralyzing grief. Then the insane roller-coaster ride of my love addiction would kick into high gear. Break up, apologize, beg forgiveness, cry uncontrollably, beg forgiveness again, no food, no water, no sleep, no peace. Days would go by with no communication whatsoever from Mike. This was his way of punishing me for breaking up with him. For Mike was clear that I wanted him back with all my tearful voicemails of apology and begging. So Mike was in total control and that's what he really wanted.

Normally this cycle would play out within a week but ten days passed and still no word from Mike. Finally, by week two Mike called and left a message yet with no olive branch to offer.

"Shanti, I received all your tearful messages but they won't work this time. You've broken up with me for the last time sister. I will never take you back." I must have played that message twenty times in a row, praying it wasn't true and hoping I missed some subtle peace offering. But there was none.

I spent the next few weeks in bed because I could. With no job to go to and Rebecca vacationing with her Dad in Hawaii for the rest of the summer, I could stay under cover, literally. There were days when I would not shower, bathe, or brush my teeth. Eating was a once a day event and only because the hunger pains bothered me too much. I missed Mike desperately. I even lost my desire to avoid pain by screwing someone else. Guess all that therapy worked. Band-Aid sex lost its appeal, finally. Anyway, I promised Mike that I would not have sex with anyone else for a month if we broke up. If I ever thought we might get back together, I had to keep this promise. Only this time, keeping the promise was easy. I had absolutely no desire for anyone but Mike. Not even Lenny. Not even Yigal.

While completely dysfunctional over our break-up, generating a party atmosphere for my Dynamic Dating Parties was impossible. My friends tried to get me to come out but I never answered the phone. I was emotionally bereft, financially strapped, and completely paralyzed by it all. Even got into a huge fight with Iris, my best friend from the law firm, who didn't seem to understand my pain and spewed her harsh judgments on me.

"Leaving the law firm was the stupidest idea you've ever had Shanti and you've had many stupid ideas. I'm sorry but it's your fault that you're in this horrible place. I can't feel sorry for you. I won't."

Fair-weather friend took on a new meaning. I had never known her to be so cruel and couldn't understand why. But, I had no strength to butt heads with anyone so I stopped contacting her, tough love was not helping me. I needed compassion and told her not to call me for a few months until I was back on my feet.

One morning I heard a voicemail message from Didier Bellamy, my short-lived French romance at the start of the new millennium. Though we both knew that romance between us was impossibly complicated, we had remained friends, though no longer with benefits. We had tons of friends in common from the fashion industry and our on-going connection kept the heydays of the 80s alive for us both. The message was brief and upbeat.

"Hey Patty my baby! I am in New York for a few days and would love to see you. Please call me."

178

Though I was tempted to ignore Didier, I decided to do something I rarely ever did: show my pain to someone other than a current lover. Didn't work too well with Iris but maybe Didier would be different.

I called Didier back, and spent the next half-hour on the phone explaining my plight. The following day we met for lunch. Didier was shocked that I left the job I loved so much.

"You wouldn't even leave that job to marry me! This new boyfriend must have been special. I am sorry I did not stay in touch but when you told me we could not be intimate with one another any more because you entered a monogamous relationship, I felt it best to leave you alone. I was happy for you. However, I was also sad for me. I hope you understand."

I replied, "Of course I understand. But I did not leave my job for Mike. I left my job because I wanted to focus on my Dynamic Dating Parties and my dating coach practice. But now I am devastated, it's impossible to function." I began to cry.

"Oh my baby I feel terrible for you."

"It's okay Didier. It is not your fault."

"But how will you pay your bills? Did you save money before you quit your job?"

"No, I did not save more that a couple thousand dollars and I've used that up already. I am going to sublet my apartment for a few months, I guess. At least I won't have to pay that overhead."

"But then where will you stay?"

"I can visit with my parents for a little while, stay with friends. I don't know, Didier. I can't even think that far."

Didier took a long pause and stared at me.

"Didier, I am sorry to lay this on you. I am sure you thought you would have a fun time with me in New York and instead I am bringing you down."

"Don't be ridiculous baby. I want to help you." He continued to stare at me.

The waiter brought our food but I couldn't touch it.

"Come on baby. You have to eat. You are too skinny." Didier pulled out his wallet.

"Take these few hundred dollars in cash and I'm going to write you a check for $2,000 right now. Then I'm going to mail you a credit card with a $2,000 limit. This will allow you to stay in your apartment for a few months and get back on your feet. You can't sleep on people's couches like a teenager, you have a young daughter."

I began to cry again.

"Baby listen, I know you much better than you think. I know you are a very proud person and would never ask for money. But you need it right now. Please take it."

The torrent of grateful tears came pouring down. Didier became uncomfortable. As the waiter passed Didier assured him, "I swear it is not me that is making her cry. I am the good guy."

Crying and now laughing through my tears, "Yes, Didier, you are indeed the very good guy."

Didier's emotional and financial support did indeed get me back on my feet. I even tried to get my old job back but of course they hired and trained someone else during those two months. Yet now, free from my emotional love withdrawal, I got clear that I did not have the kind of strength to run a business on my own. It was an expensive experiment. So I revamped my resume and started looking for work. I got several temp assignments that carried me over nicely. My main goal, however, was gaining a permanent position again. I was confident that I could.

While healing and rebuilding my life I was happy that I did not look for men to fill the void. No dating or hook-ups in the two months apart from Mike and no contacting Yigal. All the deep work with my core energetics therapist, Ala, was truly paying off. I was grateful that Mike had introduced me to this incredible form of therapy. With Ala I was learning to feel my pain and not cover it with sex or attention or love. I was actually happy being single for the first time since, well, forever. This was truly a miracle to me.

Chapter 27

Reunion and Engagement to Mike

After two months of detox from Mike, I was feeling strong again. My temp jobs were pulling in enough money to keep me afloat and Rebecca was back from Hawaii and ready to start the new school year. How many days and nights did I sacrifice our mother/daughter times to run for my man fix? Her Dad was always a yes if I needed to work late. He would come right over. However, I didn't usually work late. It was merely a cover for a hot date. Now I was going to be the full-time Mom that I dreamed to be. I was happy to devote my time and attention after work to Rebecca with no desire to meet a man.

Then, something terrible happened. Mike called. When I saw Mike's name flash on the caller ID I completely froze. I was terrified to hear Mike's voice. Praying that he called only because he left something at my place, I still could not play the message. Maybe he is still angry? I was hoping for that. But my worst fear came true when I finally did play the message.

"Shanti, my greatest love. I have been a total basket case without you. I am so sorry that I was cruel to you. You didn't deserve it. I know I am a tough customer and you have stuck by me. I don't deserve another chance with you, I know that. But if you ever thought it might be possible, I would do anything to have you back. I am devastated without you. Please think about it. You don't need to call me right back. I know you. You're probably with some new handsome guy already. But if you are open, I would love to see you, talk to you, maybe even hug you."

Mike just showered me with a huge dose of love and sweetness. That was the dangerous drug, that wiped out all his cruelty. I was in serious risk of running back to him. I immediately called Ala, my therapist, for a session. Through the session I finally got clear that this was Mike's pattern and mine as well. I could not go back to that insanity. It felt great to be in my power. I waited a few days before calling Mike back and left him an equally sweet message.

"Mike, thank you very much for your message. It is terrible to end a relationship with so much animosity so I am happy that we can be peaceful and loving again. I am not dating anyone and I do not intend to date anyone for quite some time. I have to get back on my feet financially. Mike, I cannot go back with you. Two years of this roller-coaster relationship has been enough for me. We both trigger one another in ways that are truly destructive. I wish you all the best and pray for our healing as we continue to go our separate ways. Take care of yourself Mike."

But within a couple weeks, Mike's unannounced visits outside my apartment and inside my spiritual communities wore me down. I had no defense against his sweetness and his hug sealed the deal. By mid-September we were back together again. Only this time we got engaged and moved in together. There was no ring for neither of us could afford it, but the commitment was there. We spent four blissful weeks living together and I was in heaven.

With a solid, steady stream of temp jobs paying the bills, I was now ready and able to go back to my date-coaching practice a couple times a week during the evenings. Mike so loved this skill I possessed and was always willing to help when I needed him. I had started a women's group in August and was embarking on my first men's group in October. I invited Mike to join me in the front of the room for the men's group and he was honored. We both felt as though we were a good example of a healthy relationship. Where I got that insane notion, I had no idea. But the day of the first men's group, Mike woke up with a monstrous face like I had not seen in months. When I asked what was wrong he brushed me aside.

"Mike you have every right not to talk but I cannot have you co-leading this men's group with me sporting this angry energy and no communication with me."

Mike replied in a sharp tone, "Well, I am now living with you Shanti. Where do you expect me to go while your men's group is here?"

"You can go to Starbucks two blocks away."

Mike stormed out of the apartment immediately, many hours before he needed to leave. I was quite relieved actually. I didn't want to start my men's group with his angry vibe. My first men's group was a success and Mike returned the exact moment I had told him the group would be done. He entered the apartment without talking or looking at me and retired to Rebecca's room since she was with her Dad that night. He slammed the door.

Doing my best to ignore Mike's tantrum, I lost the stand off and opened the door.

"Mike, you are acting totally childish. Tonight was my first men's group. I could not have you around with your dark cloud enveloping us all. When will you get that the world does not revolve around Mike? You need to grow up!"

That was the trigger that set him off. Mike flew off the bed and started aggressively pushing me around Rebecca's bedroom. He was snorting loudly like a bull and staring me straight in the eyes. But he uttered no words. He looked like an absolute lunatic.

I screamed, "Mike, stop pushing me! You are hurting me! Stop!!"

But he kept pushing me and then pushed me into the bathroom. I felt trapped.

I screamed again, "Mike, let me out of here right now!"

I was afraid that he might bash my head against the sink or the bathtub and hurt me. I was extremely frightened. Mike had never manhandled me before and he was very strong.

I told Mike, "You let go of me here this instant Mike. Right now!"

But instead of releasing me he dragged me to our bed and threw me down.

I was being strangled by Mike and gasping for air. After my initial panic I somehow got calm. Perhaps that's what lack of oxygen does? Realizing I could no longer breath, it became apparent that I would die.

I remember thinking to myself, "I can't believe I'm going to die this way."

I soon began to drift up out of my body through my head. It was such a strange experience but I was no longer scared. I didn't even feel the need to breathe. It was wild. Then I heard Mike scream. He started shaking me.

"Are you going to yield? Are you going to fucking yield?"

I did not want to yield to this monster, no way. I was so fucking angry with Mike that my ego wanted to respond to his request by saying, "NO, fuck you! I am not going to yield to you, asshole!"

But I could not speak. I couldn't even move.

At that moment I thought of my daughter and how she would grow up without a mother if I did not surrender to Mike's will. I felt grief-stricken with the notion, and with that I came back into my body. Perhaps Mike's shaking allowed some oxygen in, I don't know. But I decided to give him an affirmative gesture to his heinous request of yielding. I wanted my daughter to grow up with a mother! I blinked my eyes several times and attempted to nod my head in the affirmative. I knew holding onto my pride would only bring injury or death upon me. So I swallowed my pride and managed to nod my head as best I could and blink my eyes. Mike finally jumped off me.

I gasped and coughed for at least ten minutes, but not before screaming at Mike, "Get the hell out of here!"

Was I crazy? Yes! I was completely crazy because he could have attacked me again. Ladies please, do not be as dumb as I was. Swallow all your pride, not just some of it, at least until the bastard is out of your sight and you are safe.

After ordering Mike to leave my apartment he glibly announced, "I'm taking a shower first."

While Mike was in the shower I called several friends but no one answered. I was terrified but frozen at the same time. I should have left the apartment but I was stuck in the entryway. Then I heard a knock at the door.

"NYPD may we come in?" spoke the voice on the other side of my front door.

I found out later that my neighbor heard us fighting and called the police. Love thy neighbor as they self. Thank you Joseph, my precious neighbor! Thank you NYPD for your instant response.

The police officers stood at the doorway, one male and one female. The male officer asked, "Are you okay Ma'am?"

My response, "I don't think so."

"Can we come in?" he asked.

I nodded and they entered.

He asked, "Are you having a domestic dispute?"

"Yes," I replied sheepishly.

Within moments we heard a crash in the bathroom and loud cursing, "Fuck! Fuck! Fuck! Fuck!"

The cop asked, "Has he been drinking?"

I told him, "No."

Then he asked, "Does he often curse like that or get angry on a regular basis?"

I told him, "Yes, Mike has a very bad temper but this was the first time that he got physical with me."

He asked what happened and I told him.

Then he warned me, "Statistically, once a guy crosses the physical violence threshold, they almost always continue. Then the physical abuse escalates."

We then heard something drop on the bathroom floor again.

Mike shouted, "Shit! Shit! Shit!"

After Mike's rant we heard loud huffing, snorting, and growling. It was loud enough that we all got quiet and looked towards the bathroom. Mike truly sounded like a wild animal. I saw the male officer cover his gun.

I thought, "Oh my God, is he going to shoot Mike?!"

Though I was enraged with Mike I still loved him and did not want him to die. I started feeling light-headed, like I was going to faint.

I took a few moments to digest the officer's information. Mike and I were living together and engaged to be married. It was a terrifying concept these officers laid on me - the violence would escalate. I barely made it out of this situation alive.

Breaking through my quiet quandary the male officer asked softly, "Do you want us to arrest him?"

Still feeling frozen I was not sure what to do. I was terrified of the ramifications of having Mike arrested. Then both the officers spoke with me about filing a restraining order against Mike to protect myself. Yet all I could think about was how angry Mike would be if I did that, and how final our relationship would be after taking these legal actions. I didn't know what to think, what to do.

Mike emerged from the bathroom, half naked with a towel around his waist. I couldn't look at his face. I was certain that I would see that angry Mike glare, that he would believe I called the police on him.

"But I didn't call them," I wanted to tell him.

What a crazy thought. Thank God someone did call the police! The male officer took Mike into the bedroom immediately and the female officer stayed with me in the living room. My frozen state melted and I began shaking uncontrollably and crying hysterically. I had to sit down as I was about to fall over. I had no strength in my legs.

"Ma'am, would you like us to arrest him?" the female officer asked.

"I don't know, What will that do? I'm afraid!"

She was the epitome of calm, thank God, and explained, "You can file an order of protection against him if we arrest him. That is the only way. We'll take him in, book him, and we'll take you in and have those marks on your throat photographed."

I tried stretching for the mirror to see what she was talking about but couldn't reach since I could not stand.

She said, "You have some redness and bruising around your neck. There are also a few scratches."

I automatically held my neck, the place where my life almost ended. "What if I don't have him arrested?" I asked.

"You won't be able to file an order of protection at this time then. You'll have to wait until another incidence."

Since I couldn't think straight I thought about my daughter. I couldn't have this maniac around her. For Rebecca's sake I gave the officer the go-ahead. "Yes, arrest him. But I cannot be in the same police car with him please!" I begged.

Just the thought of sitting in the police car with Mike got me to shaking even more uncontrollably.

"Why am I shaking so much?" I asked her.

"You've had a trauma ma'am."

Hearing those words echoed in my head, "You've had a trauma. You've had a...traaaauma."

She broke my trance and said, "We will call another car for you. Stay here, I'm going to tell my partner of your decision."

As she began to walk away from me I grabbed her arm. "Wait, please! Please don't let Mike in this room. I can't see him! Please!"

"Yes, ma'am," she replied.

Facing the windows to avoid seeing Mike leave the apartment in handcuffs, I felt total relief as the door closed behind him and I ran to turn all the locks. Returning to the living room I began to cry again, even more intensely. The female officer was very kind with me.

She said, "You are doing the right thing. If he has a history of rage issues, this first incidence of physical violence will not be the last."

I knew she was right. I had put up with years of Mike's emotional abuse. However, physical abuse, I had zero tolerance. Though it was my fear that Mike might hurt my daughter one day that gave me the courage to have him arrested, it was what I needed. On that violent night in October of 2006, I made the firm decision to leave Mike for good.

And I never saw him again.

Part IV: **Orgies**

When monogamy fails miserably, Shanti looks to Lenny to keep her from love withdrawal. When two alcoholics meet at a bar they end up drunk on the floor. When two sex addicts meet at a polyamorous workshop they end up at an orgy.

Chapter 28

PTSD, Lenny to the RESCUE

What is going on with my body? Whenever I heard a very loud sound or saw violence on TV or film, my body would shake uncontrollably and I'd have no strength in my legs. I would have to sit down immediately. The experience would last for 10 minutes upwards to 30 minutes. A friend told me that I had Post-Traumatic Stress Disorder (PTSD) and I should get myself to the doctor. For some reason I felt it would go away eventually, that it was a natural reaction to being strangled. Sure enough, all the symptoms of PTSD disappeared when I started dating Lenny a few months later. Who needed drugs? I had my favorite drug - the comfort of a man's embrace.

After brief Happy New Year text messages back and forth, Lenny and I reconnected on January 11, 2007. I knew I was playing a dangerous game being with an openly polyamorous guy but Lenny was so sweet. I told myself that this would be a short-lived affair, long enough to heal from the trauma of being strangled by Mike. I had no intention of staying with Lenny long term. Little did I know!

Lenny took me out for a lovely dinner and then he invited me to his home in Williamsburg.

I replied, "I am afraid to run into Mike. It is too fresh, too scary. I don't know what he would do if he saw us walking together."

"No problem my Princess. We will take a taxi right to my door. Would that work for you?"

I flashed Lenny a huge smile.

Making out for much of the cab ride, when we arrived at Lenny's abode he took the time to show me around. He then proceeded to light several candles and burn a stick of incense. He wasted no time in removing my clothes but he did it in a slow, methodical way. It was a big turn on. Lenny then proceeded to give me a fabulous orgasm with his fingers and tongue stroking my clitoris, as he had done the year before. Now I wanted intercourse. That was usually the order I liked it, orgasm first, then intercourse. Since the majority of women do not orgasm with intercourse, we are usually left high and dry because men fall asleep after their orgasm. But when I pulled Lenny on to me, his cock was soft. I said nothing but I was surprised.

Lenny interjected, "Mr. Happy has difficulty when he likes someone too much."

I knew exactly what he meant. It was often difficult for me to orgasm when I really cared about someone. I would be nervous that they might have performance anxiety or what not and I would clam up. Feeling Lenny's anxiety and wanting to make him feel better, as any good love addict would, I said, "You can objectify me."

Lenny looked shock and asked, "Excuse me?"

I repeated, "You can objectify me. I don't mind. I actually like it."

Lenny smiled, "Really?"

"Yes really," I assured him.

I then rolled over to present my backside. Lenny became instantly hard and we had a hot and hard ride together. However, there really is such a thing as too much of a good thing. Lenny woke me five times during the night for more sex. As Mike had often been uninterested in sex, I didn't want to deter Lenny. That said, when Lenny hit me up for round six at dawn, I stopped him.

"AFO," I said, "All Fucked Out."

We both laughed and went back to sleep, or so I thought until I heard the sheets moving in a rhythmic pattern to discover that Lenny was masturbating.

I thought, "I am waaaay too tired to service this guy. Good he is handling it himself. He is a bottomless pit!" I had never experienced a guy so insatiable before. But I was too tired to think any more and I fell asleep while he whacked off. At 1 p.m. we both woke to another round of sex.

190

Lenny was the exact opposite of Mike in all ways. Mike was angry, Lenny was peaceful. Mike had no financial stability, Lenny had been in the same well-paying job for eight years. Mike only wanted sex on his terms, Lenny wanted sex on any terms. Mike wanted monogamy, Lenny wanted polyamory. With the exception of Lenny's polyamory persuasion, I was greatly enjoying the change. Of course I didn't put together all the pieces of Lenny's sexual prowess for another five years. Should have paid closer attention to that first reunion night of sex on January 11, 2007. It foretold a life riddled with constant flirting, sensual exploits, kinky exploration, and an overdose of sex. Originally the sex was mainly with me but it soon branched out to sex with many, both men and women.

As my love addiction would mandate, I soon fell in love with Lenny, even though my intelligent self knew better. But my constant obsession was now focused on Lenny. Being with him took away those three years of emotional pain with Mike and his recent attack of domestic violence. Though Lenny's desire for a life of polyamory did bother me, I somehow hoped he would outgrow it with me, see the error of his ways. Surely I would be enough for any man! Ah, how we delude ourselves. Addiction will do that. Denial is a warm blanket that keeps us cozy within our private dungeon.

After a month with Lenny I was hooked and I told him so. He was flattered and expressed the same.

So I asked him, "Since we are both hooked on one another, how would you feel about being monogamous with me?"

I probably should not have asked him this question while he had food in his mouth for he nearly choked. I should have taken his coughing and sputtering as a No but my denial was too strong. I fetched Lenny a glass of water and asked, "What is your main stop about being monogamous?"

"I feel that I have not yet explored enough."

"How old are you again?" I asked.

"I'm 39, 40 next month."

"And, not to sound condescending or anything, but what have you been doing all this time?" I inquired.

Lenny laughed, "I know, sounds silly but I was a super late bloomer, very shy. I only recently had my first couple of monogamous relationships in the past two years."

"You mean with your Mexican girlfriend?"

"Yes, Carmelita lasted a few months. Now she's my live-in platonic roommate."

"Yeah, that's so weird," I interjected, "but anyway, you said a couple of monogamous relationships. Who was the other one?"

"Tammy, you met her with Mike last New Year's Day."

"Oh yes, right. That was awkward. I realized then that I still had deep feelings for you."

"Yes, me as well," Lenny confessed.

"So, how long were you with Tammy?"

"Six months. She made it easy for me though. She presented it like one month at a time. At the end of each month we would negotiate and see if we wanted another month of monogamy."

"Interesting. Why did she break it off?"

"I broke it off," Lenny replied.

"Oh, sorry to assume that. Why did you break it off?" I asked.

In a matter-of-fact manner Lenny replied, "I wanted to have sex with other people."

If I was in a healthy emotional place, I would have run away right there. But my love addict already planted her roots and was determined to do whatever it took to keep this guy. Not even Lenny's declaration of bisexuality deterred me. Since I clearly had bisexual leanings myself, I felt comforted in knowing Lenny was part of the LGBTQ community. Lenny was also grateful that I accepted this aspect of him.

I remember when he first told me of his bisexual leanings I had reassured him: "Honey, I know fag hag is no longer a politically correct term but back in the 80s, the majority of my friends were gay men and I even slept with a few of them. I used to watch gay porn in bed with my gay roommate. I loved it. I was a flaming fag hag. I find man-on-man sex very hot so I'm not telling you that it's cool with me that you are bisexual to make you feel better. It's a turn on for me."

When I was done with my fag-hag speech Lenny pulled me in close and started making out with me intensely. Such soft lips, he was such an amazing kisser. After several minutes of hot making out, I pulled away.

I also made clear, "Being bisexual is cool but what is not cool with me is a life of polyamory. I lived it already for three years with Yigal and it led me down a dark path, into a life of continuous promiscuity."

Lenny quickly responded, "You see, that is what I have not yet lived. I want to have my time in promiscuity."

When Lenny made this so crystal clear, my denial hit the wall. His licentious appetite so resembled my own out-of-control promiscuity that I could not stand it. I broke up with Lenny right then and there, amidst a torrent of tears.

He begged, "Shanti, please, I'm in love with you. I don't want to lose you. I have never been in love like this before."

"I have fallen in love with you too Lenny but I can't go back into these polyamorous waters. I nearly drowned before."

"Was it any more difficult being polyamorous with Yigal than it was to be monogamous with Mike?"

I hated that Lenny brought this up because my relationship with Mike was indeed extremely painful. In fact most of my sexual relationships had been painful roller-coaster rides. Some twists and turns were exciting, others calm and pleasurable, yet too often the steep drop had threatened to kill me.

I explained, "Lenny, I know my relationship with Mike was treacherous. But I did not choose well when I decided to settle down to monogamy with him. He had a lot of mental problems that triggered my issues of abandonment. But he was the only guy asking for monogamy and so I went with it. But I can't do this again."

"Do what again?" Lenny asked.

"I can't choose a guy, like you, that is not going to be a good fit for me. I know what you want. You have made it very clear. It is not what I want. I was hoping against hope that you might change your polyamorous leanings if you fell in love with me. This hasn't happened so I have to go."

On a frigid Friday night in February, I walked to the L train in Williamsburg, struggling to manage a torrent of tears. All the hipsters were out with their funky knit hats and mittens. I wasn't aware that adults wore mittens any more. I was sad that I would not be visiting this odd and interesting place again and the joy from their faces reminded me that I would not partake in that feeling for some time to come. I was surprised by how intense this loss felt. But this was more than a one-month romance gone sour. I had met Lenny in the spring of 2004, only a couple months before meeting Mike. We kept in touch off-and-on over those three years and even got together for sex during one of my break-ups with Mike. So this break-up had all the earmarks of a long-term relationship and the pain went deep. Only a few days to Valentine's Day. This loss felt unbearable.

Grateful that it was the weekend and Rebecca was with her Dad, I did what I always do when smacked with intimacy pain. I climbed into bed and sobbed for hours. But somehow, I felt strong in my self-esteem. I was happy that I had not allowed myself to be with a man who would not be good for me. This knowledge was of great solace and by Saturday night I took a shower, made dinner for myself, and watched TV. I did not go onto a dating website to fill in the pain nor did I contact any old lovers. My work with Ala, my therapist, was truly working. I was finally able to be alone and content, even happy, dare I admit.

On Sunday afternoon I saw a call from Lenny coming in. I did not answer. He left a message but I did not listen right away. That would have been the old me. I finished my lunch and started my laundry. When I felt calm and settled, I listened.

"Hello my beautiful Princess Shanti. I have been very sad all weekend without you. (pause) I, (pause) um, I have been thinking about my needs verses your needs in a relationship and it seems really crazy to me that two people that get along so well, and love one another so much, cannot make it work. If you would be open, I would like to discuss some options for us. Please call me back when you get a chance."

Clearly these options were not monogamy so I attended to another load of laundry and pondered what he might possibly propose that I could accept.

After all the washing, drying, and folding was complete and I felt solidly in control of some portion of my life, I called Lenny back. "Hey Lenny, got your message."

"Thank you for calling me back. How are you feeling my Princess?"

"I felt like hell all weekend but I'm getting back on my feet tonight."

"Well that's good. (pause) Um, if you are open, I would like to speak with you in person. You know, I am not so great on the phone."

Certain that a meeting at my place or his would land us in bed, I agreed to meet in a coffee shop nearby. Lenny poured out his heart and his fears of feeling trapped in a relationship. What he proposed was a semi-monogamous relationship - we would be a monogamous couple but with occasional guest stars.

"What the heck is a guest star?" I asked.

"Well, I know you also like women sexually so maybe a few times a year we could take a woman or a couple to bed with us."

The idea was instantly titillating but also frightening. "I don't know Lenny. How would this work out? How would we even find this person or persons?"

"Oh you don't need to worry about that. I am in touch with several people in the polyamorous communities."

"Oh yes, of course you are," I replied.

Lenny chuckled and I took a long, hard look at him. Damn, he was hot. Nine years my junior and draped in Costa Rican gold skin with long black hair. When I first met Yigal he looked very much like this, I am a sucker for that look. I was done for. Clearly my loins were running the show for I agreed to Lenny's wild proposal.

"Okay, I will agree to this crazy proposal but I am only willing to have others join our bed a couple of times a year. It can't be our main course, only a decadent dessert once in a while. If that will work for you, that will work for me."

Lenny smiled brightly, "The minute it does not work for either of us we will communicate. I am so happy my Princess is going to stay with me!"

Lenny hugged and kissed me so intensely I could barely breath. He chuckled and declared, "Now that we are in a semi-monogamous relationship, I shall call you my Queen."

We celebrated our official union on Valentine's Day evening. As it was a school night, I asked Rebecca's Dad to watch her at his place. He was almost always a Yes for unscheduled Rebecca time. Ladies, if you're going to get pregnant, be sure to find a guy who will make a great Dad. I don't know how parents who are married manage to keep a relationship alive with little to no non-child time. Being divorced with a great father to team with, I was able to have the joys of motherhood plus the excitement of being single. It was the perfect combination for me.

Lenny arrived at my place with a dozen red roses and a big duffle bag. He informed me the night before that he would be bringing the entertainment to be enjoyed after we ordered in a delicious meal.

"Gorgeous flowers. Thank you. What's in the bag?" I asked.

"Nah, you'll have to wait until after dinner and no peeking." Lenny made clear.

He knew me so well already. After dinner and dessert Lenny pulled out what he called a second dessert, a joint.

"Oh my, it's been quite some time that I have not smoked a joint," I said.

"How long?" Lenny asked.

"I don't know, a couple of years. I think I smoked once or twice with Mike."

"Would you like to smoke tonight?" Lenny asked.

I replied, "Yes, as long as smoking weed is not a regular thing. Like the guest stars, weed should also remain an occasional dessert, a couple times a year."

"As you wish my Queen."

After a few hits from Lenny's joint, I was reminded how horny marijuana got me. Not that I needed any help with Lenny, he was hot enough just the way he was. We made out intensely until I felt something icy cold on my neck and jumped.

"Oh! What is that?!" I asked.

"It is the beginnings of our entertainment," Lenny replied with a sly smile.

Lenny buckled a black leather collar around my neck with a red dog tag that read, "Property of Lenny."

He explained, "Since you have such a great desire to be possessed by me, I thought you would enjoy being collared with me as your owner."

I smiled. I did indeed want to be owned by Lenny, as long as I would be his only slave. I had been asking Lenny for over a month to show me some of his kinky BDSM moves. The back of his bedroom door was laden with bondage-domination-sadism-masochism (BDSM) equipment.

Yet whenever I asked Lenny to go there, he'd reply, "Nah, did that for years but not into it any more."

As I had never had any guy use BDSM equipment on me, I was incredibly curious and turned on by the idea of it.

Lenny attached a heavy metal leash to my collar and gently pulled me over to the bed. He slowly removed all my clothing and bound my wrists and ankles to the bedposts with leather straps. It was scary and titillating at the same time. He went on to torture me with pleasure using a leather glove with the palm side covered in fur. He caressed my naked body oh so slowly. It was such an intense sensation to feel all this attention and sensuality and not be able to reciprocate. I was wet before he touched my pussy.

Chapter 29

Fireworks and The Sex Party

July 4th 2007 brought our first sexual encounters with guest stars and plenty of fireworks in bed. Feeling as though six months together was not enough time for me to want anyone else, Lenny lured me in by way of our newfound costume craze. Recently enamored by our star performance at the Mermaid Parade in Coney Island, Lenny told me of a sex party in Brooklyn that required all players to dress in patriotic costumes. He had me at costumes.

However, once I agreed to attend this sex party, all my resistance also came up.

"Wait, so how is this going to work? What if someone comes up to me that I don't like?" I asked.

"You don't have to accept any offers. I would be happy just to attend this party with you my Queen and have sex with only you while others watch us. That is a big turn on."

Contemplating Lenny's offer a moment I replied, "Okay, but what if some woman comes up to you that wants you and I don't like her, for whatever reason, but you like her?"

"I will always defer to you my Queen. If Mama ain't happy ain't nobody happy."

We both burst out laughing.

Lenny created a set of incredible costumes for us. We looked like American super heroes in our red, white, and blue Spandex outfits, complete with capes, stars, and stripes. I thought he couldn't possibly trump the Mermaid Parade outfits but he did. We were the toast of the party. Everyone came up to us and complemented our outfits. It was a great icebreaker, for otherwise I was frozen in fear much of the night.

Yet I was relieved that, in most ways, this sex party was like any other club party. There was a bar, a dance floor, and a lounge area. However, what was markedly different was an area behind the sheer silks that barely disguised the room full of beds. The beds stayed fairly empty for the first hour and became increasingly more crowded as the night went on. Lenny was attentive to me throughout the evening and his intense attention I very much enjoyed.

At several points along the way Lenny asked, "How are you feeling, honey?"

"I feel great as long as I am dancing."

With the flip of his cape Lenny announced, "So then we shall dance my Queen!"

It felt so good not to be pressured into something that I didn't want to do.

When thinking about being pressured, Mike's improv acting disaster immediately came to mind. Mike knew I had scars from sexual harassment *à la* casting couch and yet he still pushed me to coach him in acting. He got very angry when I declined. How relieved I was not to be with Mike any more and his horrible angry temper. Of course at the time, I had no idea that although Lenny wasn't pushing me to be a swinger, he was instead grooming me to be one. He had all the time in the world to wait for me. Invite, invite, invite, shower me with attention, but never pressure or judge. Pushing me into this swinger lifestyle would have caused an instant rejection. Smart man. He even attended a polyamory support group where they discussed ways to "safe-port" a partner who was not yet on board with multiple partners. Maybe they prescribed Grooming 101 for homework.

As the bedded area became more crowded, Lenny asked, "Would you like to take a walk in there, just to look? We'll be voyeurs."

Scared but totally curious, I nodded my head. And with that gesture I entered a world I never imagined. There were several couples having sex next to one another that did not seem to be interacting with anyone else. That was a great relief to see. Then there were a few beds where I couldn't figure out who was with whom: men and women caressing, sucking, and fucking one another, moving from one body to the next in a massive rhythmic flow. When I saw this scene I panicked.

"Lenny, I don't want to do that."

"Of course not. Whatever my Queen wants. Would you like to sit on that couch over there? No one is sitting there."

Lenny began massaging my neck and shoulder and soon we were making out intensely. Within a few minutes we were sexing with our costumes on, enjoying one another and the crazy freak show surrounding us. Some guy came over while Lenny was entering me doggy style, rather aggressively, from behind.

The guy announced in a loud voice, "Hey, these guys even fuck like super heroes!"

I felt I had entered the wildest world I could possibly imagine. Yet I also felt strangely safe, knowing that no one else would be touching us. We were voyeurs and exhibitionists and that suited me just fine. I didn't want to touch anyone else sexually... or so I thought.

We hung out at the sex party for a few hours more, back on the dance floor, sitting at the bar, and chilling in the lounge. We even started speaking with some of the other players. One of them offered us a joint and we accepted. That's when the entire tenor of our evening changed. We meandered our way back to the beds and this really cute African American girl name Tramecia started fawning over me.

"Hey tall beauty. Can I touch those gorgeous breasts of yours?" she asked.

I gave Lenny a smile to see if he approved and he smiled brightly back at me. Before I knew it some guy that Tramecia knew had joined us and we were cross-pollinating. Although I would not allow myself any contact with the guy, Lenny and I played with Tramecia and her friend joined in to play with her too. Lucky girl. With this one simple action we had become official swingers. Wow, smoking that joint really got me crazy wild with desire. Dangerous stuff.

At various points during the night we connected with Alex, a highly regarded leader in the tantric community where we often hung out. Alex was impressed with our loving connection and freedom of sexual expression. We had met Alex before but never

200

spent too much time with him, as he was usually the leader or host. That night, Alex invited us to be quests at some of his events. We both felt honored and privileged. I was surprised how many leaders of various tantric groups were there that night, promoting their workshops. Guess it was easiest to market Tantra to those already open to sexual exploration.

Yes, in my first six months with Lenny, he managed to introduce me to several Tantric and sensual communities. With each new group or event that he brought to the table, I would resist.

Yet I always ended up going anyway, resistance and all. No, Lenny never strong-armed me. But he killed me with his soft puppy-dog eyes. I knew I had to be open to these communities or he would either cheat on me or leave me, and my love addiction could never bear that. Please my man or lose my man.

As early morning sunbeams permeated the club, it was time to leave the sex party. We packed up our condoms, lube, cum rags, and super-hero capes, jumped in a cab, and headed home to our perfect Gotham where all good super heroes lived. We sat back in the cab without a word to one another. I stared at the approaching skyline with memories of my wild nights as a super model dancing in my head. Yet nothing I ever did in the 80s was nearly this wild. It became clear to me that I had entered a world I may never recover from. It was one thing to have spent years in promiscuity. But that was one person at a time. I now entered the orbit of orgies.

As we approached Manhattan I watched the sun rising over the East River and pondered with dread, "Who am I? What have I done? And what will become of me?"

Chapter 30

My Year of Living Lustfully

I was falling deeper in love with Lenny as each month passed. I felt emotionally secure in our semi-monogamous relationship even though it had a flexible edge that allowed for our kinks and guest stars. We surely had an all-star cast at our fingertips. Hot and sexy players from the greater New York area were lining up for a chance to join our sensual lair. The conundrum was finding a couple where both individuals were pleasing to us both. Since that was a difficult order to fill, we often settled for a single lady or gent to join in on the festivities. One day Lenny expressed his quandary:

"I can't understand why I never found this many sex partners when I was single."

Lenny was serious in his question but I was seriously baffled by his naiveté.

I replied, "Uh dah, not to toot my own horn honey. But having an attractive partner changes the game completely."

"Ooooh, I see, I see. My beautiful Queen, thank you for waking me to this truth. How unconscious of me to not see it."

Lenny had a formal, old world manner of speech that at first I interpreted as jest. But he really did speak this way much of the time, perhaps because Spanish was his first language. I found it endearing.

It seemed like a perfect relationship that first year. Even though Lenny was laid off from his steady eight-year job as a web designer, a few months after we became a formal couple, he told me it had been over a decade since he had any real break from work and he desperately needed one. Lenny was not planning to look for employment for several months. I trusted he knew what he was doing as his unemployment checks were ample enough to pay his bills and our recreation, so I didn't worry. And Lenny, he was all about recreation. Unfortunately, I could not partake in all of Lenny's festivities because shortly before Lenny was laid off I acquired a full-time position in a new law firm. However, this law firm was nothing like my first one. There were no after-work drinks with co-workers, schmoozing and sexing with clients and other office inhabitants, nor were there any Christmas party dalliances. It was all work, work, and more work, I worked an average of 60 hours a week. Granted I was well paid for the overtime but it gave me little time to enjoy Rebecca or Lenny. I was exhausted and this was difficult to digest against the backdrop of Lenny's constant happy party parade.

Lenny had plenty of free time to research new guest stars to invite into our bed, new swinger parties, and new Tantra courses. We studied with a famous Tantra teacher from Hawaii that year who taught us, among valuable healing skills, the art of the "happy ending." Though we didn't come to rely on that massage technique for nearly a year, it became a viable option when the recession hit, and our bank accounts were happy indeed.

Soon after the high of my first swinger party wore off, I was feeling less like a social outcast and more like a super cool 48-year-old. I could not have imagined in my 20s that my life approaching 50 could be this fun and this wild. We attended Burning Man dance parties on a regular basis that usually required some form of creative costuming, which Lenny was delighted to create. He put weeks of effort into our regalia that practically earned a standing ovation when we'd enter the parties. Our costume addiction was clear to us but we had no desire to detox. We also joined a sensual group I referred to as The Sweet Spot, based on hand-genital stimulation in a group setting. They somehow found a way to market hand jobs as a spiritual experience. And of course Lenny continued to develop a core group of swinger singles and couples that often joined our bed as guest stars. Whatever happened to a couple of times a year?

Chapter 31

Burning Man, Nevada

At the end of July 2007, with Lenny's first trip to Burning Man coming up, I was getting anxious. He was going without me. Burning Man is an annual artistic event that takes place in the Black Rock Desert of Nevada for eight days, with over 50,000 inhabitants. It is a wildly creative event that features giant sculptures, 24/7 music, and radical self-expression and inclusion. Clothing is minimal and topless women are commonplace. That was the part that worried me: Lenny was a sensual force to be reckoned with and Burning Man was well known for wild days and nights of sex, drugs, and rock 'n' roll. I was increasingly anxious. Though we sexed with others a couple of times, we were always in one another's company. My possessive nature would not allow him to pursue sexual adventures without me, though he would have loved to. Funny, in the community of open relationships I was seen as tight, possessive, and controlling. Go figure. As wild as I was, in this world I was considered conservative. Really? Me?

During one of the last Burning Man fund-raising parties in early August, a couple that we both liked a lot overheard me expressing how sad I felt not to be traveling to Nevada for The Burn itself.

"So why don't you join us?" Bethany asked.

"I can't take that much time off from work," I said.

Bethany pondered, "Well...hmmm...you will get that Monday off for Labor Day right?"

I nodded.

She continued, "Maybe you can take off Thursday and Friday. This way you get a good five days in."

"Really?" I asked. "I thought you had to commit to the entire eight-day event."

Bethany replied, "Nah, however, once you've gone once you'll want to return for the full experience. But five days is a strong experience and you'll catch the tail end, which is the best part anyway."

That Monday at work I put in for those two days off, found a ticket to Burning Man, and booked my flight and rental car. Nevada here I come!

While packing up our costumes and making plans to meet Lenny on the Playa, I got a call from Alex, the sensual workshop leader.

"Hey Shanti. I enjoyed watching you and Lenny sexing at the July 4th party. You guys are great."

I replied, "Yeah, that was a big experience for me."

Alex asked, "Are you aware of the Dark Odyssey summer camp experience each September in Maryland?"

"I think I did hear something about that but not totally sure. Is it kind of like Burning Man for people into bondage and sadomasochism?"

Alex replied, "Yes, I've heard it compared that way. Well, I teach sensual massage to this BDSM crowd. They love it. Problem is, my demonstration partner recently backed out and I need to replace her. Would you be interested?"

I asked, "Would that be sensual massage with a happy ending?"

Alex replied, "Yes, I will be stroking your pussy towards the end of the demo. Lenny is welcome to join you, I have a large suite at camp. You would be able to participate in all the BDSM festivities as well. It's four days and a lot of fun."

All right! This was an appetite that I had organically but one that Lenny was less interested in pursuing. In fact, that first time Lenny had played BDSM games with me was Valentine's Day, and that was also the last time.

"Alex, I can tell you right now that I am a Yes but let me speak with Lenny to confirm."

"Wonderful! You'll be great. You're a natural. I've had my eye on you for years now. Trust me, I know a big slutty kinkster when I meet one."

Lenny agreed to join me for the Dark Odyssey BDSM experience in September. But for now, it was all about Burning Man. Lenny packed two tents and a sun flap.

I asked, "Why do we need two tents?"

He replied, "One tent is for undressing after being outside as it will get full of playa dust and one tent is only for sleeping, to keep it clean. It's difficult to stay clean there but with two tents it's more do-able. We'll want a clean bed for loving, won't we Bunny?"

"Of course my love..."

Burning Man was everything I'd hoped for and more. There was creative inspiration at every turn, 24/7 dancing, constant costuming, and spiritual magic everywhere. It may not have been everything Lenny had hoped for though, because I kept him on a short lease until I got there. The woman who created the 4th of July sex party suggested I give Lenny a sexual pass for the days before I arrived. I was not having it.

I remember our intense discussion right before Lenny left for Nevada. "Lenny, if you really want to sex with others before I arrive, then let me know right now. I'll cancel my trip and our relationship along with it."

"No Bunny. I don't want to break up. Please, don't leave me."

I pondered, "Well you are pouting like a poor deprived child. Maybe being unattached is what you really want, deep down inside."

Lenny replied, "No, I want you. I promise I won't sex with anyone until you get there. Okay? Will you please come and join me on this magical adventure?"

After a few minutes I calmed down and agreed to join Lenny. This was the extent of our fights. Lenny wanted some additional sexual privileges and I got angry and threatened to leave. Then he would see how adamant I was, and he would acquiesce. But Lenny constantly pushed the envelope and many times he succeeded, the hopeless love addict that I was.

The night I arrived at Burning Man, the greeters suggested I park my car in the parking lot, sleep there overnight, and look for my camp in the morning light. After all, there were 50,000 people to sift through. I was not okay with that suggestion. I didn't want to waste a moment of my precious time in the parking lot. Looked at the camp map, found our camp within 15 minutes. Good map training from my father coupled with strong instincts brought me right to the arms of my beloved.

However, I was shocked when I entered the main tent of our camp to see an orgy in full bloom. Yet there, at the edge of the festivities, my sweetheart lay swaddled in a white sheet, sound asleep. I remember the great feeling of love and pride that Lenny was able to resist his temptations for me.

I thought, "He really does love me after all."

I kissed my Prince on the forehead and then I whispered, "Hello my love. Thank you for honoring me. Thank you for honoring our commitment to one another. I love you so very much."

Still groggy, Lenny pulled his arms out of his cocoon and splayed them open as if to hug the orgy in progress.

"Welcome to Burning Man Bunny!"

We stayed in an openly sexual camp that included a large LGBTQ contingent. Knowing this in advance, I brought my soft latex cock with me, and walked around camp topless while packing my piece in boy's briefs. I had always enjoyed gender bending and Burning Man was a wonderful place to explore this aspect of myself.

I first enjoyed playing around with gender as a model in Paris when a famous hairdresser cut off my girlish locks. At first I was devastated but soon found a fan base of gay men that loved my look. I tried on occasion to play-up the boyish aspect of my look and personality by sneaking into gay male clubs. More recently Lenny and I would go out in cross-dress outfits, additional costume attention always welcome. But I did enjoy the exhibitionistic thrill of it. Anything taboo was enticing. My sex addict loved these kinds of adventures.

Funny enough, though we camped with kinksters and met many others along the way, we actually never sexed with anyone else at Burning Man. Maybe it had to do with the fact that showering was a difficult feat and dust was absolutely everywhere. Whatever the reason, I was happy to just be with my Lenny. It was a rare occasion and I enjoyed it immensely. Oh, and all those drugs at Burning Man? If there were any, no one wanted to share them with us. I must have asked twenty people if they had a joint. Not a big drug user, I thought this might be a great opportunity. But nope, there was no dope for us. They say you get at Burning Man exactly what is in your heart. Guess I didn't really want drugs after all.

We rode our bikes everywhere, danced incessantly, enjoyed all the creative sculptures, art performances, and burned The Man and Temple while chanting all night long. It was time for me to go. Lenny stayed on a few more days to clean camp, as we had planned. I took a red-eye flight back to New York and the cab took me right to my office. I was totally exhausted with playa dust still permeating my tangled hair. Thank goodness my boss was out of town, for I looked a total wreck. I had just come from a world where clothing was optional and money was not permitted. If anyone needed anything we'd all look around to help one another find it. It truly was a utopian interlude. But here I was, back to a world where only money mattered and conservative clothing was mandatory. I felt trapped and miserable in the routine of my 60-hour-a-week job. Thank goodness I had Dark Odyssey to look forward to, in less than two weeks. I couldn't wait to escape again.

Chapter 32

Dark Odyssey – BDSM Camp

Returning from our enlightening experience at Burning Man, we immediately began formulating our Super Hero Play Shop that we had been brewing since that 4th of July sex party. Our super-hero outfits had been a huge success at Burning Man in the desert of Black Rock. Everywhere we wore them, we felt we had something special going. I knew we needed to come up with business cards or flyers soon since, we'd be meeting new people in a few weeks at Dark Odyssey, the BDSM camp in Maryland. People there might be interested in our Super Hero Play Shop. We also needed to come up with a name for our brand and Lenny liked the name The Tantra Warriors. It fit just perfectly with our super-hero sex images. But Lenny, Lenny was not exactly the name of a super hero. Shanti worked nicely so I came up with another Sanskrit name to complement mine and I proposed Ananta, which means eternal. Lenny loved it immediately and from that day forward, we called him Ananta.

Talented graphic artist that Ananta was, he quickly created spectacular flyers with our super hero images for our Super Hero Play Shop. We scheduled our debut for that upcoming spring of 2008 in New York. Though we were only in the beginning stages of its creation, we were certain that the event would be a huge success, a time for adults to bring out their buried childhood dreams, and fly again. We took the flyers with us on our Dark Odyssey excursion. If Burning Man was the hipster ball of the year, then Dark Odyssey was the BDSM ball of a lifetime and I arrived with absolutely no warm-up. I had never been to a BDSM club, private party, or social gathering of any kind. I walked into a world that I had no idea existed, and was both repulsed and mesmerized at every turn.

Why had I agreed to attend Dark Odyssey and be Alex's demo model for his sensual massage class? I can only admit to blind curiosity. Someone without a sex/love addiction might never venture into these waters. But since I had few sensual hang-ups and boundaries, I was game. The sensual massage demo did not frighten me, it excited me.

Arriving to Dark Odyssey late at night, we didn't know what to expect with the morning light. Before leaving our suite for breakfast Alex suggested, "Since our sensual massage demo is not for another day, you and Ananta are free to roam the camp and check out the festivities. Enjoy!"

My god, and what festivities there were. As soon as we walked out of the house where all the facilitators were staying, we ran right into a naked couple having morning sex on the front lawn. The man was hitting the woman with various whips and paddles. I really was not ready for this. Ananta remained calm and seemed completely unaffected.

"Ananta, will there be naked people having sex all over this camp?!"

"Probably," he replied, with complete certainty. "I don't know, I've never been here before either. Let's go get some breakfast and check it out for ourselves."

I insisted, "Do not, under any circumstances, leave my side."

"Of course not Bunny."

There were No Sex, No Nudity signs in the dining hall, thank goodness, I was ready to throw up my eggs. After settling down with my tea and watching the show go by, Ananta pointed to a large board that listed all the events for the week. He beckoned me to follow him. That was easy, I was not going anywhere without him. Reading the board I was clear that I had just entered a world even wilder than the sex parties and I felt sick. I wanted to leave. I started crying.

Ananta was surprised, "Bunny, what is happening?"

"I think I've made a terrible mistake. I don't feel good here Ananta. I want to go home."

"Okay sweetie. Would you like to take a walk outside?" Ananta asked.

"No!" I cried, "it is crazier outside! I want to stay in here."

I sat down to read the board in detail, it listed all the workshops and social events that would be offered. There were workshops on dildo play, strap-on demo by a famous porn star, cutting workshops, branding, flogging, caning, whipping, bondage with ropes, bondage with leather straps or chains, spanking, wanking, and everything in between. Did I mention water sports? I was overwhelmed and leaned into Ananta.

I asked desperately, "How am I going to survive here for four days?"

Ananta replied, "I don't know honey. You were the one that had appetite to come here. There must be something attracting you."

I looked around at the freak show. There were men dressed as babies wearing diapers, bonnets, adult sized baby doll dresses, and sucking on pacifiers. There were morbidly obese people wearing the tiniest of G-strings and nothing else. Apparently that was not considered nudity. There were some people covered head to toe in tattoos with various ribbons and straps attached to rings sewn onto their bodies. There were transgendered men and women in various stages of transition that somehow gave the place an air of conservatism. Though I was afraid of my own appetite, I decided I had to watch the show.

We ran into several people in the dining area that we knew from various sensual communities and Burning Man. This really helped because they offered me friendship and sounding boards that I desperately needed.

Nancy, who was at my first sex party on July 4th asked, "Is this your first time here at D.O. Shanti?"

"Yes, my first time. Does it show?"

Laughing sweetly Nancy replied, "It does show. It's okay though. Enjoy your freak-out. Most everyone goes through it the first time. But no one is judgmental and if all you do is watch that is totally fine."

"Phewww. That's what I needed to hear." I replied.

Nancy continued, "And if you would like to do a private scene there is a bulletin board in the corner where you can write out your desires and ask for other players."

The three of us immediately headed over there. The bulletin board had several scenes advertised already.

Male - LOOKING FOR TORTURE TRIBE TO HURT ME IN THE DUNGEON Saturday, September 15, 8 p.m. Bring your deadliest weapons! All genders welcome.

Male - HUMILATION SCENE – Looking for Domme Women ONLY to yell and spit at me. Meet outside dining hall Sunday, September 16th 3 p.m.

Female - SLAVES WANTED to lick my boots and anything else I want you to lick. Saturday, September 15, 5 p.m. at entrance to pool. Preference for young boy types and large-breasted women.

Transgender fem - WATER SPORTS. DRINK UP and bring me your PISS! Meet outside barn Monday, September 17, 11 a.m.

Female - Bukaki Babe. Looking for 20 or more men to release their juices on me. Sunday, September 16, 2 p.m. Sex-O-Rama room.

"What the hell is Bukaki?" I blurted out.

Ananta chimed in immediately, "It's when a group of men jerk off on a woman's face."

"How do you know this Ananta?"

"It's every man's dream," he replied with a smile.

"Really? I just can't believe it's real! This entire place is crazy!"

Nancy smiled, "Oh it is very real and a lot of it is tons of fun when you let go of your judgments. But at first it is a rough landing, I know. I felt like you do when I first came here."

"How long ago was that?" I asked.

Nancy thought a moment, "Hmmm, I think like eight or nine years ago."

"Wow, you must be a pro by now."

Nancy laughed, "Actually, I used to be a pro, pro dominatrix that is. But now I just do it for fun. My man makes enough money that I don't need to work any more. But I do still enjoy the activities. You'd probably make a great dominatrix yourself, you're so tall, beautiful, and commanding. Men would clamor to have you hurt them. Have you figured out if you're more submissive or dominant?"

"I can't even figure out if I'm going to stay," I replied.

"This is the Disney World of BDSM," she said, "Pace yourself or you'll get nauseous from the wild rides." Nancy laughed and walked away.

I looked to Ananta. "Get nauseous? I've been wanting to throw up all morning!"

Feeling a need for fresh air and finally feeling the courage to walk outside again, I was immediately amused by a group of human animals parading in front of the dining hall. There were several dozen people dressed as ponies with their handlers holding the reins, along with dogs and cats on leashes and some spectacular birds. Many of these human animals were largely naked except for butt-plug tails and other accessories that delineated their animal. I found it quite beautiful. Maybe I was finding my tribe after all. I beckoned Ananta to follow them with me and we ended up at a corral outside the barn. The scene was amusing, yet quite serene. I finally smiled.

"Nice to see you smile again Bunny."

"Yes, I'm really fascinated with this."

"What kind of animal would you like to be?"

Without skipping a beat, I replied, "A horse. I love their beautiful tails and manes."

"Yes, you would make a gorgeous horse my Shanti."

That was it. It took a group of humans dressed as animals prancing about to make me feel comfortable at a BDSM camp. The remainder of the day was a blast. Though we did not fully participate in any of the workshops, we did watch several, including a cutting-and-branding class, the strap-on demonstration with a famous porn star, and various flogging, whipping, and bondage workshops. It was a fascinating education. The greatest surprise of all was how friendly everyone was. I had newbie written all over my face and everyone was super sweet in making me feel comfortable and answering my myriad of questions.

The next morning it was my turn to be on stage, serving as Alex's demonstration model for his sensual massage. There were 50 people in the room and Alex set up a camera aimed on us so everyone could get a great view. Our images appeared brightly on a huge 8x10 screen. Being a model and an actress, I've always known that I am an exhibitionist, but seeing my naked body that large and close up was overwhelming, even for me. I had to look away from the screen completely when Alex started massaging my pussy so I could get into the pleasure of his touch and not the freak out of my mind. Seeing my pussy that up close and personal was definitely a shock. But Alex's touch calmed me right down. Wow, he did indeed have an incredible touch. Ananta had a magical touch too but Alex, he was the master.

After the demonstration was over, we had a question and answer session. "How did it feel to be brought to orgasm while we watched?"

I replied, "Well, the exhibitionist in me loved it for sure."

The room chuckled.

I continued, "But after a while, Alex's touch was so divine that I lost track of everyone and it was just me and Alex. I was in a total sensual trance. I highly recommend anyone who wants to bring their woman into ecstasy to study with Alex."

I met Ananta for lunch in the dinning hall where the freak show was always blazing high. But somehow, after my stage performance with Alex, it didn't seem as freaky.

"Hey Bunny. How are you feeling?"

"I'm feeling great actually. Trying to figure out what I want to do here next.

"What are you most afraid of?" Ananta asked.

"I'm afraid of the extent of my sensual pleasure. I really loved being on stage when Alex brought me to orgasm. Going further in that direction really scares me."

Within the next half hour I mapped out with Ananta my taboo fantasy and posted it on the camp bulletin board.

Female - FEMININE FEAST! Looking for men and women to ravage my feminine body into orgasm. Positions to be filled:

-right breast

-left breast

-clitoris

-vagina

-anus

214

-feet

-mouth

Meet me in Sex-O-Rama tonight at 9 for some after-dinner delight!

In 20 minutes all my positions were filled with friends who were anxious to help me out. That's what friends are for! I reserved my mouth for Ananta – for me that is the most romantic body part.

Ananta asked, "What if others want to join in?"

I replied, "They can be audience members. I like to be watched."

Ananta laughed, "Yes, my Bunny is a bad rabbit for sure!"

Right before show time, Alex, who signed up for the anus, had to pull out. His girlfriend was not at camp but he called her and for some reason, she felt threatened by his involvement in my orgy. Why it didn't bother her that he was stroking my pussy at his sensual massage workshop, I have no idea. I lost my ass man, but felt no need to find a replacement. Three people on my crotch was a bit much anyway. But everyone else was on deck and happy to serve.

Ananta made sure that I had plenty of pillows, sheets, lube, and latex gloves. I wanted those stroking my pussy to wear gloves. It was not only safe sex, it was a divine feeling when lathered with lube. As my sensual orgy team assembled, one of my pussy strokers pulled out a huge vibrator, the Hitachi Magic Wand.

She announced, "Just in case our Queen would like added stimulation..."

"Wow!" I exclaimed. "Okay, but let's keep this for later. I don't want to cum too soon."

"As her majesty wishes."

I put Ananta in charge of communication between my pleasure team members and me. I knew that once I surrendered to my pleasure I would not want to be speaking much. So anything I wanted to communicate I would whisper to Ananta, who would stay close to my mouth, and he would relay to those in charge of that body part where I wanted some adjustments.

I had foot guy start massaging first. Hmmm...I so loved a good foot massage, it got me in the sensual mood fast. He was the only person that I did not know well so I gave him the less intimate position. Yet a good foot massage got me wet instantly.

215

Once I was warmed up with the foot massage, I called in my pussy squad and soon the breast team, our good friends Jim and Dina, and I enjoyed watching them making out together while they stroked my breasts. That said, I needed Ananta to communicate with them more often as their making out was taking their attention away from me. I felt a lopsided touch. I finally had to have Ananta stop their making-out altogether. Bitchy Queen I was.

Then there was my fidgety foot guy. He kept trying to creep up my thighs towards my pussy.

"Ananta, tell the foot guy to stay on my feet only," I commanded.

But after two tries, I finally told Ananta, "Get him off of me! If he is that turned on, tell him to drop his pants and jerk off while watching me."

My foot guy was happy to comply. He became my first active audience member.

Soon the room became filled with onlookers.

I told Ananta, "Tell the guys in the audience to drop their pants and jerk off."

At one point there were a half-dozen guys jerking off all around me. It was super hot.

My clitoris babe asked, "Is it time for the turbo vibrator your majesty?"

"Yes!" I exclaimed.

And within a few more minutes I had a room-rockin' orgasm and let out a huge howl. Everyone in the room stood up and clapped, an ecstatic standing ovation. Oh what an night...

I had just experienced the sluttiest thing I could possibly imagine. If Ananta and I did not make it as a permanent couple, how would I ever explain this to another man? I felt liberated and yet trapped at the same time. Somehow, enacting this taboo changed how I thought of myself. If attending my first orgy that summer changed how I felt about myself as a "good girl," there was no longer any doubt that I had entered the total "bad girl" world. Would I continue or would I recover, I had no idea. But I felt something sink inside me as the fear of no return soaked into my thoughts. What had I done? What could possibly come next?

I spent the next night cross-dressing as a man in the masculine alter ego that I now refer to as Shawn. Ananta was semi-dressed wearing only black combat boots and a cock cage. I had never seen this contraption before.

"Ananta, what do you do with this?"

As he attached a leash to the end of his cock cage he said, "Well, you often tell me that you suffer with jealousy. Now you get to keep my cock on a leash and control wherever it goes."

We both laughed and went down the hill for dinner. Evidently, a cock cage was acceptable dinner attire. I couldn't figure out the rules of this place, nor did I care to. I was happy to be leaving the next day, terrified of what I might become if I stayed any longer.

These BDSM kinksters were partaking in what some might consider risky behaviors, yet they were set in controlled environments with willing participants. Most of my sexually risky behaviors took place in my everyday life with friends, lovers, co-workers and often with unwilling participants. How many times did I send my boyfriends up the pole with my infidelities? I rarely thought of the consequences that my risky behaviors might have, at least not consciously. Perhaps the risk, pumped by adrenaline, is what fueled my action? As I got sober from my sex/ love addiction these risky behaviors were revealed as part of the addiction cycle.

Chapter 33

Private Swinger Parties at Home

Ananta and I were both a tad burned out on large group events. From our costume premier at the Mermaid Parade at the end of June to the July 4th Sex Party, to Burning Man in August to Dark Odyssey in September, we were both needing some quiet times at home. But that didn't mean Ananta was burned out on sexing with others. I'm not going to lie and totally blame Ananta for always getting us into sensual mischief. I did enjoy kinkiness once in a while yet I would have been happy to dine at such a feast only two or three times a year as a special dessert. However Antanta, he could have gorged on kink as a steady diet.

Ideally he would have loved to live with me and another bisexual swinger couple so we could mix and match. He also loved my best friend, Adriana, but she would never have sex with him. Adri was strictly into women, or so she thought until she fell in love with - and married - an Orthodox rabbi the same year I got into a relationship Ananta. From then on Adriana drifted away from me. It broke my heart but her new conservative life and my new wild life did not mix. Adriana had been my best friend, my lover, and my emotional rock. I would grieve the loss of our friendship for many years to come.

Ananta became my new life focus and I knew I had to feed his sexual cravings or risk losing him. I could not risk losing Ananta. I was completely in love and attached to him. Co-dependent, love addict, I was vaguely familiar with the terms but I needed what I needed. Da Nile is a wide and deep river.

By the winter of 2008 we had become warm and cozy with Barry and Sandy. They were the organizers from the Brooklyn sex party we attended on July 4th that previous summer. It began with

218

Ananta's soft request and my reluctant agreement to have them over for dinner.

I told Ananta, "Okay, but I cannot guarantee that I will be sexual with them. A party is one thing, lots of drinking, dancing, and music but in our home? I don't know, honey."

Ananta was chill as always, great groomer that he was. "My Queen, if all we do is share a meal together that would be delightful."

Towards the end of dinner, with some covert and overt sexual innuendos, I suspected that I was to be the dessert. I heard Ananta and Sandy whispering in the next room as Barry and I washed the dishes together. I could smell a plot brewing and expected some sort of sensual activities might occur but I was still new to the scene, I wasn't really sure of the protocols.

Barry started flirting with me heavily in the kitchen, at first with his glances and then his words. "I'm really happy to be here with you tonight Shanti. You are very hot. I couldn't stop noticing you since Ananta started bringing you out with him last winter. Then when you came to our party in July, well, I have not stopped fantasizing about you."

Barry was tall, dark, and handsome, exactly my type. It made me nervous to feel my attraction for him, and I still could not figure out why Ananta would want me to want another man. But since he did, I tried my best to go with it.

Barry asked, "May I kiss you?"

My mind went wild with rebellion: "Oh hell, I don't know! I still am not clear I like these guest-star sexcapades!"

But instead of sharing my thoughts I just giggled nervously.

Barry asked with his bedroom eyes, "Are those giggles saying Yes, you want me to kiss you, or No you don't?

Drying my hands from the dishwater I turned to him, "Barry, I am very attracted to you. I am. But this is a super awkward experience for me. I love Ananta very much and am not comfortable kissing another man. I know you guys must do this all the time but I really don't know how I feel about this swinging thing."

Barry explained, "Well, we don't actually do this as often as you might guess. We do organize sex parties but they are a lot of work to produce and we don't have much time to connect with other couples while we are working. I get nervous too. I am nervous right now because you are so pretty."

Barry's genuine smile had me feeling more relaxed. Then he leaned in to kiss me, though I was not ready. As fate would have it, at that moment Sandy burst into the kitchen and put her arms around my waist.

"Isn't she the hottest thing?"

Barry smiled, "Yes she is."

I excused myself for the bathroom, desperately needing to escape the heat of that kitchen. I also wanted to clean myself because sensual activities seemed imminent. After a few minutes there was a knock at the bathroom door.

"It's Sandy. Can I come in?" I opened the door. She asked if I was okay.

I wanted to scream out loud, "No I am so not okay! What kind of insanity is going on here where my husband wants to touch you, and you AND your husband want to touch me?!"

Instead, trying to be cool, I said, "I'm okay but I'm very nervous. I am not used to this kind of thing, you know? I feel really awkward. I don't know what to say or do or not do."

She grabbed me by the waist again, "Well that's okay honey. You don't have to do anything you don't want. Is it okay for me to hug you like this?"

It really wasn't okay but I said, "Yes," trying desperately to fit into this crazy swinger world.

Sandy pressed onward: "Is it okay if I kiss you?"

I really wasn't sure about the kissing but I squeaked out, "Okay."

Sandy was tiny, probably no more than 5'2". All I could think about in that moment was how strange it was to bend down to kiss someone. I usually looked up to a guy or at least eye-to-eye. Adriana was more like 5'5" but still, we rarely ever kissed, she would have loved to kiss me more often but I was not into romance with her. It was strictly sexual for me with Adri.

Though I would have preferred Sandy to stand tall on the toilet to kiss me, I went with this strange difference in height and enjoyed her enjoyment of me. I really did prefer kissing men but when I got aroused sexually, I did love me some pussy. That makes me bisexual. I know that. However, I had not been bi-romantic. I was only romantically attracted to men.

When Sandy pulled away from her swooning kiss she asked, "Can I lead you to your bed while we talk about what you might like to happen there?"

I was a woman of few words at this point, rather frozen really. Happy that Sandy was taking the lead.

She led me by the hand from the bathroom to my bed. We passed Ananta and Barry sitting at the dinner table and their faces lit up watching us recline together.

Sandy then announced, "Guys, Shanti is a bit nervous and uncomfortable right now."

Then she looked at me and said, "Okay, so I'm going to ask you some questions and see what you would like to do now. Will that work for you honey?"

What happened for the next ten minutes was much like a game of sexy charades. Everyone asked me questions, hoping to uncover my sensual appetites so we all could get under the covers. They also asked questions about my boundaries. I started with the boundaries, as they were my greatest concern: Intercourse with Barry was off limits for me and intercourse between Ananta and Sandy was off limits. I was sure Ananta would have loved to screw Sandy but I would have been too jealous to observe that. However, hand-genital touching between any of us was fine with me. Turns out, a few hits of marijuana and most of my inhibitions magically disappeared. I rarely smoked, but on this night, it was a welcome relief.

Sandy and Barry became our most frequent guest stars. Sometimes we'd visit them in Brooklyn and other times at my place. We soon added several other couples to our tribe. But, Sandy and Barry were our regulars. After several encounters of hand/genital touching, I felt safe enough with Barry to go all the way, but I didn't like it. Intercourse, especially in the missionary position, was too intimate for me. I reserved that for my husband, who I was in love with. Barry sensed my upset and stopped rather quickly.

Then I watched Ananta penetrating Sandy, and it was titillating for me to watch my husband entering her. I began kissing her breast and Barry joined in to kiss her other breast while Ananta slid into her. She seemed to be in heaven.

I wished I could be as free as Sandy but I was not. I became a swinger to keep Ananta happy: co-dependent love addict. I was indeed a reluctant swinger but did my best to get with the program. There were times when I enjoyed it more than other times but I would have been much happier if my husband had desired only me. But since I knew that would never happen, this was second best. At least this way, he would not cheat on me to get his kink on. That was the agreement anyway. Or so I imagined.

Chapter 34

Leaving Legal Again

I left my life as a legal secretary in June of 2008 to join forces with Ananta in the unemployment brigade. Ananta had been laid off from his web design position a year earlier. He had enjoyed a year of relaxation, social networking, costuming, and sexing. Against this leisure backdrop I was grinding away in an intense 8 a.m. to 10 p.m. position supporting a busy attorney who, unfortunately for me, was a work-a-holic. This was nothing like my first job as a legal secretary. That was a dream job, it often included a blow job on the side, great place for this sex addict to work! But with my new work-a-holic boss, I had to keep his train running smoothly at all times of the day or night. On top of these outrageous hours of work I was working with Ananta formulating The Tantra Warriors. We were creating a relationship-coaching practice and offering several unique and colorful workshops.

I had been offering dating-coach sessions for singles after work and on weekends for a few years. But now that I was in a solid relationship, I felt I could coach couples as well. Ananta had been studying for several years with many of the same teachers I had studied with, so we felt we would be the perfect coaching team. We were deeply in love with each other and our relationship was founded on the principles of these various camps where we both studied. Now we wanted to coach others on how to have an outrageously happy relationship like ours. We felt we were relationship super heroes and had the costumes to prove it.

Ananta's happy-go-lucky lifestyle only magnified the oppression I was enduring at work. However, instead of encouraging or insisting Ananta get a job, after all he was out of money, I decided to quit my high-paying, well-positioned job and join in on the "fun." I had recently dug myself out of over 50k of debt with a few thousand to spare, and I was certain our new business would be successful and thriving within a few months. Delusion can be so seductively grand.

I took the month of July off to enjoy the summer and join my boyfriend's fun parade. We went to several parties and sensual social gatherings, the nude beach (Ananta didn't like the "regular" beach), and of course swinger parties. Wake-up call number... one, two, three that my boyfriend might have a sex addiction? Going to kinky events was my end of the bargain, if he would promise never to cheat on me. He accepted my terms, at least outwardly.

Ananta's unemployment ran out, so I was paying for most of the entertainment expenses. Wake-up call number... four, five? But since we were building a life together, I told myself it was fine. Making a temporary sacrifice until income from our new business kicked in. Ananta moved into my apartment to cut down on his expenses. Bye-bye hipster haven in Williamsburg.

Come August I'd had enough frivolity and was getting anxious to create our website, workshop outlines, contact lists, and business cards. While Ananta grunted and groaned about all the fun we were missing out on, including a trip to Burning Man that year, I became the slave driver. Wake-up call number...six, seven?

During September 2008, I felt unsettled by the news that such a giant financial institution as Lehman Brothers filed for bankruptcy. Then there were the projected collapses of many other banks. Yet I had a new business baby to care for and took only minimal notice. However, by the end of September it became painfully clear that our new baby could not thrive in this financially bankrupt environment and there would be little financial future for anyone.

One day, after ignoring the headlines no longer, I started to panic. I called my one loyal coaching client, Heinz, to see if he wanted a tune-up session. I had been coaching Heinz before I met Ananta and could always count on him for some stable income. He was wealthy, smart, and patient in his efforts to find Mrs. Right. This day, however, instead of a session he invited me out for drinks. A social invitation with clients was not a practice I normally accepted, but I was desperate. Maybe he wanted to introduce me to possible new clients? Maybe he wanted to make an indecent proposal? I had no idea, nor did I care. All my carefully constructed professional boundaries went out the window with my financial panic attack. After three glasses of merlot, a cup of olives and two cups of nuts, I finally received the message all too clear.

Heinz said, "Shanti, I have no disposable income to offer you now. I will be filing for bankrupt. Most likely I will have to give up my apartment and move in with my son for a while, in Texas."

Soon after Heinz' declaration sunk in, he put me in a cab and handed me a $20 bill for the fare. This would be the last sliver of income from our coaching practice for many months to come.

When I got home I saw an open bottle of merlot on the kitchen counter. Though already quite drunk, I poured another "healthy" glass, an unprecedented move for me. I curled up in bed with my goblet and called Ananta. I needed some calm from this devastating financial distress. But Ananta did not answer. Next, in my drink-and-dial mood, I called my ex-boyfriend, Yigal. He answered from the comfort of his home and was more than happy to chat. In the middle of my flirtation with hunky Yigal, Ananta called to say he was on his way home. I was high on the combo of merlot and ex-boyfriend attention.

When I got back to the call with Yigal I let him know I needed to get off the phone soon because my "man" was arriving. Yigal, all too aware that Ananta had been unemployed for the past year and a half, laid into me.

"Shanti, what kind of guy has no job? What kind of guy lets you pay for him? What kind of guy takes you to sex parties? Shanti, you are the most loving, beautiful, spiritual woman I have ever met. What are you doing with this loser?"

Yigal's blast was the deafening chime of truths I was too paralyzed to embrace. Then his flirtations escalated to the point of great discomfort so I hung up. We were entering the danger zone of reconnecting, all too familiar.

I lay on the bed, completely hammered, terrified, and outraged that Ananta had not stepped up to the plate to take care of us financially, as Yigal just reminded me. I was stewing in my angry sauce when there was a knock. I opened the door to find Ananta's smiling face and a white bouquet of mums. I somehow managed to let him in before I beat him over the head with the flowers.

Though I did not say it I thought, "That's what you get for giving me cheap flowers you lazy out-of-work, good-for-nothing freeloader!"

My next move was back to the kitchen to grab the open bottle of wine. I left my goblet by the bed and just guzzled it right out of the bottle. I remember Ananta's feeble attempt to take the bottle from my hand but I was determined and finished the half-bottle in one long swig. I saw Ananta's eyes widen and that was the last time I remember seeing his face for the rest of the evening. I was totally plastered.

The remainder of that night was a blur. All I remember was crawling around the floor crying in despair.

"How will we live? We are going to starve! No one will help us! We are going to die!"

I do remember carrying on in French, crying out to my dead grandmother, Odette Owen, a lovely French Canadian who I completely adored. We lived with Gram for a couple years when I was very young, and now I was desperately craving to be taken care of, safe and warm, like with Gram.

Eventually I threw up two bottles of merlot on the hardwood floor. All I could see was a sea of red wine. At first I panicked, thinking it was blood. Though I could not hear Ananta, nor see him, I felt his loving hands and arms guiding me to bed. When I awoke the next morning I was silent for many hours, numb from terror, hopelessness, and nursing a horrible hangover.

Chapter 35

Dumpster Diving for Dinner

When my head cleared from the hangover and the terror of being broke, I rolled up my sleeves as always and figured out plan B.

I spoke to Ananta very matter-of-fact: "We have no income and hefty bills. The biggest is rent so let's sublet this place a couple weeks a month and stay with your parents."

Ananta looked puzzled, "In Costa Rica?"

Ananta's parents were currently staying on their little farm in their homeland of Costa Rica. They spent about 1/3 of their time there.

I clarified, "No, in the Bronx. We can stay in the attic where we always stay when we visit."

I could see Ananta's wheels turning, "And... what about Rebecca? She will be very far from her school."

"Well, we will have to shift her schedule. She will have to stay with her Dad Monday through Thursday when we sublet, and stay with us in the Bronx on week-ends."

Ananta did not respond but his silent nod emoted much.

"Rebecca won't be happy about this but we have no choice Ananta. We are totally broke with no money coming in. What do you suggest?"

"Okay Bunny."

Ananta often called me Bunny. It was a term of endearment that I hated at first because I felt more like a lioness than a damn rabbit. Yet Ananta was so cute when he said it that I let it stick.

I went on, "Next biggest bill is food. Going out to eat is out of the question but even groceries are pricey. I asked Rebecca's Dad earlier today if he could give me extra child support money for a few months just to carry us in groceries but he refused. I figured he thought I might be lying so suggested that he just give us the groceries. He still refused. Nice guy eh?"

Ananta stayed silent. I was waiting for some brainstorming on his part but there was nothing. I replayed in my head the sharp words from Yigal. Anger returned to my spirit. Since Ananta had no ideas on how to get us out of this financial mess, we would follow my plans, since I was the only one that had any!

I continued, "For food, we will get our food from the garbage bags outside the grocery stores."

Ananta's face convulsed.

"Yup, I did it once with Mike as a funny ha-ha but starving is not funny so ha-ha, this is how we can get our food."

"Okay Bunny. Whatever you want."

"This is not what I want Ananta! What I want is for us to be able to earn income to buy groceries and stay in our apartment and not have to live in the attic of your parent's house. But it doesn't look like that is going to happen.

"Yes Bunny."

As soon as it was Rebecca's night to be with her father, we packed up our granny cart, backpacks, plastic bags, rubber gloves, and headed for the grocery stores after 10 p.m. At night the grocery stores throw out expired produce, dairy, meats, canned goods, breads, pastas, and any foods that have passed their expiration dates. Most of the food is still perfectly good, only the freshness date is up. I learned with Mike how to retrieve these foods from the grocery store garbage bags and dumpsters through a grass roots organization whose aim is to salvage good food that would otherwise go to land fills. That night was our lifeline. Not only did we discover there was ample free food to feed us for the entire week, but there was an over-abundance waiting to be had. From that next night forward we took huge suitcases with us and filled them so that we could share our newfound wealth with family, friends, neighbors, and the homeless.

Dumpster-diving was our new job and like any job, it had its perks and its pains. The winter months were long and hard after the Second Great Depression of 2008. On bitter cold nights I longed for the luxury of shopping inside a warm grocery store and picking the foods of our choosing. With dumpster-diving you get what you get and we did our best not to get upset. That was our motto. We became great creative chefs, concocting new recipes with our plentiful bounty. We both gained a bunch of weight that penniless year.

Chapter 36

Stripping 101

Though we made good money renting out our apartment a week or two each month - thank God for Airbnb - it was not quite enough to pay all our bills. There were still utilities, phone bills, toiletries, transportation, and occasional medical bills. None of us had medical insurance back then except Rebecca, who was part of the New York State run program, Child Health Plus. Sure America, take care of the children. But if the parents die, then what? Stick the children in foster care? Thank God for Medicaid and Obamacare.

Why not use my credit card to pay our bills? After the legal bills from my divorce from Jeremy, then four years of college, I was nearly 50k in debt. It took me five years to bail myself out of debt and I wasn't going back. So we needed to find another solution besides moving in with Ananta's family full-time. They were the sweetest people on earth but I did not want to give up my autonomy just yet. There had to be another way.

My friend Vinny was a dear friend in his mid 60s who had bailed me out of tough spots in the past. He was a trader but mainly, his wife paid the bills. Vinny wasn't handsome but he always had women around him; it didn't hurt that he was financially generous. Vinny was friendly with several strippers and one of them, Chrissy, was a cute 20-something from Brazil that he was particularly found of. The three of us often dined together, a free meal during the frigid dumpster diving nights was a slice of heaven. One night, after hearing my financial woes, Chrissy made a suggestion.

"Why you don't be a stripper?"

I nearly spit out my wine.

Laughing along with Vinny I replied, "Chrissy, I am 49 years old. They are not going to hire a 49-year-old stripper."

"My beauty, you look like 30 years old. And I have seen you dance at parties, Vinny and me. You are gorgeous and you got the moves."

Still in disbelief I asked, "Are you serious?"

"Shanti, there are couple women at my club in their 40s that don't look hot like you. I swear. I can get you an audition. Just tell them you are 30."

"No way!" I protested.

Chrissy looked surprised, "Why not? You make lots of money and stop eating from the garbage! This is too much for a super model to eat out of the garbage. Vinny, tell her."

I clarified, "No Chrissy, I meant no way I can say I am 30. I won't pass for 30. I am open to auditioning but I will tell them I am 39, okay?"

"Okay *amore*! You are going to love it!! You are so natural for this job."

Chrissy spent the remainder of dinner going over what to wear and the ins and outs of auditioning with her boss, who was a bit of an asshole.

I told her, "I need a few weeks to get in better shape and feel more confident."

"You crazy! Excuse me if I insult you but Vinny tell me you and your husband go to orgy parties, no? So, this is no problem you do that but you are naked there, no?"

I smiled, "Yes, I am naked there but the lights are dark and honestly, I am not trying to impress anyone. Half of me doesn't even care to be there so I don't try to impress."

"Vinny, what she say?"

Vinny, who had been quiet during our exchange, chimed in, "Shanti is a cursed co-dependent, just like me. We go along for the ride even if it makes us throw up."

Vinny laughed hysterically at his own joke. He often did that. He really was funny and his metaphor was precise. I piped in to clarify for Chrissy, who looked lost.

"Chrissy, I go to these orgies to please my husband. He likes them. I don't really like them but I do it so he won't cheat on me." Chrissy looked confused. "You know, sleep with other women?"

She started speaking loudly in Portuguese to herself until she grabbed my arm, "*Amore*, what you do with your husband, okay, is your business. But if you want make money, you make lot of money stripping. I promise you."

The conviction coming from Chrissy gave solace to my frightened soul. It was two months since the economy tanked and no one was hiring in corporate America, they were only firing.

With my newly restored enthusiasm I told Chrissy, "Yes! Thank you sweetness for this opportunity!!"

"No problem *amore*. You so gorgeous. You make big money stripping. I kill my boss he don't take you and I make him big money. He no can say no."

I spent the next few weeks dieting, getting buff, and shopping for a stripper dress and platform heels that I could afford. Chrissy offered to let me borrow one of her outfits but she was a foot shorter than me, with tiny feet. She assured me that the money I would make stripping would pay for the outfit in less than an hour. I was getting excited, though I was a tad nervous that someone from the corporate world might recognize me and then I'd have trouble going back there. But at this point, all I wanted was cash. I lost all concern for my reputation when dumpster-diving paved the way. This was about survival.

Once my outfit was in place and I felt good about my body, I called Chrissy.

She said, "Tell Vinny bring you to the club for dinner tomorrow night. Dress very sexy. You have nice dinner, watch the girls dance, and then I introduce you to my boss. Okay?"

"Should I bring my stripper dress?" I asked.

"No, no, auditions in afternoon before work. You just come tomorrow night meet my boss."

That next night I normally had Rebecca so I asked her Dad to watch her. At first he protested but then I explained that I had a business dinner with several attorneys, hoping one might hire me. It wasn't a total lie. It was a business dinner, and likely many attorneys would be in attendance.

Full of excitement and anticipation, I enjoyed my pre-audition night. Vinny walked me around and I felt many men staring at me, even though naked women lined the aisles. Sex/love addicts crave attention almost more than sex, almost. I watched intently how the women danced and how they held the men's attention.

I thought, "Oh yeah, I got this."

Then I felt a tap on my shoulder. It was Chrissy.

"Listen, my boss is in the office. He's no coming on the floor tonight. Are you okay meet him in his office downstairs? Just knock the door and tell him I send you. He knows you are beautiful and you were a big super model. His name is Ivan."

Chrissy led me to the office door and walked away. I knocked. No response. I knocked again.

"What?" replied the grouchy voice behind the door.

"Hello, it's Shanti. Chrissy told me to come see you."

The door opened to reveal a man with dark hair, average height, average weight, and average looks. There was nothing unattractive or remarkable about him except his aggressive energy. He seemed quite annoyed that I was disturbing him.

"What do you want?" he barked.

"Chrissy told me to see you about dancing here."

He seemed confused then a brief light opened in his eyes, "Oh yeah, I'm really busy right now but you can come in for a minute."

Ivan's office was very small, not what I imagined, and his desk was covered in papers. The legal secretary in me wanted to help him organize everything.

He sat at his desk and asked, "So where do you dance now?"

I panicked a moment trying to remember the strip club in Miami where Chrissy told me to tell him I worked. I hate lying, but here I was about to spew a line of lies.

"I just moved here from Miami. I worked at Felix's," I told him, sweating all the way.

"Yeah? Felix's is a good club. Why you move up here?"

"I have family here."

"How old are you?

233

I felt the burn of another lie about to be born, "I'm 39. Is that too old?"

"Well, most of the girls are in their 20s but some of the older girls make more money then they do. Depends the girl, you know?"

I nodded. Then I felt him look at me more closely. Was he looking for wrinkles, fat, saggy skin? I wanted to run out of the room.

He leaned back in his chair. There was no chair on the other side of his desk so I remained standing. I felt nervous, more nervous than any acting audition I had ever had.

Ivan began to speak, which eased my nerves. "Here's the thing. Since this economy crashed, all my corporate clients have pulled out. You see the club tonight? It's empty for a Thursday night. Dead. Even my regular girls can't make a decent living."

I felt as though Ivan was about to give me the brush off until I remembered Chrissy's parting words, "Make sure he gives you a dance audition this week. Don't let him say no."

I was nervous because I knew I was living a lie so I told myself to pretend this was an acting audition and I was playing the part of a woman that had been stripping for years. Instantly my nerves disappeared and I started improvising.

"Sure I understand. We had the same problem in Miami but I never lost income. Guess that's the beauty of being older. We don't take no for an answer. I could always get the $20 G-string customer into the private rooms. I'd still be there but my mother's not too well. They're in NJ. I need to be living closer to them."

"Look, I can't promise you anything right now," he paused to look at me again. "Can you come back tomorrow for an audition?"

"Sure," I replied.

Ivan got out of his chair and walked to open the door. "Okay, bring your dress and be here at three for hair and make-up."

As the door closed I felt intense excitement and nervousness all at once. I was incredibly proud of my performance. Now to go back to the dance floor and do more acting research.

I joined Vinny, who was in the middle of a hot lap dance. I watched closely as she spun her sensual web, knowing I would be doing the same tomorrow. Vinny seemed embarrassed to see me. Vinny and I were never lovers but super great friends. We had similar mother abandonment wounds and that bonded us. I excused myself to let Vinny have his private time. I searched for Chrissy to tell her the good news. I saw she was busy talking to a client so I waited at the bar. Then a handsome man struck up a conversation with me.

"You working here?" he asked.

The actress kicked into gear again, "No, not working here yet. Just moved back here this week. Have an audition tomorrow."

"You'll get it. You're their style," he told me.

"Oh really? What is their style?" I asked.

"Tall gorgeous women."

"Awweeee, you do flatter!"

Chrissy came bounding up at that moment, "So what happened sexy mama?"

Our stranger interjected, "Great! I'll take both of you to the private room!"

Chrissy then sat on his lap and replied, "You can have both of us next week. But tonight, she is mine!"

She drank his drink then grabbed my arm and pulled me to an open couch.

"So tell me, what happened?" Chrissy asked. I told her every detail. Chrissy stood up and clapped, "*Brava amore*! Let's have a drink to celebrate."

She pulled me back to the bar where our stranger was still seated. Frankly, she didn't seem like she needed another drink but I was happy to appease her. Chrissy sat on the gentleman's lap again, "We need drinks my love."

He seemed happy to oblige, "But of course. Waiter."

As Chrissy got more cozy with our stranger it became clear that he would not be a stranger for much longer, he would be her new client. So I gracefully eased away from them and headed back to Vinny's table, to ask him to take me home.

I often called Vinny my GA, for Guardian Angel. Vinny was always looking out for me. He was my greatest protector, always there when I needed him. My GA, how I adore him.

I slept in the next morning, since Rebecca was with her Dad and I had a nasty hangover. However by 11 a.m. I knew I could linger no longer. It was time to prepare for my big audition and my bacon-and-eggs hangover breakfast with coffee would get me started. I always craved a heavy greasy breakfast when nursing a hangover. Screw the calorie counting, I had to wake up.

I arrived at the club, 3 p.m. sharp and headed for the make-up room back stage where Chrissy told me to find her. There she was, cheerful and radiant as always. Chrissy was fascinating. She was not strikingly beautiful and not in the best shape either, a tad plump for a stripper. But she had a way with men. They all adored her. Her real name was Maria Luiza but the club manager gave her the more American name, no idea why. She had a thick accent and the men loved that she was Brazilian. Strip club protocol was clearly not something I understood, I was a total newbie.

Chrissy had a son at age 17 who lived with her parents outside of Rio. She worked eight to ten months a year, sent big bucks home and went home for a few months to be with her son. Chrissy was always ready to help anyone in need. She made stripping look like a savior occupation.

For me, stripping was not a big deal. After all, I was a regular at orgies. But here perhaps I would be paid for my sexual prowess.

The make-up artist was also a good hairdresser and she did an amazing job. I looked like I was ready for the red carpet. My pink sparkle halter-top gown, silver G-string, and acrylic-and-silver platform shoes were ready to waltz me out to the stage. I knocked on Ivan's office door.

"It's Shanti, I'm here for the audition."

"Um, okay, I have a phone call to make. Have the bartender make you a drink and tell the DJ what song you'd like. I'll be out when I'm done."

Mister warmth Ivan surely was not. Good thing Chrissy warned me about him or I might have taken his cold demeanor personally. I ordered a margarita on the rocks and it did the trick. I was feeling nice and warm and bubbly.

Ivan emerged and slammed the door. He yelled to the D.J. to play the music. My nerves rekindled. I reminded myself, "You've been dancing all your life. Just get into your own sensual space and you'll be great."

I took center stage but Ivan instructed me to go to the corner with the pole.

"Shit!" I thought, "I don't know how to pole dance!!"

Thank goodness I had been at the club the night before and watched the girls on the pole. They didn't do real hard-core pole dancing either, more of a casual swing and tease. So I did the same and added my own Shanti magic. I relaxed into the song and my nerves disappeared. My gown slid off of me like a waterfall and I was dancing topless in my G-string. It was such a rush.

Before the song was over Ivan barked, "Okay come down."

Ivan explained, "Look, you are obviously beautiful, have a great body and you move well. Three months ago I would have hired you. But like I said to you last night, my regular girls can't even make a decent night's pay. This economy is killing my business. Why don't you come back in a few months and if business picks up I'll give you a couple of nights."

Though I was disappointed not to be making money immediately, I was full from the excitement of living out a fantasy - to be a stripper, even if only for one night.

Chapter 37

Tantra Massages with Happy Endings

With stripping now off the table, Ananta and I looked for other ways to make money in this barren economy. During the previous summer, when we were blissfully unaware of the crash to come, Ananta and I had taken a course on Tantra massage. My goal in taking this course was not to learn a new sensual technique, but to learn the art of deep sensual intimacy. Ananta and I had plenty of sex, together and with others. But I felt we lacked intimacy. We had tons of sex but making love... that was a rare occurrence.

Though I was not looking for new sexual techniques during this three-day workshop, I did find some, along with some of the intimacy I was looking for. However, it was not how I pictured it. At the end of day one we were asked to go home and practice the Tantra massage technique with our partner. Though the technique required hand/genital touching; I was not prepared for the surprise outcome. There were also specific breathing exercises and a well-planned set-up of sensual foods, drinks, music, and decorations. It gave me the idea that this would just be a nice, sensual experience. So I was not prepared for the emotional release that ensued. Both Ananta and I had similar releases that involved intense fear and grief, likely what was in the way of our true deep intimacy.

The notion of a Tantra massage often conjures up a sexy spark of the illicit in most people's mind. Yet if they had any idea what was a true Tantra massage, often confronting yet deeply healing, they would probably opt out. However, when our economy tanked and I tried unsuccessfully for months to return to my career in law, I took to Tantra massage and my new career in the lawless. But not the real Tantra massage, that was too intense for most men. I took to the cheap version and offered a sensual massage with a happy ending. This type of Tantra massage put an instant smile on the man's face and gave my wallet a hard-on.

I asked Cammy, a woman in our sensual tribe who offered Tantra massages, how she found her clients. She showed me several of her websites.

I responded, "Cammy the sites are very beautiful and you look absolutely gorgeous in these photos. But I do not want to go to all the time and expense of creating several websites if I end up not liking this gig."

Cammy then shared, "I found many clients surfing the sugar daddy websites. These men are used to paying for women so a Tantra massage is an easy sell. Just be careful, never mention anything about Tantra or a happy ending. If you've contacted an undercover cop your ending will be anything but happy! Say you are offering a deep sensual massage."

"OMG Cammy, Tantra massage is illegal?"

"Yes, illegal everywhere in the U.S. but easier to get away with in California and Hawaii. Ananta cool with you doing this?"

"Oh you know Ananta, the kinkier the better. Plus we are completely broke. Good incentive right?"

Cammy looked at her watch, "Oh crap, I'm late! I have a client in half an hour. Listen, call me tomorrow. There are safety precautions you need to take with clients. I'll explain tomorrow. Ciao bella! You'll be great at this. The men will think they died and went to heaven."

The next day Cammy emailed me a litany of questions she suggested I ask potential clients to be sure they were not psychopaths or cops - or both. She also wrote how to dodge questions about the happy ending in case it was a cop. This was looking far more complicated and dangerous than I had anticipated.

"Shanti, you have to be especially careful with first-time clients. Never acknowledge that you will give them a happy ending. If they ask, tell them that in the end they will indeed be happy. That is one of the codes. I also suggest you meet them in person for a drink if at all possible. You can usually sift out the creeps at a face-to-face. Plus the cops rarely do a face-to-face."

I grimaced, "There is so much to know. This is not going to be as easy as I thought."

Cammy cut me off, "Hey, I think you're going to like it and you can't beat the money."

"Oh right, how much can I charge?" I asked.

"Varies, whatever you feel you can get, go for it. Pull the super model card, they'll love that. But I wouldn't offer your services for less than $300 for an hour and a half session, especially if you're providing snacks and booze at half time."

Cammy continued to school me and I absorbed everything. There was much to learn.

"Now, one more thing," she said. "It's important. If you don't rent a massage space where others are around and you use your home, make sure that Ananta is somewhere nearby. Text him when the client arrives and when he leaves. If Ananta does not hear back from you in two hours from when the client arrives he should text you. If you don't answer he should come home."

Starting a new career offering Tantra massage was not as easy as some of my Tantrika friends made it out to be. I was hoping for an easy quick fix to my financial woes but alas, no. I joined several sugar daddy sites, some were free, and others I had to pay. Once registered it took days before I received even one response. Apparently, in the sugar daddy/sugar baby world, the men are the hunted since they have the cash. I contacted nearly twenty guys before I got one response. In the typical online dating world women are bombarded with emails as we are the hunted. For the first time in my life I had sympathy for how hard it is to be a single man without a decent income. Now I was in the position of most single men without much green. We sugar babies are the hunters. We are ignored, dismissed, and not treated with much kindness.

In the midst of my frustration came a sweet email from a rather handsome sugar daddy who was close to my age.

Looking at his profile I thought, "Why is this guy on this sugar daddy site? He doesn't need to pay to find a woman, he makes good money, not too old, and he is good looking."

I was puzzled. But I was more broke than curious and made a date to meet with him.

I joined Trevor Griffin for coffee one evening after he got off work. He was an investment banker and indeed, as sweet as his email correspondence suggested. But Trevor was also smart, funny, and even better looking in person.

I remember coaching myself, "Shanti, you are not dating this guy, you just want his money. Who cares about his personality?"

I found it difficult to be so calculating. I needed to like someone that I was being so intimate with. We set a massage date for the next week at my apartment and I had Ananta go to a nearby Starbucks, texted him when Trevor rang the bell. Unbeknownst to Trevor, he would be my guinea pig Tantra massage client. I could not let on that he was my first, I felt that I needed to sound knowledgeable and experienced to command such a high fee.

I brought Trevor into the bedroom, handed him a robe and towel, and showed him to the shower. By the time he came out, the soft, sensual, Middle Eastern music was playing, the candles were glowing, and the incense was burning. It was time. First order of business, get his cash. Cammy told me to get the cash as soon as he walked through the door but that felt too rushed and cold. I wanted him to feel comfortable first. After I took his drink order, I brought him to the bed to sit. Then I returned with his beverage and a beautiful jewelry box.

Trevor looked at the box and asked, "What is this?"

I replied, "This is my treasure box," and I opened it. "This is where you put your money."

Trevor stood up immediately, "Oh I'm sorry. I didn't realize I pay you up front. Let me get my jacket."

As Trevor retrieved his jacket I thought he too might be a newbie to this Tantra massage business. Whether that was true or not, it put me at ease. Trevor returned with $350 in cash, three hundred-dollar bills and one fifty-dollar bill. Seeing that crisp cash lying there so gracefully in my velvet-lined jewelry box had me feeling like a royal. I relaxed some more.

As Cammy had foretold, I did get into a meditative trans during the massage. Though I was working hard to relax Trevor's muscles, at the same time I was stretching and breathing. Felt like a strong yet relaxing workout. When I finished his backside I had him sit up, threw the robe over his shoulders, then gave him a sip of his drink. Next I brought over a tray of fruits, cheeses, and chocolates. I asked him what he desired, then took his food and fed him. He really liked that. When he had enough I had him lie on his back.

I massaged his front side much like I had the back, with long, strong stokes. But when I saw that there was only 15 minutes remaining of our session I lightened up on the strokes and moved closer to his groin. Without any touching, his cock started to get erect. I took an extra dose of massage oil and began to stroke his cock. It was not long before he released and I had towels, both dry and wet, at the ready. In all my years of sexing with men there was only one that actually enjoyed the feeling of cum on his skin. The odds were likely that Trevor would prefer to be cleaned.

As soon as Trevor came and I cleaned him off, I covered him with a sarong and tucked it in tightly around his body like a swaddling baby. Then I lay next to him for a few moments and hugged him. Soon I whispered, "Lie here and relax while I clean myself up. I will come back to let you know when to wake."

Trevor was not steady on his feet so I helped him to the bedroom and suggested, "Would be good to bend over and touch your toes a few times with some deep breaths. Get dressed slowly. This was a deep massage. You will need to be gentle with yourself on your way home."

Trevor replied, "Deep, yeah. God, I felt like I was on some other planet and I'm not back yet."

I started to laugh, "Good! This is real relaxation. Enjoy!" I left him to dress in the bedroom and sat on my bed in the living room. I felt at peace, knowing I gave this man pleasure and that I had handled my money fears. I knew then that this was a way I could earn money to supplement our subletting the apartment. Finally, the crash of 2008 could no longer bury me. I gave Trevor a hug as he left and as soon as I closed the door I texted Ananta to come home.

Between dumpster-diving for food, renting our apartment, and Tantra massages, we were able to keep ourselves afloat. I don't know how other people survived the great depression but I am guessing many also resorted to drastic measures. However, someone without a sex/love addiction may not have taken to such intimate measures to make money. Little did I know that this was just the beginning of my "intimate" financial endeavors.

Chapter 38

Super Heroes to the Rescue!

Not long after the economy crashed, a major TV network came knocking at our email door. They had seen our super hero outfits and workshops online, and asked if we'd be interested in being on their reality show. It was a no-brainer for me: we would make great money and the fame would generate even more money. However, I was met with some surprisingly fierce opposition. Ananta was neutral, he would do it if I wanted to but he was not particular excited. However Rebecca, now 15, was dead set against it.

"No way Mom. I do not want to be on TV, especially not with you and Ananta in your super-hero outfits. All my friends will laugh at me!"

"Oh come on honey. You don't have to wear the outfits. They like that you don't like our outfits. You can totally be yourself."

"No Mom. No way."

I was beside myself with disappointment. This seemed like the opportunity of a lifetime and I could not get Rebecca on board. Sadly, I declined the network's invitation, citing resistance from my daughter. A couple of months later I get another email from the network, asking if my daughter might like to speak with one of the producers to get a better idea of her role. But Rebecca flatly refused. I understood that she was not up for being embarrassed, but we really could have used the money.

A few months later I received yet another email from the network. They sent links of their previously produced segments to present to Rebecca. I knocked on Rebecca's door.

I said, "I got another email about having us on the TV show and they sent a few links to show you."

"Mom, I told you, I do not want to be on the show. I wish you would stop asking me."

Jillian, her best friend from boarding school and a child actress, was staying over for the weekend. She chimed in.

"What show?"

I explained, "We have been asked to appear in an episode of a well-known reality show but Rebecca is not interested. They keep asking us but..."

Jillian broke in, "Are you crazy Rebecca? You should do it. You will be the most popular girl in school."

There was a silent pause in the room. Jillian and I looked at Rebecca.

She replied softly, trying to cover her growing smile, "Okay."

Jillian's endorsement was gold. That's all it took. Within days the network sent us a contract and a questionnaire that was three inches thick. They asked intimate details about our lives together. We had to tell them our life's story and it took weeks to complete, especially with Rebecca dragging her feet. Next we had several rounds of medical, psychological, and drug testing. You'd think we were applying for a position at the Pentagon. They asked us to videotape segments of our lives together including the dumpster-diving. Ananta wanted to film us at a sex party but I nixed that immediately. Prime-time TV would never go for that. Plus, I didn't want to be known as the hedonist I surely was. The entire interview process took several months.

Finally, on June 18, 2009, my 50th Birthday, we began shooting. It was a great birthday present, so why was I crying? Because of copyright laws, nothing in our apartment that was not created by us could be shown. That meant that all the artwork had to be taken down, my fashion photographs put away and all the books turned around so we could not read their spines. I never realized how much I loved my home until those details were stripped.

Ananta asked, "Bunny, why are you sad? Isn't this what you wanted?"

Explaining myself through a torrent of tears, "If I were playing a role I wouldn't care where I played it. But this is my home, our home, and we are not acting, we are being real, playing ourselves. This place looks nothing like our home any more. I hate it!"

The director came over. She was concerned and very sweet with me, she gave me a big hug and sent an intern out to get me a cake. But there was much to do so I dried my tears and reapplied my make-up. No time for a pity party, even though it was my birthday.

As Ananta and I sat in front of the cameras and lights, I felt a calm wash over me. This was a world I knew well and it felt like coming home. Then the producer approached us.

"Guys, we know you are relationship coaches but your name, the Tantra Warriors, is a bit too racy for prime time TV. We need you to change it, just for the show."

Blow number two! We were hoping to use our brand to generate more clients. My God, I was sinking deeper into my emotional mire.

The producer then said, "Let's resume in five minutes."

Five minutes? What the fuck? I had forgotten about this aspect of TV, all hurry up and wait. Ananta was frozen but since our logo was TW I looked for a "T" word that would go with Warriors. I loved the warrior aspect of our brand but never much liked Tantra for the same reason the network did not like it: too racy. But Ananta really loved that name so I went with it, co-dependent that I am. I was actually delighted to shed some of this overt sexuality, it was rather a relief.

"The Transformational Warriors!" I blurted out.

Ananta gave me one of his surprised and delighted looks and we kissed until I heard the director announce, "Places everyone."

She then reminded us to refer to our company as The Transformational Warriors and if we forgot she would cut and start again. We were on our way, with great financial hopes for the future. The super heroes would rescue us from bankruptcy and homelessness.

After two weeks of intense shooting, we wrapped up our segment with high hopes for a bright financial future. The producer told us it might take several months to air. In the meantime, we produced more workshops, took on new clients, and continued to dumpster-dive, rent our apartment a couple weeks a month, and offer Tantra massages. Ananta tried to market himself as a Tantra masseuse too, but women rarely pay for such services and he was not comfortable delivering happy endings to gay men, even though he himself was bisexual. I never understood this. But then again, there were so many aspects of Ananta that remain a mystery to me even today.

Chapter 39

Marrying My Super Hero

Note to self: When someone tells you who they are, believe them. Ananta was a confused man, confused about his sexuality, confused about who he was and how he wanted to relate to the world. But I had enough clarity for us both, so I thought. I loved Ananta intensely, I wanted to marry him. For all his constant need for sexing with others, he did love me and I felt it deep in my heart. I had not felt this kind of unconditional love since my great love story with Yigal. Within weeks of dating Ananta I knew he was The One and I made it clear that I would participate in his swinger life only if he would marry me within the next few years.

Well, those few years had gone by so I delivered the dreaded ultimatum: "Marry me or I will leave you."

Ananta hemmed and hawed for a few more months until one weekend, during a workshop we were participating in, the facilitator pushed him for an answer.

Ananta looked at me with fury in his eyes, "Okay fine. You want me to be unhappy? Then let's get married!"

Gwen, the facilitator, and I both looked at one another in shock and disbelief. Ananta was usually a quiet and peaceful soul.

She asked him, "What does marriage mean to you?"

Without hesitation Ananta replied, "Marriage means boredom and feeling trapped."

I butted in, "Excuse me, but you'd be married to me and I am sooooo far from boring. If there is any boring to be had in this relationship it would be on you, not me."

Some of the participants chuckled and Ananta cracked a smile. Gwen spent some time going over the stereotypes of relationships

247

and marriage that we carry deep within, but do not examine. She acknowledged Ananta for digging up his hidden beliefs so that they could see the light. By the end of the workshop, Ananta agreed to marry me and the room exploded in rapture and congratulations.

Though I was thrilled that we were engaged, the whole wedding thing did not thrill me. I remember planning my first wedding with my mother, I got so sick of all the decisions and choices that I handed the entire ordeal over to her. Fortunately, Mom felt honored and she took over with gusto.

I thought maybe it was because I was not in love when I married Rebecca's father that had me feeling so blasé about the ceremony. However, here I was again, getting ready for wedding number two and still not wanting to plan for it. This time I was indeed very much in love and yet still no wedding mojo. By then Mom was in her late stages of Alzheimer's disease and could barely remember a conversation we had two minutes ago. So there went my wedding planner. With no money to pay for a professional wedding planner, we picked a date in late June of 2010 at the same loft in Brooklyn where we had attended several swinger parties. It was all we could afford. We booked our friend Bill's Band. The remainder of the planning we put on the shelf.

During this period it became blatantly clear to my sister Janet and me that Mom's Alzheimer's was taking a downward spiral. She needed far more care than Dad could provide. They were living on Cape Cod, a major haul for us to visit. Our older brother Paul lived in CA so he was no help. On one particular visit over the winter, Janet arrived to find Mom gorging on cereal drowned in Bailey's Irish Cream. We needed to do something. We had been begging Dad for years to move closer to us so we could better support them. But he stubbornly refused as he always did. When that man didn't want something, nothing would change his mind, nothing.

As fate would have it, Dad developed a urinary tract blockage from bladder cancer that landed him in the hospital. We had to call in visiting caregivers for Mom. Dad was in the hospital for two weeks. He got the rest he desperately needed from caregiver burn-out, and Mom finally got the nutrition and TLC she desperately needed. When Dad got home from the hospital he was still weak and could not do chores so he kept the visiting caregivers coming, he liked the support.

With this new scenario showing Dad how nice life can be with support, Janet and I convinced him to move to New Jersey. Months of work to sell the house on the Cape, packing decades of Dad's hunting/fishing gear and tools, literally the entire basement and garage, and then months to find a house in New Jersey. All this consumed my entire wedding planning time. With only one month to go, Janet and I were unpacking Mom and Dad in their new home. It was then that we realized just how far gone Mom really was. She couldn't be left alone nor could she do much of anything for herself. We started the interview process to find caregivers in New Jersey. Wedding plans? Who had time?

Luckily I found a fabulous Sottero wedding gown at a thrift store, with a lace-up corset back. Since the wedding gown had never been worn it was also uncut so it was plenty long enough for this tall me. Best of all, it cost only $130.

It was now three weeks before the wedding. We had the space, the band, my dress, and no money. I still had no time to prepare so I put Ananta in charge. Told him to send out an email to the guest list that we would be doing this wedding potluck style, so either bring food or a check toward our honeymoon. It was an old-fashioned barn-style wedding and that suited me just fine. I told Ananta to find a few people to put in charge of decorations, set-up, serving, and cleanup. We would order the flowers, wine and beer, and make a few main dishes.

On the hottest day of the summer, Saturday, June 26, 2010, we got married on the roof of that swinger loft in Brooklyn. As the minister pronounced us husband and wife we heard banging in the background: spectacular fireworks launched just at the moment when we kissed. It must have seemed planned, the timing was uncanny. Luckily the sun had just set to cool us down but the loft downstairs, where the reception was being prepared, had been cooking all day. We never inquired if there was air conditioning. Oh well, it was a sweet sweat-fest to remember. My sister and my parents stayed to eat and for the one special dance with father and daughter. Then they split. They were roasting.

I had a wonderful time, even though it was like celebrating in a sauna. All our dear friends and family were there and Rebecca gave a moving speech that had us all in tears. We danced the night away and left with the sunrise. But we didn't sleep for very long as that Sunday was the Gay Pride parade. We planned to switch outfits, me wearing Ananta's tuxedo and he wearing my wedding gown. Actually I had made a second wedding gown for the end of the evening, to be more comfortable. I don't know where I found the time or the genius design, but I put it together so that it would accommodate both my figure and Ananta's. Gay Pride was an extension of our wedding celebration and we had a blast, a splendid cross-dress ending to our bisexual celebration.

Chapter 40

Our Reality Show Airs

We spent a good part of early July in 2010 resting from the wedding sprint and the ordeal of moving my parents. But the ordeal wasn't over yet for my sister and me. Each passing day brought a new set of problems. We had to find new/better grocery stores, hardware stores, doctors, barbers, auto mechanics, and caregivers for Mom and Dad. Then there was teaching Dad to use a GPS and a cell phone. A stubborn 80-year-old alcoholic does not a patient student make.

We took it one crisis at a time. In between the disagreements, blaming, crying and screaming, we had some great laughs too.

Then in mid-July I got that long-awaited call from the reality show network.

"Your segment is going to air in August as the season finale. It's a great honor. Congratulations!"

"Are you sure?" I asked in disbelief, for we would not get paid until it aired. "Did you see the segment yet?"

"I did indeed and you guys are incredible. You're going to love it. It's time to celebrate."

Eighteen months of preparation was about to bear fruit and I could hardly believe it. I thought I'd be dancing around the apartment but instead I got very quiet.

Ananta asked, "Bunny, are you okay?"

I started to cry, "I don't know if I'm happy or sad or relieved or all three. These past few months have been so intense with my parents I don't even know how to enjoy this moment."

Ananta hugged me softly and started gently massaging my arms, my hands, my thighs, my feet. He had incredible hands. He didn't utter a sound for a long while, just let me be with whatever was going on. I cried without sobs, gentle streams of warm tears flowing down my frozen face. Then Ananta broke the silence.

"Hey Bunny, would you like to have a party in honor of the show? We can find a bar that has a large TV screen and invite all our family and friends."

Instantly I woke from my tearful trance. "Oh wow, I love that idea."

Attention and more attention, the bottomless pits that most sex/love addicts need to constantly fill. And so we set out in search of a viewing spot and found the perfect place in the East Village. We promised that a hundred drinkers would be in attendance, and so they gave us the main room without a fee. They even allowed us to display a constant stream of our photos and videos on the huge screen, while we waited for the show to air. We prepared photos and videos of us on a DVD loop in various costumes, most notably our wedding costumes that ended with us cross-dressing for the Gay Pride parade. Everyone clapped at that part.

The reality show was even better than I imagined and I assumed our family and friends felt the same as each commercial interruption filled the room with a chorus of disappointed ughs. When the show resumed there was then a chorus of shshshshsh. It was so much fun to watch everyone, who we dearly loved, enjoying our ride. Alongside our wedding, it was one of the greatest highlights of my life that year.

Being the most popular couple of the night, we were approached by all the swinger couples and wild singles to put them on our sensual calendars. I saw how delighted Ananta was with this type of attention, it made him glow. I did enjoy seeing him happy, so we took all the names and numbers.

Chapter 41

Ananta's Betrayal and the Honeymoon

In late August we prepared for our upcoming honeymoon in Paris. We received enough money from our wedding guests to fund the entire trip. Our flight left on August 30th and we started the fun a few days earlier with Jim and Dina's wedding, our dear friends from Vermont. Ananta referred to them as his kinky parents because they were in their 60s and they loved many of the same sensual activities as Ananta. Indeed, Ananta had sexed with Dina while Jim watched on a few occasions but that was before Ananta and I met. After I came on the scene, all of that stopped although we did dabble in some light sensual touching with them.

Their wedding was one of the best I had ever attended. The country air was warm during the day and cool at night. They married by the river next to a dairy farm and said 'I do' just as the cows came to bathe. It was as picturesque as one could ask for. They were our dear friends who had found love later in life and most of their friends were our friends. It was a remarkable two-day event and when we got in Ananta's parent's car to return home, we were full of joy and contentment.

Not paying much attention to my phone that weekend, I used the car ride home to catch up on correspondences. I came to a very odd message from Lauren Harrison, a fellow relationship coach that I was not close to. Lauren sent me a private message on Facebook:

Dear Shanti:

Thank you for graciously sharing your husband with me. We felt your divine presence with us.

Much love,

Lauren

I turned to Ananta and read it aloud. "What is she talking about?" I asked.

"Ooooh, yeah, last week I had a very long conversation with Lauren about her husband, her health, and her business."

"But, why would she thank me for sharing you with her?"

Ananta seemed as confused as I was.

"I don't know Bunny. Maybe she was thanking you because I felt kind of guilty that I spent two hours on the phone with her? I finally told her I had to get off the phone before you got jealous. She understood even though she is not a jealous kind of person."

I replied, "Yeah well they have a totally open relationship. We do not. They sleep with anyone they want to sleep with and they do not even inform one another. Maybe you should have married Lauren if that is the type of marriage you want."

"No Bunny. I married you. I want you. And we are about to have an amazing honeymoon in Gay Paree!"

It took several hours to get home and I used this time to catch up on sleep. The jetlag from New York to Paris is a killer and I wanted to get a jump on my rest.

After unpacking from the wedding I made some last minute adjustments to my pre-packed honeymoon luggage. Then I sat at my computer and caught up on Facebook. I looked again at that message from Lauren. I read it over and over again. Though I accepted Ananta's answer without question, now her message just didn't make sense. Why would Lauren thank me for a phone call? This woman was known for sexing with several people. They must have sexed together and Ananta must have told her I was okay with that. Why else would she thank me? I felt ill, knowing this had to be the truth.

I yelled to Ananta in the other room, "Ananta, come here."

"Yes Bunny."

"Don't fucking Bunny me. What does this message from Lauren really mean? Don't you dare lie to me again," I insisted.

Ananta hung his head, "I'm sorry Shanti."

"You slept with her."

"Well, we didn't have intercourse," he said.

"No? What did you do?"

He replied, "We had oral sex."

"Oh like that makes it all better? Is this your Bill Clinton excuse - I never had sex with that woman! God damn you Ananta, I fucking hate you! I have sucked and fucked more pussies and cocks to keep your God damn libido happy and you still had to cheat on me?"

"I'm sorry Bunny."

"I am not a fucking bunny I am a fierce lioness and I am going to tear you to shreds with my teeth! God damn you Ananta. We are supposed to go on our honeymoon tomorrow. You have destroyed everything."

I sobbed uncontrollably. Ananta made a motion to hug me but I slapped his arm away. "Don't you dare fucking touch me!"

I ran upstairs to the attic of his parent's house where we were staying that night. We had rented out my place for the next two weeks while we would to be in Paris. "Paris?" I thought, "How can we possibly go to Paris now?!"

After such a romantic betrayal, the situation couldn't be graver on the eve of our honeymoon. I cried, I screamed, and I didn't care if anyone heard. Ananta's mother was in Costa Rica but his father was here. Ananta's father had cheated on his mother several times. I was sure he understood the drill - where else did my husband learn machismo? After yelling out my initial rage and grief I lay in bed staring at the ceiling, wondering what to do. My mind was running short sprints and hurdles around the track of my life while my heart was gushing pints of blood from this deep emotional wound.

My initial impetus was to cancel the honeymoon. But when I thought about how much money we'd be flushing, money that our beloved friends and family had given us, it felt unfair. Then I thought to go by myself. But everyone would find out that I went solo, because all my photos would be selfies. Questions would soon abound and Ananta's infidelity would eventually be public knowledge. If I decided to leave Ananta I would not care, but I was not sure I wanted to leave him yet. I wasn't thinking clearly and this was no time to make a rash decision. The only other choice was to go together. We'd have two weeks to deal with the issue over there. Then, we could either stay together or divorce.

I vacillated between grief and rage with a few respites of feeling numb. "So this is what betrayal feels like," I thought.

All those years in my 20s when I cheated on my boyfriends, I never understood why they got so upset when they found out. I was in love with them. The cheating was just sexual. But here it was happening to me and I was devastated. Karma's a bitch.

I finally fell asleep, hoping to wake and find this had all been a terrible nightmare. Then I awoke to Ananta's footsteps mounting the stairs. My rage rekindled. This nightmare was real. Ananta entered the room with a tray of food and a flower. I looked away as soon as I caught a glimpse of him and his peace offering.

"I thought you might be hungry," he said.

I did not answer, nor did I look at him.

"I'll just leave it over here," he said.

Soon I heard the door close and his footsteps descending. I started to cry. It was impossible to hate Ananta for he was so sweet and kind. But he fucking cheated on me! I hated that I could not hate him! I wanted desperately to call Jim and Dina but how cruel to ruin the high from their magical wedding weekend. I couldn't do that to them. I needed to talk to someone else who knew us both, someone who could understand my rage.

I decided to contact the relationship coaches in California that we both studied with. We set up a Skype coaching session for us both that afternoon. It didn't leave me much time to make a decision about the honeymoon but it would at least give me an hour breather before we would need to head to the airport. That would have to do.

I had taken several classes and private consultations with Candice and Briana over the years, and trusted their expertise. I was sure they would be on my side, the side of the justice, but boy was I wrong. Since Ananta cried throughout most of the Skype session, I guess they felt sorry for him.

They told me, "Ananta acted out by cheating on you because he is not having enough sexual expression in your relationship."

"You guys have got to be fucking kidding me! I go to all Ananta's swinger parties, orgies, and private sex parties. No, you are feeling sorry for Ananta because he is sobbing and I look like the bad guy here because I am raging like a lunatic. Yes, I am ballistically angry but I have been lied to and cheated on and it is normal to feel this way. No, I am not going to give any more room for his sexual needs. I know what he wants. He wants to have separate relationships with other women while I am not present. I won't accept that so we should just divorce already."

They made some other suggestions but they had lost me already. I was shocked. In the past they had given us such great coaching. Could the experts be wrong?

When the session was over Ananta asked timidly, "Are we going to Paris?"

"I don't know," I barked.

"I just need to tell my father if he needs to take us to the airport."

Shooting Ananta a hundred daggers I spat, "He can wait. Your father who cheated on your mother for decades can fucking wait in the car until I am ready." I don't think I have ever felt this angry in my entire life. My whole body was shaking with rage.

Ananta left the room and I lay on the bed thinking about my beloved Paris. How I would miss her if I stayed. Fuck it, fuck him, I'm going to Paris! I began to gather my bags and bring them down the stairs. Ananta, hearing my footsteps, met me half way.

"Where are you going?" he asked.

"I'm going to Paris. You are coming with me but I'm not going to be interacting with you. You spend your days by yourself and I'll spend my days by myself."

Ananta replied, "Okay. Whatever you want."

"That's what I want. I'll meet you in the car."

Our trip to the airport was blanketed in total silence. I imagined that Ananta's father suspected what was up. But since his mother was in Costa Rica at this time, and she was the social voice in the family, we got to keep this situation quiet. I didn't even thank his father for driving us, blaming him for Ananta's cheating ways. But unlike his mother, I was not going to stand for it.

I did not speak to Ananta throughout the boarding process, not even on the flight. I slept for several hours and didn't even speak with him during the meals. As we got closer to Paris I began imagining the honeymoon with Ananta that I had longed for, and started crying. I looked out the window, not wanting him to see the crack in my anger. It was so difficult to be angry with Ananta, he had such a tender soul.

Just then I was hit with a lightning bolt of an idea. I ran it around my heart and my brain and they both seemed satisfied so I shared my plan with Ananta. I turned to him, "I want to enjoy this trip to Paris like the romantic honeymoon it was meant to be."

This was the first time I looked at Ananta's face in several hours. He seemed devastated with grief and guilt. I continued, "I am going to get up and go the bathroom in a moment. When I return, I want you to wipe that sad and guilty face of yours and I will remove my armor of anger. We are going to pretend this incident never happened."

Ananta looked shocked, "What?"

I replied, "Yes, we will not speak of it during our honeymoon. But don't think I will have forgotten. I am just putting it on the shelf to be dealt with upon our return. Is this acceptable for you?"

"If this is acceptable for you, it is acceptable for me."

"Okay good. Remember, when I return from the bathroom, we will resume our relationship as it was when we were at Jim and Dina's wedding. Anything after that does not exist, for now anyway. We simply went straight from Jim and Dina's wedding to our honeymoon."

"Yes Bunny."

Upon hearing Ananta address me as Bunny again, I felt the warmth of love return to my heart.

We had an unforgettable honeymoon in Paris. I loved every second of it. From biking around the city, to the romantic dinners, the wine, pastries, cheese, porn shops, and the swinger club, we had a blast. Yes, we were the same people after all, even in Paris. We were two sex/love addicts sharing ourselves with each other and the world. On the flight home, like a forgotten blanket reeking of mold, the stench of his infidelity pervaded my mind again. Good-bye Paris bliss. Hello hell.

Chapter 42

Sugar Daddy December to Remember

Upon returning from our honeymoon in Paris, the ugly infidelity was waiting. Losing faith in our relationship coaches, I listened to my own gut, for once.

I made it clear to Ananta: "I can forgive this one transgression of infidelity. But I will not accept another. Two strikes and you are out. If this is unacceptable to you, then you know where the door is."

"Okay Bunny."

I told him, "Look, I don't want to torture you if being married to me is painful and not what you want. There are tons of polyamorous women out there for you to play with."

"But none of them wanted me," he replied.

"Ah, so I am the leftovers? Nice."

"No, that's not what I mean," he said, "I believe we attract what we truly want, not what our head wants. I like that you are possessive and jealous and want only me. Makes me feel loved. I just need to handle the 'poor me' who wants it all, and realize that I truly do have it all with you. I love you so much my Queen. I want to make this work."

"So will you communicate with me when you are feeling deprived instead of acting on it?"

Ananta nodded.

"Good, then we can talk about your desires and I will check in and see if I am up for a swinger night, okay? I love you too, so very much. I want us to work."

With our renewed declarations of love and fidelity, as much fidelity as two swingers could have, we had ourselves a colorful autumn season. We attended more swinger events than before and Ananta seemed happy. I also stepped up my Tantra massage practice, to pay off the wedding bills. I got a pass on sexual activity in side relationships, without Ananta present, because Tantra massage was a moneymaking digression and not an emotional involvement. I made it clear to Ananta that my Tanta massages did not give him a license to cheat, though if he wanted to offer Tantra massages for money he was more than welcome. He never did.

In early December, as the last of the autumn leaves lost their grip, our colorful life got even more vibrant. Bianca Orchid, one of the women that Ananta and I sexed with, made me an offer I could not refuse. We reconnected at a loft party that chilly December evening though our conversation was anything but cold.

"Shanti my love, you are looking gorgeous as ever!"

"Thank you Bianca darling, and so are you *ma belle.*"

Bianca pulled me into a corner and lowered her voice. "I have a business proposition for you. I know you have expressed a desire to earn more money. One of my dearest clients saw a photo of you and me together on my Facebook wall and wants to meet you. Would you be interested in earning $1,000 for 90 minutes of pleasure?"

Bianca was a high-class prostitute and Ananta and I felt special that she didn't charge us. "Bianca, I don't judge you for your profession, you know that. But I could not screw a man I did not love. I already tried with the swingers. Tantra massage is good money. It's only an upscale hand job, not too intimate."

Bianca replied with subtle confidence, "My client is willing to do or not do anything you want or don't want."

"For $1,000?" I asked.

Bianca smiled, "Yes. You would also be with me and play with me as always, only my client would be fucking me at some point. You are welcome to watch or make out with me."

"So what would I do with him?" I asked.

"Whatever is interesting for you," she replied.

I thought about it briefly, "Well, I don't know how happy he will be with me. I won't kiss him, or suck him or fuck him, I'll only give him a hand job."

Bianca smiled, "He would be fine with that. Would you allow him to stroke you as well?"

I thought out loud, "Hmmm... well... Ananta and I already do a stroking practice with The Sweet Spot and we do it for free so I don't see why he would mind. Ananta's resistance might be envy, he wishes he could get paid for his kicks too."

Bianca moved closer and began stroking my hair. She was a stunning woman in her early 30s, naturally blonde and absolutely beautiful without a stitch of make-up. I found her irresistible. She explained, "My love, in most arenas of the world, men earn far more money than women and they are in greater demand. The reverse is true for prostitution. Women rule here. We make the big bucks and are in constant demand. Why do you think I do it?"

We both laughed and then started making out, which instantly drew a half dozen men around us. It's crazy how turned on men get to see two women being sensual with one another. Bianca's client wanted to experience this up close and personal, real personal.

"Oh wait. Bianca, is your client attractive? How old is he?"

She replied, "Honestly, when I first met Ron, no. He was not very attractive. He was fat and smelled horrible. I got him to change his diet, lose weight, start working out, and get his teeth fixed. I told him I would stop working with him if he didn't."

Bianca gave me another long kiss. "Goodbye gorgeous, work calls. I'll let you know about my client very soon. He is quite eager."

All my girl friends that were Tantrikas, strippers, and prostitutes had to leave parties early because they worked mainly at night. I am already a Tantrika, attempted stripping, so now a prostitute? I was not comfortable with that. I called Bianca within a few minutes of her leaving.

"Hey listen, I really don't like the idea of being a prostitute even though everything you described feels fine to me.

"Baby, this gig is not with a standard john. Ron is my sugar daddy. He is a regular. I see him every week, sometimes twice. He loves taking care of women and he showers us with cash and presents. I know you baby. I know what would work for you. You would not be a prostitute, you would be a sugar baby. So think about it and get back to me, no rush."

I left the party soon after Bianca departed and went home. Ananta was in school that night at Hunter College. With no job, I pushed him to finish his art degree. He was a great artist. Ananta was only a semester away from graduation when he left college to design websites. It was time for him to finish.

I went straight to the computer to look up the definition of sugar baby – "a slang term for a young female or male who is financially pampered/cared for by a 'sugar daddy' or 'sugar mama,' usually much older, in exchange for companionship." Well, that didn't sound so bad, except I was not young. I guess it depends on how I feel the first time. I should give it a shot. How else will I know? $1,000 for 90 minutes sounded insane. I never even made that much money as a model!

After getting Ananta's support and a few more conversations with Bianca, I found myself with an appointment at the Warwick Hotel in midtown at 11 a.m. on a Thursday.

I asked Bianca, "Why in the morning?"

She told me, "Ron has to go home to his wife at night. He goes to his office at nine, handles some business, then meets me for some fun."

"Wow, I never imagined doing this in the morning."

"Oh I have tons of clients that want me to address their morning wood," Bianca explained with glee. "We'll have a blast together. You'll see, baby, and Ron is masterful with his hands."

I found it endearing that Bianca referred to me as baby when I was nearly 20 years her senior. But she did feel older than me, more advanced in the sensual arts.

"Wait!" I yelled before she hung up, "What do I wear?"

"Whatever you want. I usually come in sweat pants."

Confused I asked, "But I thought they like…"

Bianca cut me off, "Garter belts and high heels? Prostitutes sometimes get asked to wear that kind of outfit and I do that too, for one night only sizzle sex. But Ron is a big hippy. He likes his women au natural."

I decided to wear an elegant fitted cream-colored dress, from my days in legal. It made me feel professional and sexy but not too outrageous, even though this was an absolutely outrageous thing for me to be doing.

I was nervous as I approached the hotel desk and asked for Ron's room. My paranoia said they had to know I was a prostitute. I felt ashamed. Even though Bianca said I was a sugar baby, it felt like prostitution to me. I was terrified.

When I got to Ron's door, Bianca answered with wet hair wrapped in a huge white towel. She gave me a big kiss and welcomed me in. The room was nice, not too extravagant but attractive.

I asked quietly, "Is Ron in the bathroom?"

"Oh no, he's not here yet. You want some of my breakfast?"

"No thank you. When did you get here?" I asked.

"About ten last night. Ron only uses the room for a couple of hours and he has to pay for the over night so I come the night before. Sometimes my boyfriend stays over. It's nice. You can come too, the next time."

I was officially feeling overwhelmed. Just then I heard a knock at the door. Bianca directed me to answer and as I walked to the door I prayed that Ron would be at least decent looking. He didn't need to be handsome but decent would be nice.

I opened the door. Quelle relief! Ron was tall and had a beard and long hair – he looked better than I had anticipated. I began to relax.

"Good morning. You must be the beautiful Shanti."

With a tinge of shyness I replied, "Yes, I'm Shanti."

I didn't know if I should hug him, kiss him, or shake his hand. It was such an absurd moment, everything felt awkward! But Ron seemed at ease and took command. First he kissed my hand. Then he led me to the bed and we both sat while Bianca reclined and finished her toast.

Ron stroked my arm and said, "It is so lovely to have you join us this morning. There are so many things I want to ask you. Do you mind if I take a quick shower first?"

I shook my head, relieved, thinking that the longer he showered, the less time we had to get sexual.

"Do you want to take a shower with me?" Ron asked.

"Oh hell no!" is what I wanted to say. But instead I uttered, "Oh, no thank you. I took a shower right before coming over here."

"Okay honey, here is a robe so you can get comfy though."

Bianca was busy on her phone. I wanted her to help me feel more comfortable but that was not happening. I would need to make myself comfortable. I disrobed and cloaked myself in the white hotel-style robe.

Bianca popped off the bed, completely naked, and poured the last of the breakfast tea. She had a phenomenal body. I hope I looked that good at 32; I did feel pretty good for 51. She sat down next to me.

"Are you nervous?"

"Fuck yeah, doesn't it show?"

Laughing, Bianca replied, "Totally! But it's so cute on you. I guess this is why men like virgins. Can I help you feel better?"

Just then Ron came out of the bathroom. I was relieved to catch a glimpse of his underwear as the robe parted. I was not at all ready to see this stranger's cock.

Bianca spoke up, "Ron, our dearest darling Shanti is a bit nervous. She has never done anything like this before. Let's help her feel more comfortable."

Part of me was not happy with Bianca's declaration but I was also relieved that my state was finally being acknowledged.

Ron replied, "Well, we have a virgin on our hands. How often does a man get that?"

They looked at one another and cackled, then Ron went over to the table to fetch his satchel.

"I have all kinds of goodies here for us. First, let's find some music that you like."

We settled on R&B as he scrolled through his playlist.

As soon as I heard Teddy Pendergrass singing *Turn Off The Lights* my entire body started relaxing.

Ron pulled out a pipe, "Anyone for a little hit?"

Bianca went for it but I rarely if ever smoked pot during the day, never mind in the morning. Sometimes I smoked at swinger parties to loosen up, help break the ice. Yes! This is exactly what I need right now!

Bianca passed the pipe to me. I took a hit and instantly started coughing.

"I see we have a virgin pot smoker too," said Ron. "Me thinks we are corrupting this delicate flower, are we not Bianca?"

Ron turned back to me. "Would that be okay with you Shanti, if we corrupt you a little?"

I was already feeling stoned and enjoying their sensual advances, though only from an energetic place at first. Then Bianca opened my robe and started fondling my breast. "I just love this woman's breasts."

"Good," Ron replied, "you can tend to them while I tend to her pussy. Would you like that Shanti?"

I panicked a moment, not wanting him to go down on me or try to screw me. Then I remembered my boundaries. Bianca said she would make them clear to Ron and I trusted her, so I relaxed.

"Yes, I would like that," I replied timidly.

Ron guided me down onto my back. He did not open my robe all the way but he was scanning the parts of my body that were exposed.

I was feeling very stoned and enjoying how they both took charge of me. It was hot. I was becoming aroused. My nervousness was completely gone. Within moments Ron pulled out the lube and started stroking my pussy. While he did so, he asked me all sorts of questions about my life, as if we were having a cup of tea. I don't know if he did this to relax me but it worked. I completely surrendered to his touch, to my pleasure, to this wild experience. My orgasm was intense and I let out a loud moan.

"Wow!" they chorused, which made me laugh.

Ron then turned to Bianca but she said, "No, no, I'm good. I'll play nurse to Dr. Shanti while she operates on you."

Ron lay on his back and stripped off his underwear. This was the moment where I wanted to stop. But then I remembered that

I only needed to touch him with my hands, no different than the happy endings of my Tantra massages. I began to massage his cock with lube. Bianca was kissing his lips. Odd, I was much happier in my position than hers. Felt far less intimate. I always felt kissing to be the most intimate act. I could only kiss someone when I was in love or in lust, and I felt neither for Ron.

Ron kept asking me to slow down as he was close to cumming. I saw Bianca glance at her phone then she nodded to me. I figured time was nearly up so I got him off.

Bianca curled up by his side so I took his other side. The sexing was fun but the romantic stuff was not. I started to crash and long for my husband. I questioned myself, "What are you doing Shanti? Is this the kind of life you want?"

My downward spiral broke when Ron said, "I am so sorry ladies but I have to jump in the shower and run out of here. I have a meeting in 20 minutes."

He kissed us both on the forehead and went into the bathroom. I took that opportunity to get dressed and Bianca did the same. When Ron came out, Bianca was kissing me.

Ron said, "Hey wait a minute. This is not fair. I have to get to work." We all laughed.

Then Ron said, "We must do this again if you would like, Shanti. I would be honored."

I was not sure I would ever do this again but to avoid an awkward moment I told him I would.

Before leaving, Ron slipped an envelope into my handbag. I stared at the envelope before opening it. There were ten crisp 100-dollar bills. Now that took away all my discomfort. I had an orgasm, hung out with one of my hot girlfriends, gave a guy a happy ending and in 90 minutes I made $1,000. I compared that to $350 for a Tantra massage. Sold! I had just accepted my first sugar daddy and he was oh so very sweet.

Chapter 43

Wedding #2: Catholic in Costa Rica

In mid-December of 2010, Ananta and I flew to Costa Rica for wedding ceremony number two with his extended family. A Catholic priest would be performing the ceremony, thereby making it the "real" wedding. Both Ananta and I had been married before but since neither of those marriages had been performed by a Catholic priest, we were allowed to marry in the Catholic Church. I thought you couldn't get married in the Catholic Church if you were divorced, but maybe the rules were different in Costa Rica.

With copies of our passports, birth certificates, baptism records, Holy Communion and Confirmation certificates, we headed to the church to see the priest. Once he looked over all the papers, we had confession. I had not been to confession in over 30 years. How on earth would I confess all my sins in less than an hour? Did having sex with multiple partners count as a sin? What about taking money for sex from a sugar daddy?

I panicked the night before when I learned we had to go to confession and asked Ananta's brother, Reuben, for advice. Where his Costa Rican mother found two old-school Jewish names for her Catholic sons, I will never figure out. Leonard and Reuben, two guys from Costa Rica, NOT!

Reuben's advice to me was simple, "Pick only one issue going on in your life and talk about that. The priest doesn't speak much English anyway."

And just like that, I was absolved of my sins. But I was not absolved of my hostess duties. Everyone in Costa Rica wanted to meet me - the tall, beautiful, blonde American. Funny, I had been blonde for a decade but it was the first time I wanted to go back to my natural color. I stuck out prominently in Costa Rica as a blonde but I wanted to be one of them, to fit in. I nearly dyed my hair brunette while I was there but my good friend Sorya, my maid of honor, talked me out of it.

She said, "Are you kidding? Every woman wants to be blonde but you can actually pull it off, people think you are natural. There is no way I'm letting you dye your hair brunette. I won't do your hair and make-up for the wedding if you do!"

"Geez alright," I replied after her fiery Latina blast.

I adored Sorya. She had no problem laying out the law of the land.

In the next few days more of my crew arrived. First was Jim and Dina, our newlywed couple. Then my daughter Rebecca and her girlfriend Hannah. Finally, my dear friend and former modeling agent in Paris, Marie-Josée and her husband Christophe. It felt wonderful to have some of my family and friends at this wedding, for I was greatly outnumbered by the Hernandez clan and their entourage of cousins and friends. They were the sweetest people on earth but my Spanish was not great and I often felt left out. Sorya was my liaison between both camps. She would fill me in on the gossip, which was only good, everyone was impressed with Ananta's choice of bride. Of course in Costa Rica he was known by his birth name, Leonard. Terribly rough for me to call him that but I did my best. Leonard Hernandez.

The wedding was at their gorgeous ranch with orchids growing everywhere. The reception required a casual clothing change and everyone got the memo. I had such a blast. Mama Hernandez pulled out all the stops and we danced until the wee hours. Our hangover brunch of eggs, sausage, and plantain required mucho coffee and some added a shot of rum. I was fried yet content but Ananta, he was somewhere else.

Ananta had been distant during the whole trip, guessing it was a big responsibility for him since none of my crew, except Sorya, spoke Spanish. Years later when reading about sex addiction, I discovered that those who act out intensely with sex over the Internet go through withdrawals when they cannot connect online. The Internet was spotty at best at their family ranch. Ananta must have been detoxing. He just didn't seem like himself.

A week after the wedding we all celebrated Christmas together. Rebecca and her friend Hannah were having a great time. There was a fabulous pool and plenty of animals around the ranch, the countryside was magnificent. After Christmas we did tons of sightseeing. Everyone was in awe of Costa Rica.

Right before New Year's Eve, my clan returned to the States. Ananta and I stayed for some long overdue alone time. Of course tons of his family and friends were there for New Year's Eve but we stayed on another week to chill. We only had sex once during that time. Between Ananta's infidelity right before our first honeymoon in September and this asexual December honeymoon in Costa Rica, I was starting to feel that I might have made a grave mistake in marrying Ananta, twice at that!

Part V: **Prostitution**

Can the end ever justify the means? Caring for her elderly parents and poverty stricken since 2008, Shanti decides to leave dumpster-diving to catch bigger fish. Sugar Daddies and johns become her new food source, with plenty of leftovers.

Chapter 44

My Parents Decline

Back home, I took a few days off to unpack, pay bills, and do laundry before heading to New Jersey for a belated Christmas reunion with the Owen clan. It was as if all the fun and relaxation of Costa Rica disappeared the moment I approached my parents' threshold and rang the bell.

Dad's voice, "Kay get the door. No, the door, the front door! Where are you going? Jesus Christ, just a minute!" Dad continued barking as he opened the door: "Your mother deliberately went into her room when I asked her to get the door."

"Belated Merry Christmas to you too Dad."

"Catherine! It's Patty and Ananta. What are you doing in there?"

I walked in to find the house a complete shambles. There was clothing, food, glasses and empty bear cans everywhere.

I asked, "Dad, where is Mary?"

"She has a cold or flu or something. I didn't want her coming over here and getting us sick."

"No, no of course not," I replied, "but, what about Karen? Couldn't she take the extra days?"

"I don't know. She was busy or something."

Then I asked, "What about that new woman. I forgot her name. She was supposed to come one or two days a week. Monica?"

"I don't remember. She left. I told you, your mother is difficult to handle."

Dad looked wiped out, and more agitated than usual.

He screamed, "Catherine, Patty is here for Christ's sake. Come out here!"

I replied, "Dad, it's okay. Let her be."

Ananta sat on the couch only to jump up immediately.

Dad said, "That was your mother. She just spilled her glass of wine."

"Dad, the doctor told you Mom should not be having alcohol. It interferes with her meds and makes her more confused."

"Good, then he can live with her all day long. She gets into the liquor cabinet when I'm not looking."

I suggested, "Maybe we should get rid of all the alcohol in the house. Would do you some good too."

Dad turned back to the football game but I know he heard me. Dad stop drinking? No way!

Mom came down the hallway. She seemed surprised and happy to see me. I was relieved that Alzheimer's had not yet destroyed her long-term memory.

She hugged Ananta and me tightly, and said, "A fra when is so frr."

I asked Dad, "Has Mom's speech been getting worse or is this the alcohol talking?"

"It's terrible. I never know half the time what the hell she's saying."

Mom was about to sit on the couch but Ananta scooped her up in time. She started to giggle.

"Mom it's wet. Hold on while I get some towels." I went to the linen closet but there were no clean towels. All gone. "Dad, where are the clean towels?

"Well, I guess they're all dirty," Dad replied.

I went to the kitchen to get paper towels but they were gone too. I looked around the filthy kitchen to find 2 napkins. Then I opened the refrigerator. There was beer, wine, soda, butter, lettuce, bread and a few condiments.

"How long has Mary been away?" I asked.

"I don't know, a week?" Dad said.

It looked like she hadn't been here in a month. The house was a mess and there was no food or clean laundry.

Dad said, "I don't know, maybe two weeks. I'm trying to watch this game. Christ, can you just let me watch this play?"

I wanted to escape this madness but I knew it had to be handled. I went into the laundry room to retrieve some dirty towels, anything to soak up the wine on the couch. After blotting the couch I announced, "Ananta and I are going to the grocery store. Then we'll pick up a pizza. Are there any special toppings you want?"

"Oh boy, pizza? That's great!" Dad exclaimed. "Pepperoni is fine. There's a liquor store right next to the pizza place. Get me the big bottle of Jim Beam and four bottles of merlot."

As soon as I got in Ananta's family car I burst into tears. "I hate my family! I hate my life! I just want to go home but we don't even have a home!" Torrents of tears came cascading down my face.

I continued my rant, "Half the time we live in the attic of your parents' house, or with my parents, or with Jim and Dina. We are roving gypsies and not because it's fun. We keep saying how much fun we are having because we are trying to make the best of a shitty situation. It is not fun any more Ananta. I want our home back!"

"Okay Bunny. We will start to work on project 'get our home back' as soon as we get back to Manhattan."

I burst out laughing, "That is not funny. Why am I laughing so hard?"

Ananta had this magical way of getting me to lighten up. He replied, "Then we should get more serious. Let's drive to the grocery store and be uber serious. Let's see who can be the most serious."

"Stop, I got it. Really though, you don't have to deal with parents like mine. Your parents are a dream. They are not only self-sufficient, they continue to create a wonderful life for themselves. My parents are a mess and it's getting worse."

"Bunny, how old are your parents?"

I had to think, "Ummm... Dad is 80 so Mom must be 76."

"Oh okay. My parents are in their 60s"

With a huge sigh I replied, "I know your parents are much younger than mine. I'm just barking and thrashing, feeling victimized and alone."

"What about your sister?"

"Oh shit, you're right. I have to call her."

I called Janet and recounted the horrors I walked into that night. I could never have survived my parent's decline without her. She was my rock, my screaming buddy, and my shoulder to cry on.

After giving her the full picture she replied, "Dad is such a fucking asshole. When I get down there tomorrow I'm going to put a lock on that liquor cabinet."

Though I had softened towards my mother in the past couple of years, I was totally a Daddy's girl and often took his side. Janet was close to Mom and had major issues with Dad. But as Mom continued to slide deeper into Alzheimer's, Dad slid deeper into alcoholism. He began drinking right after breakfast and carried on throughout the day and night. He must have spent at least $500 a month on alcohol. Even I could no longer defend his out-of-control behaviors.

The next day I told Ananta to go back to his parents and thank them for the use of their car. I knew there was more work to be done here than I could handle in only two days. I did not want to tie up their car.

First on the list was to hire more caregivers. It was clear that Dad could not watch Mom, even in the night hours, because he was hammered. While Janet got onto the Internet searching for caregivers, I did ten loads of laundry and cleaned the bathrooms.

I was in the laundry room when I heard Janet cry out, "Shotz, look at Mom walking down the hall, will you?"

I peeked around the corner, "What do you mean?"

She pointed out, "Watch her from behind. See, she is leaning towards one side."

"Yeah, she is."

Janet said, "She walks straight normally."

I replied, "Well, let's keep an eye on her, see if it gets worse."

Janet erupted, "Girl, I am exhausted. I need to get home soon. I have a two-hour drive. But I will call Monica to ask why she stopped coming by."

I watched Janet on the phone call with Monica. I knew her well enough to know something bad had happened. She was silent for a long time, then I heard her say, "I am very sorry you had to experience that. I wish you had called one of us."

I looked at Janet who stared at the wall in front of her.

"I want to fucking kill him. I swear to God. Fuck!"

"What? What happened?" I asked, with my heart in my stomach.

"Dad made sexual advances to Monica but she said she was a big girl and could handle that. However, what she could not handle was how aggressive he was towards Mom. One time Dad tied Mom's hoody around her neck so tight that Monica was afraid he was going to strangle her. She had to pull Dad off of Mom."

Janet started to cry, "I have to get out of here or I am going to kill Dad as soon as he walks through this door. I will call you from the car."

My sympathy and compassion for Mom was growing by the minute. Dad was clearly bullying her. Sure, he had caregiver burnout and his drinking was off the charts, but what could we do about it?

Janet called back, still crying. She said, "Mom has to have 24/7 care now. We cannot trust Dad for a second."

I replied, "You're right. But that is going to be so expensive."

"Tough!" she exclaimed, "We'll use up all his damn money caring for Mom. If he had not moved her from Amherst to the Cape in the first place, none of this would have happened."

"Girl, I know you think Dad created Mom's Alzheimer's. We don't know that and I don't want to go down that tunnel right now. But I agree, she needs 24/7 care. Problem with spending all Dad's money on caregivers is that there will be nothing left to care for Dad after Mom passes."

"Fuck Dad! He can die in a gutter for all I care!"

Janet began to cry harder. I could no longer protect my fallen hero and we needed to protect Mom. I told Janet to get home safely, get some sleep and call me in the morning.

When Dad returned he was clearly drunk already, but he asked for more. Enabler that I am, I reminded him of the rum we brought from Costa Rica. I gave Mom her meds for the night and tucked her in. When I came out, Dad was sitting at the kitchen table with the bottle of rum, already half empty.

I thought to myself, "How can we get an 80-year-old man to admit he needs help, let alone to an AA meeting?"

I took the bottle away from him, put it in the liquor cabinet, and locked it with Janet's lock. We told Dad the key was on top of the refrigerator. But I kept the key with me that night. He had far surpassed his limit.

"Hey wait a minute. I am not done with that," he protested.

"Yeah Dad, you are done with it."

I sat across from Dad just staring at him, wondering what to do about this situation. Then he picked up a ruler lying on the table.

"You see this?" he asked. "This is what I use on your mother when she refuses to take her meds."

Horrified by the images going through my mind I asked, "What do you mean Dad?"

"You know how God damn hard it is to give her those meds. Half the time she spits them out, just to be a pain in the ass."

"Dad, she can't help it. Mom doesn't know what she is doing."

"Oh yes she does. She does it to piss me off! So I have these wooden rulers all over the house. When she acts up I whack her really hard, just like she hit you with those wooden spoons when you were a kid."

Dad had such a sinister look on his face. I almost forgot that I had told him about Mom's abuse towards me as a child. It was several years back, after she was diagnosed with Alzheimer's. The image of his face back then, full of shock, indignation, and guilt, came back to me now. Part of me felt validated by his current actions, like he was taking care of me now because he never knew about it back then. For a few guilty moments I reveled in Dad's retaliations. But I could not let it persist. Calling Janet about this would send her over the edge, I knew that, but she had to know.

Dad pointed out where he kept the rulers. I easily found five of them and my heart sank. I threw them in the garbage and started to cry and pray to God for help. I was lost and forlorn. But nothing could have prepared me for what happened next. Dad was slumped over the kitchen table and I went over to help him to bed.

He asked, "Who are you?"

"I'm your daughter Dad, I'm here to help you get to bed. You're drunk Dad."

"Well you are very beautiful," he said. Then Dad pulled open my blouse.

The horror I felt in that moment could not be equaled. He crossed the line to incest. How would I ever get back from this? But like most of my sexual traumas, I swept it away.

"Dad, stop, I'm your daughter."

"Who? I don't know who you are but you are very pretty," he said, groping for my breasts again.

The only solace I had in this horrific situation was the knowledge that he really was too hammered to know who I was. I tried to lift him off the chair but a 260-pound drunk man was dead weight.

As he made a motion to get up I pulled him up at the same time. He walked one step and fell on the floor. He howled in agony. I was terrified that he broke his hip. Not knowing if I should call an ambulance, I sat near him in a chair, waiting to see if his groans subsided or escalated. Eventually they did subside but then Dad's groans turned into moans and took on an entirely new tone, one that I wanted no part in hearing. Then he puked.

I fetched a blanket to throw over his lecherous and putrid body to keep him warm during his cold night on the hard kitchen floor. Then I called my sister.

I told her about Dad's drunken lechery and his bed of puke on the kitchen floor. I knew if I told her about the wooden ruler torture she would hear nothing else and sure enough, when I got to that part she screamed.

"Fuck! I'm going to kill him with my bare hands, I swear to God!"

"What are we going to do?" I asked hopelessly.

"Well I can't have Mom here. We don't have enough room and I surely can't watch her 24/7. You remember the last time she stayed with me she peed all over your modeling photos?"

"Yeah, I always wondered if that was personal."

Janet burst out laughing, "Oh my God. Thank God we can still laugh because this is as bad as it gets. Fuck! Can you stay this week and interview people? I'll screen them on the phone first."

I replied, "I'm calling Mary in the morning. Hope she's feeling better. I am sooooo not cleaning up Dad's puke."

Dad was still passed out on the floor in the morning, but breathing. I went to check on Mom, who was in the process of changing her underpants. In my shock and horror, I saw a deep, dark purple bruise on Mom's hip the size of a soft ball. Just when I thought it could not get any worse.

I left her and went to the front of the house to call Janet.

"Girl, forget the extra caregivers. We have to get Mom out of here. She has a huge bruise on her hip where Dad has been hitting her."

"OH MY GOD! FUCK!!" and she started to cry. "Is she okay? I mean, how is she?"

"Well, she seems the same as yesterday, chipper but totally confused."

Janet continued, "Remember last night how Mom was walking funny? That must be where Dad whacked her. Fuck! I'm going to whack the fucking shit out of that asshole when I see him."

I knew better than to defend Dad. There was nothing to defend.

I told Janet, "We need to find a home for Mom, one that takes Alzheimer's patients."

She replied, "Dad is never going to sign a release for that. Remember we tried that before."

"Yes, but he is abusing Mom now. Can't we prove the abuse and take his marital rights and power of attorney away from him?"

The phone got quiet. Then Janet said, "What is Dad's greatest fear?"

I thought a minute, "Running out of booze?"

Janet laughed, "Okay, after that?"

"I have no idea."

"Going to prison," Janet declared with certainty. "He's done enough shady things in his life that he's afraid to go there."

I replied, "I never got the impression that Dad feared going to prison but let's say you're right. So what? How does that help?"

Janet continued, "Let's tell Dad that Monica called to tell us that she is going to have him arrested for sexually harassing her and abusing Mom. However, if he takes Mom to a home, Monica will drop the charges."

"OMG you are a genius! This might just work! Okay, let's get Monica on a conference call and see if she would be willing to go along with us if Dad calls her. If she is genuinely concerned with Mom's welfare, I think she will."

As easy as that, Monica agreed to back us. I was with Dad when Janet called to tell him of the unfortunate situation. She did a great acting job. Dad was visibly shaken and had no resistance. He never even asked to speak to Monica. I did my best to keep his mind off losing Mom and to focus on the great care she would get, also how Dad would get a much-needed break. His health had deteriorated severely in the past couple of years, starting with the bladder cancer.

Once in a while Dad would protest, "But I didn't abuse your mother. What the hell is she talking about?"

"Dad, you did. I don't want to go over this any more, it is too painful. You were drinking and don't remember but I have photos of Mom's bruise and the wooden rulers that Monica saw you using on Mom."

I embellished the crap out of this story, blaming it on Monica, the caregiver. Janet and I figured we'd get more cooperation from Dad if someone from outside the family was to blame for taking Mom away from him.

For the next week we worked around the clock. During the day we visited assisted living homes that took in Alzheimer's patients. At night we researched more assisted living homes. Mary came back to work and was clearly not happy that her job was about to be terminated. She tried desperately to convince Dad not to allow this, which was not helping matters. But we needed Mary at this juncture for Mom could never be left alone with Dad, it was too dangerous.

By the week's end we found a great place that was semi-affordable and had a bright and cheery staff, not to mention the food was pretty good. On Valentine's Day, February 14, 2011, we moved Mom into her new home. That day I saw Mom as the innocent victim and had great love and compassion for her. Mom had been my monstrous abuser when I was a child but I could not allow Dad to bully her any longer, not even in retribution. Assisted living was our Valentine's Day gift of love to Mom. We had high hopes that she would be happy there.

Less than a week into her stay at assisted living, Mom broke her leg. Of course Mary, our parent's main caregiver for the past eight months, tried aggressively to convince Dad to bring Mom back home, citing the dangers of assisted living. We had kept Mary on part-time to help Dad with the transition, cook his meals, do his laundry, clean the house, and keep him company. However, we had to get rid of Mary after we got clear about her stance. We upgraded Christie, the weekend caregiver, with more hours.

Once I got the call about Mom's fall, I went to the hospital in New Jersey immediately. Looking at Mom in the E.R., I saw how frightened and frail she was.

I spoke with the doctor about the nature of her injury.

He explained, "The ball at the top of her leg broke off."

I asked, "Is this from a fall she took at her new home?"

He said, "It is unlikely. This type of break is usually from an injury that affects the leg but does not show up immediately. The ball of the leg joint gradually loses blood supply and breaks off."

Then I remembered Janet's observation that Mom had been leaning to one side while she walked two weeks earlier. I told this to the doctor.

Then I asked, "If Mom had a fall or a hard hit to this area a couple of weeks ago when she was home, could that do it?"

"I cannot say for sure but most likely yes," he replied.

The doctor went on to explain how to care for Mom since her Alzheimer's would not allow her to understand she had a break. She would continue to try and get out of bed. Though I heard him speak it was like a distant voice. All I could see was Dad hitting Mom with that hard wooden ruler, the likely cause of her injury. The man who was once my hero, my protector, was now the villain in this sad story.

I called my sister to tell her what was going on. I knew she would not take the news well.

Chapter 45

Sugar Daddies and Other Sweet Men

Looking at my poor frail mother in the emergency room, I flashed on my next move. I needed more free time to care for her, and more money. I instantly made the decision to become a prostitute.

I had a taste of it with Bianca and Ron and it wasn't too bad. As I thought this over I realized I would have to give more service than with Bianca and Ron. They were the ideal situation. But this was the only way I thought I could afford to care for Mom. Prostitution paid big bucks and therefore allowed me to take more time off. Of course a woman without a sex/love addiction might never consider such a sordid profession. But I didn't care about the social stigma. My mother was deteriorating. I promised myself I would quit once she passed. But an addiction is not easy to put down once it takes hold and prostitution was about to strangle me.

Mom stayed in the hospital for quite some time then went to physical rehab for several weeks. In the meantime, I went back to those sugar daddy websites where I canvassed my Tantra massage clients. This time I made myself available for everything. I did not ask Ananta how he felt about this. I announced it to him.

I said, "Unless you know a way to earn $4,000 a month only working four to six days a month, then I'm prostituting myself. Screwing, blow jobs, and kissing will now be happening."

Ananta replied, "If you want to do this Bunny, I want you to be happy."

Getting sharp with Ananta, "I would be happier if you made $4,000 a month so I could focus on caring for my parents but I have been asking this of you for over two years. I doubt it's going to happen now."

Ananta hung his head. Of course I knew the economy was tough and finding work was challenging. But he had plenty of time to find new swinger couples for us to sex with. Yes, I was pissed.

I also made it clear, "Just because I am having side relationships with men now, don't think that gives you permission to do the same. These men are paying our bills. If you find a sugar mommy or sugar daddy to help, that would be the only way I would accept you having sex on the side too. Do you understand?"

"Yes Bunny, I understand," he replied.

But understanding and adhering to the boundaries were not the same. I should have been even clearer.

I contacted Bianca to meet with her and Ron. It was a guaranteed $1,000 and all I had to do was jerk him off and be touched myself. He was a dream sugar daddy. But Ron was Bianca's client and I felt that I shouldn't push this too often. I asked her about ways to generate more clients and she was super helpful, giving me more sugar daddy and prostitute websites.

My first target was Trevor Griffin, my virgin Tantra massage client. I asked if he might like to take me to dinner to discuss our relationship. He was eager to oblige. Within the week we met again for dinner and afterwards returned to his apartment for sex. Wow, and what an apartment he had! A three-bedroom duplex in a doorman building with a fireplace, terrace, and all modern appliances, not to mention a spectacular 360-degree view of Manhattan.

Trevor agreed to give me a $3,000 "allowance" per month for my time, meeting him once a week. I tried to get him up to $4,000 a month to cover all my expenses but he declined. No problem, I would canvass others for the extra income. I had no idea just how much time and effort it would take to find those fill-in-the-gap guys. I was lucky to find Trevor. He was steady, committed, and fun to be with.

Adolfo was my first fill-in-the-gap guy. He was a really hot and handsome 40-year-old from Spain who was not as steady as Trevor but we did meet about once a month. He was married with young children and did not want to leave his wife or hurt her, but he also wanted more sex in his life. We met first for coffee in the afternoon and when we parted he gave me a gift bag of chocolates and cookies along with a $50 bill. He apologized that he did not have a lot of money to give me, only $450 for the hour, but I was so hot for him that I did not mind the discount.

All married men want to meet for sex in a hotel room and meeting Adolfo was no exception. I wore a classy yet sexy outfit because he was a well-dressed man that wanted more sexual passion in his life. I wanted to match his style.

When I got to his hotel door he welcomed me in a robe. I figured he wanted to get down to business quickly. But I was wrong. There was samba music playing in the background and all around the room were flowers, fruits, nuts, cheeses, breads, sausages, wine, champagne, and chocolates. I was astonished.

I said, "I just had lunch not long ago. I wish I had known, I would not have eaten so late. Is all this for us?"

Adolfo replied, "No, it is for you. I want to pamper you. You are special."

I almost started to cry and did my best to hold back the tears. Adolfo held up a bottle of Champagne.

"Would you like a glass of Champagne with strawberries?"

The Champagne was chilling in a bucket and the strawberries were pre-cut to perfection. I could see all the planning and preparation that he had put into this afternoon delight.

Adolfo asked, "May I take off your shoes and massage your feet while you drink?"

When my glass of Champagne emptied, Adolfo asked, "May I give you a full body massage?"

"Wait," I asked, "is this a dream? Because if it is I don't want to wake up!"

Adolfo smiled, "This is your dream come true. May I take off your dress now *mi amada*?"

"Yes. *Mi amada*? What does that mean?"

"It means my darling, my beloved."

For the next 15 minutes Adolfo massaged my back. Then he turned me over to massage my face, my breasts, my thighs, and soon there after he went down on me and brought me to orgasm.

Politely he asked, "May I enter you *mi amada*?"

"*Si amore, si...*"

Adolfo did not have sex with me. Adolfo made love to me. It was something even my husband rarely offered any more. I found myself tearing as he came inside of me. Of course he was wearing a condom but I felt the intense force of his orgasm throughout my body. After he came he lay next to me caressing my hair.

"I hate to leave you *mi amada* but I must return to my office. Can we meet again and again?"

I wanted to scream, "Hell yeah!" instead I said with a soft smile, "Yes, again, and again."

As I dressed, Adolfo gathered the flowers, food and drinks in two large gift bags. As I approached the door he handed them to me.

"Oh no Adolfo. I barely touched them. You should take them home with you."

"No *amada*, I got them for you. My wife, she would not appreciate these sentiments."

At that moment I felt sad for Adolfo. I saw how he was not only lacking sex but also romance. Then I realized that I too was lacking both sex and romance from my husband. This had been going on for many months. All our sexing was with others, rarely one-on-one. Though Ananta was always sweet with me, he had stopped romancing me. As my heart sank with these sad thoughts, Adolfo handed me a gift card.

I opened it. It was a black and white photo of a romantic couple embracing. Inside he wrote, "Thank you for this most beautiful experience."

There was also $450 in cash. Gosh, I almost forgot I met Adolfo to earn money. It felt as if we were a new romantic couple, enjoying our first lovemaking.

"I will call you tomorrow to make sure you are feeling good, okay?"

My God, I never dated a guy who was this attentive and considerate. This was a peak experience in my life and I made $450 to boot. I was overwhelmed with gratitude and my eyes began to fill with emotion.

Without speaking, Adolfo kissed my cheek where a tear had fallen. I felt as if I was living inside a romantic film. Was this real?

I left the room, and then the hotel, feeling loved and cherished, not at all what I had expected. I did not know how to process this. I texted Ananta that I was out of the hotel and I was safe, and jumped in a cab. When I got home I was relieved that Ananta was not there. I jumped into bed for a nap, leaving my over-flowing gift bags on the table. When I awoke, Ananta was home.

He asked, "How was your date?"

I pointed to the gift bags. I could see he felt intimidated. I was honest, giving him all the details including my discomfort with all that loving attention, compared to our current life together. Ananta always touted himself as not jealous, yet I felt a wave of it as he went through the gift bags with me. He had a way of minimizing nice things when he was jealous.

Ananta asked, "Will you see him again?"

"Yes," I said with glee.

"But he does not pay that much, right?"

"True, he is not the highest-paying client but he makes up for it with sweetness."

Ananta tried making light of the situation by chuckling, "Well, that's a sugar daddy, right? Sweetness."

Still emotionally raw and feeling deeply connected to my new sugar daddy, I felt uncomfortable being with Ananta. I told him, "I am going to the gym for a little while before dinner. See you soon."

I didn't want to be around him. That was a first. This sugar daddy business was starting to feel emotionally dangerous. If my clients gave me more than I got from my husband, why would I want my husband? With my clients I felt loved, adored, lavished with sex, gifts, glamour and of course, money. None of these treasures I was getting from my husband.

Chapter 46

My Months in Prostitution

Trevor, Ron, and Adolfo were my only sugar daddy steadies. Even though I met other clients via sugar daddy websites, they were not in long-term relationships with me. A guy that meets for sex only once or twice is clearly a john and I am clearly the prostitute. But hey, if it makes a man feel better to call himself a sugar daddy and not a john, or a woman to call herself a sugar baby and not a hooker, so be it. But I knew the difference as a business model - being a prostitute was far more work than being a sugar baby. It required constant canvassing to keep the men coming. I didn't much like it. Then, after two months of financial security, Trevor did the unexpected: he canceled his $3K subscription.

He announced his decision in a short monologue, "Shanti, I really enjoy your company. But, my son is coming to stay with me for the summer. How would I explain who you are? I don't want to lie and say you are my girlfriend. It's not like I can take you out to meet my friends and family. Let's take the summer off and have dinner in September and see if we want to reconnect, okay?"

But nothing about this situation was okay. Just like that, my steady income vanished. Not only did Trevor pull out, in more ways than one, but Ron also vanished - he went away for the summer with Bianca. I tried desperately to find another steady sugar daddy but it wasn't happening so prostitution became my main source of income. Most of the men I met that summer were from out of town and I saw them once: prostitution soon lost its romantic appeal. Handsome and romantic Adolfo was truly an anomaly and I was so grateful to see him once a month. This sexing with men for money however, was now a job and I spent all my free time, when not with my parents, canvassing new johns. None of them matched the fun, romance, or high earnings of my sweet sugar daddies. This was a straight one-hour deal and some of them had the nerve to ask for a discount. My fees ranged from $450 to $800 an hour, depending on what I thought the client could pay.

Initially I ran into a string of jerks, mostly because I was not comfortable asking for the money up front. Doing that made me feel like a street whore. I never had to ask with the sugar daddies. I trusted them. We had an on-going relationship. Trevor paid me once a month and Ron and Adolfo paid me before they would leave. Live and learn - I sure did learn the hard way.

Bill seemed like a really nice guy at first. Average looking man in his mid-60s, originally from Tennessee. We met in the early evening at a strip club in Times Square. Everyone there seemed to know him by name, he was clearly a regular. Bill ordered me a drink then a lap dance from the stripper of my choice. Next we headed back to his place, not far away. I was surprised to find two other women there. They both greeted him with great glee. He presented me to them like he brought home a new puppy. They were both extremely effusive with me. I had no idea what was going on.

Bill ordered a pizza and we all shot the shit for over an hour. They were fascinated that I was once a model and had fun Googling all my modeling photos. I got they were Bill's regulars, but was not sure if they were looking to add on a new regular or just to spice it up for the night. I could have asked but instead I sat in my discomfort of not knowing.

I had already spent two hours with Bill. The clock was ticking and I was nervous about being paid so when they pulled out a joint and started stripping for one another, I could smell the money. They were making out with each other and then Bill joined them. He pulled me in with them and entered me. Then as soon as he came he passed out. I tried to revive him.

However, one of the women explained, "Oh no, when Big Bill passes out, he is out!"

They laughed then got dressed quickly and left me alone with Big Bill, listening to him snore. I sent Ananta a text message to let him know I was having a working sleepover and would text in the morning. I also gave him the address, just in case I showed up missing. This night was creeping me out and I wanted to go home, but I also wanted my money. As soon as the sun came up I jumped in the shower. I must have waken Big Bill for he joined me and sexed with me in the bathroom. When I was dressed and ready to go, he handed me $300. I was livid.

"Three hundred? I spent 12 hours with you and your friends last night."

Bill smiled, "I know and we all had fun didn't we?"

"That is beside the point Bill. This is a business for me. I am a prostitute."

That was the first time I ever acknowledged that out loud to any john.

I continued, "I get paid by the hour. I spent 12 hours with you. You just paid me $25 an hour. I got paid more as a legal secretary."

Bill appeared calm and pensive as he gathered his thoughts. He said, "Well, I do understand all that and I am really in a tough spot here. I pay Holly and Cindy $300 each, every time they come here. It wouldn't be fair if I paid you more, now would it?"

I replied, "Yes, it would be fair because I slept over and we had sex again this morning."

"Well, that is true. I was not expecting you to sleep over, that was a great surprise for sure," Bill acknowledged.

Bill opened his wallet. He pulled out $26, all that was in there.

"I'm really sorry but this is all I have left. I don't get paid until next week."

I grabbed it and left. I was not about to come back for round two. On this day, I realized that I was a whore and I hated myself. I hated Ananta for not working and I hated that Ananta was okay with me doing this. When I got home I ranted and screamed at him, then I packed my bags for New Jersey to see my parents. At least this horrible experience would have a happy ending and not a Tantric massage happy ending: I would get to spend time caring for my parents.

Chapter 47

Dad Moves in with Mom?

I was hoping to find some solace in New Jersey but there was no solace to be found. After Mom left rehab and returned to her new home in assisted living, the director told us that we would have to relocate Mom to a nursing home if we couldn't keep her in bed while her leg healed. Technically, assisted-living homes are not allowed to use guardrails on their beds. It is one of the ways they distinguish themselves from a nursing home. No one wanted Mom to go to a nursing home. Nursing homes were like hospitals - cold, impersonal, and depressing. Assisted living was a dream compared to a nursing home.

I always stayed with Dad at his house. Even though his alcohol consumption was at an all-time high and he clearly had abused Mom these past few years, I still loved him dearly. During my rough childhood days enduring Mom's beatings and cold shoulder treatments, he was my knight in shining armor. Dad always came home with a smile on his face and exuded a genuine enthusiasm to be home with us. Mom, on the other hand, was usually in some state of rage. I believe my brother and sister and I all became successful because we pursued our passions outside the home. Who wanted to come home to Mom?

But now, all my grudges against Mom melted. She was frail and frightened. Dad and I went early the next morning to speak with the director of the assisted living. Janet joined us soon there after.

She told us again, this time in person, "If we can't get your mother to stay in bed at night while her leg heals, we are going to have to release her to you or to a nursing home."

Dad immediately chimed in, "Then let's bring her home for Christ's sake!"

I asked Dad to go upstairs and be with Mom so Janet and I could speak with the director privately. I had a crazy brainstorm and wanted to flesh it out with her.

I asked, "What if we got a twin-size bed for Dad and pushed it right up against Mom's bed when the aide turned her in for the night? She would not have the strength to climb over Dad and she would be pinned in by the wall on the other side."

Janet chimed in, "Oh great, let's put Mom's fucking abuser right back in there."

"Dad is not going to hurt Mom with tons of people around. Remember, Monica already threatened him with jail time so he is not going to go there again. Besides, he doesn't have to feed Mom or dispense her meds, which spark his rage. Also, he won't be drinking here. He would mainly be alone with Mom at night when she sleeps."

"This is crazy," Janet protested.

"Okay, so what do you want to do? Have Mom go to a nursing home or go home with Dad?

Janet broke down and cried, "I hate all of this. I wish I could take her home with me but I have a business to run. I will go bankrupt caring for her."

The director spoke, "Let's give it a try. You can order the bed for your father or we can. Just let us know. Since the room is already paid for, your Dad only has to pay for his meals."

Janet and I went upstairs to speak with Dad.

"Dad, would you be willing to sleep here at night with Mom?" I asked.

"What? I don't understand," he said.

"If we get you a twin-size bed and push it up against Mom's bed at night, she won't be able to climb out of bed," Janet explained.

"Of course I would do that. I would be happy to do that."

Holding Mom's hand, Dad began to cry. I knew he loved her deeply. His abuse was, I want to say, a combination of caregiver burn out and alcohol. But Janet had no sympathy for Dad what so ever. She left the room.

That night the assisted living gave Dad a temporary cot because the convertible couch we ordered took a few days to arrive. We thought it best to get him a couch since he would be sitting on it to watch TV as Mom slept a lot. With one click it turned into a full-size bed. Now the entire corner would be one oversized bed with nowhere for Mom to go.

Chapter 48

Jerky Johns and New Sugar Daddy

I continued to have unpleasant situations with my johns. After one more experience of me being too timid to ask for the money upfront, I learned my lesson.

A French business man that I met online told me he would pay me $600 for one and a half hours. I agreed and met him at the hotel, first for drinks and later up to his room. We ordered dinner from room service and chatted for nearly an hour in English and French before sexing, and our entire time together in the room was two and a half hours. He paid me $500.

"You owe me another $500 dollars," I told him.

Mr. French replied, "I told you $600 but we ordered dinner and Champagne. I don't need to pay for your meal."

I was shocked that he would assume I pay for the meal. No man, let alone a john, ever expected me to pay for my meal. I made it clear, "We agreed on $600 for one and a half hours. I have been here for two and a half hours."

He replied, "Hey, is not my fault you lose track of time."

I was livid but in the end it was my bad. I never accepted payment after sex again and never returned his calls again either. Some men lose all tact once they've got what they want. Hard lesson learned.

My next encounter was not completely horrific but still, not desirable nor was I prepared for it. I was starting to get referrals from other sugar babies and prostitutes when their sugar daddies or johns requested a *ménage-à-trois*. Lily asked me to join in with her and her regular john. I had never met Lily before but a stripper friend recommended her. It would be an hour and a half for $1,000. I liked those numbers. I said yes immediately, asking no questions.

I met them the next day at their hotel suite. He was a good lucking British guy in his 40s, fun, gregarious, and sexy. Lily was a tall, beautiful, Russian brunette in her 40s but in super great shape. She was smoking hot. Mr. Brit wanted to see us playing with each other in the living room. That was easy and a turn on. He watched us for quite some time, stroking his cock, smoking his cigar, and drinking his Champagne. Seemed like all the johns drank Champagne. This scene went on for quite some time.

Then all of a sudden, in a stern voice, he ordered Lily, "Take her to the bed."

His demeanor made me uncomfortable. However, Lily guided me over to the bed gracefully and we all lay next to one another. I was in the middle. She was sweet with me and so my fearful mind relaxed. But then Mr. Brit pushed my face into the pillow, lay on my back, and shoved his cock up my ass before I could stop him. I couldn't move. It hurt like a knife and I started to scream but Lily pushed the pillow deeper into my mouth.

She then spoke to me softly while she stroked my hair, "I know honey, it hurts. But it will be over soon, I promise."

She must have known all along this was going to happen. But she was right. It was over within minutes. It's not as if I never had anal sex before, I had often enjoyed it, but it took time and a good amount of lube. This was forced entry with no consent, and no lube: a rape. So what, do I file a complaint with the police? I was a prostitute now. We are outlaws with no laws to protect us.

When it was all over, Mr. Brit jumped off the bed and into the shower without looking at me or saying a word. Lily acted like nothing was off. She brought me the $1,000 in cash and several wet wipes.

"If you would not mind wiping yourself off instead of taking a shower, we want to be alone now. I'm sure you understand. It is our romantic time."

I didn't understand anything about this world and the more I participated, the less I liked it. But true to their word, they paid me $1,000 in cash and it was even less then an hour and a half. The money made it all better.

But before leaving I had to ask, "Did he wear a condom?"

Lily searched and pulled out the used condom, full of sperm, from the bedding.

"Thanks." I said with great relief.

"Of course honey. We have to protect ourselves. I hope to see you again when we are next in New York. Bye now."

Seemed whenever I was not with my sister or my parents, I was in the sexual underbelly of New York City. Rebecca spent the summers with her Dad so this allowed me time to focus on work. I was still shy $2,000 that month so I spent more time than usual fishing on the Internet and caught myself a big little fish. He was a tiny man in his late 60s, only 5'2" but with an ego the size of a whale - a textbook case of a Napoleon complex. I met him on a millionaire-dating site that one of my prostitute girlfriends told me about. She said the site was merely a cover for prostitution. She was right.

I met my extremely arrogant Napoleonic real estate tycoon for dinner only because he pushed it, saying he would pay me $300 cash for the meet and greet plus the meal. I usually only met potentials for a quick drink. I was wearing five-inch heals so when he stood up at the table the top of his head barely made it to my breasts. He said he was 5'9' on his profile. I had no issue with his height, but his personality was already driving me nuts. However, I needed the money so I agreed to stay for dinner. This time, I was smart: I asked for the money before dinner began.

His response: "It is terribly *gauche* of you to do business that way my dear."

I got up to leave, "Nice meeting you Napoleon."

"What? Oh my God! Sit down please. I will pass your request to you under the table, okay?"

I smiled then sat down. He pulled out his wallet, and started counting, then passed me the cash. I counted it.

Napoleon said, "You are tough. Did you know that?"

I replied, "I am smart and I know that. Thank you."

He spent the entire dinner telling me how successful and rich he was.

"Yet what is so amazing to me is how women flock to me wherever I go, even if they know nothing of my wealth. I am just that attractive I guess. I'm married so I do try to keep my liaisons to a minimum in case my wife ever finds out. I don't want to hurt her, I love her very much."

I was about to leave, I was that nauseated. But then I remembered I was very low on cash so I stayed, I can withstand anything for a couple hours.

I asked him, "So, if women flock to you everywhere you go, why do you have to pay for sex?"

"Great question," he replied. "I don't always pay for sex. But it's a kink I like once in a while. What about you? Why do you like getting paid for sex?"

Finally, Napoleon appeared semi-interested in me.

I told him, "I am taking care of my mother, she has Alzheimer's, while doing my best to keep my alcoholic father from abusing her. I like big wads of cash fast. Allows me to hop to them on notice."

He started to laugh, "You are funny on top of being smart and gorgeous. I like you."

"Oh I am a laugh riot," I replied, dripping in sarcasm.

"What would you like for dessert?" he asked.

"Nothing. I have to go now."

I stood up to leave.

"Wait, where are you going?" he asked and then whispered, "I paid you for dinner, remember?"

I whispered back, "I remember. We had dinner. Dinner is over. I never agreed to have dessert."

"But I am not ready to go," Napoleon said in his commander-in-chief-voice.

"So stay," I said, gathering my purse.

"Hold on, please, sit down for just two minutes." I sat back down. He explained, "This looks a little embarrassing for me. I know people at this restaurant. If you leave ahead of me, it looks like you are disrespecting me."

"Really? So I'm leaving now. If you want to save face with your friends then forget dessert, pay the bill, and get the fuck out of here when I leave."

We walked out together and he hailed me a cab. A minute later he called me.

"Hey, I like you. Can we have sex this week?"

I wished I could have told him to go to hell but I really needed the money. So I quoted him a high price, assuming he wouldn't go for it. But he did, $1,000 an hour.

We met at his place on Park Avenue in the 70s since he said his wife was out of town. I didn't like the idea but he said he was unwilling to spring for a hotel. As soon as I got to his place, he paid me the $1,000 up front, saying he only wanted to pay for one hour. Great, I thought, I'll be out of here soon. But of course, his arrogance still showed through.

While screwing me he remarked, "Isn't my body incredibly toned for a 68-year-old man?"

I replied, "So what if you don't get me to cum."

"Ouch," he gasped. "What makes you cum?"

"Fingers," I said, pulling the lube bottle from my purse and passing it to him.

He got it and proceeded to perform, he was quite good at it too. Finally, I was beginning to enjoy Napoleon and I had a really nice orgasm. Not long after, he came as well.

We lay in bed and he told me how much he enjoyed my company. I couldn't say the same of him but I was feeling warmer towards him since my orgasm high. Then I heard a door slam.

"Fuck, what is that?" I whispered with my heart in my stomach.

"Shshsh. Be quiet. Go into the shower, quietly."

I knew I shouldn't have come to his home. I had visions of his wife pulling a gun on me.

"Hey Maria. I'm in the bedroom. I'm going to take a shower and be out of here in 10 minutes."

Napoleon joined me in the shower.

"Is that your wife?" I asked in terror.

"No, I told you, she is out of town. That's the maid."

I asked him, "What if the maid is your wife's watchdog?"

"My dear, I pay all the bills. If the help rat me out, they are out of a job, so they never go there."

We managed to slip out of his home without running into the maid, he dropped me off at my place and headed to his appointment. Yes indeed, married men have their liaisons during the workday.

I met Napoleon one more time but refused to meet in his home, too risky. I stuck to my $1,000-an-hour rate and he accepted but told me that it would be the last time while paying for a hotel. I stuck to my guns and he stuck to his, I missed the money but not the wretched little man.

My next work encounter was through my friend Billie, the same stripper that recommended me to Lily and the ass-rapist. She asked me to join her and her 75-year-old sugar daddy.

I protested, "Oh Billie, come on. I appreciate you hooking me up with clients and all. But seriously, I don't think I can do a 75-year-old man. He's nearly my father's age. Yuck!"

"Honey buns, I resisted Joe for 2 years. He was always hanging out at the strip club and one night I got so drunk I went home with him. You know what? He didn't even have sex with me. Said I was too drunk, didn't want to take advantage of me. But he paid me $2,000 as he had promised me at the club and then he sent me home with a to-go cup of coffee. Now that's a great sugar daddy."

"Ooooh, you are making this hard to turn down," I told her.

Billie replied, "Joe also has a phenomenal body. I swear, I'm not lyin'. He just has grey hair but at least he has hair."

We both laughed.

"And," Billie continued, "I will be right there with you girl. Try it once. I promise you will be happy with him. You'll make $2,000 dollars for the night and he will be a steady client, I know you have been looking for that."

"But I don't want to take your client from you."

"Girl, I have so many clients I don't have time for them all, seriously. He is my present to you."

We met a few days later at Joe's penthouse apartment on Park Avenue. Joe greeted me at the door.

"Oh my God, you are very handsome!" I blurted out.

"Well, thank you my dear. You are absolutely as gorgeous as Billie said." He sent a smile of approval to Billie. "Please, come in."

I was so relieved. Joe really was handsome and tall to boot. Billie really did down-play him. I was not trying to make him feel good by my compliments, I was actually making myself feel good. It was such a relief to see that he was not some decrepit old creep. He looked a little like Cary Grant in his later years, he was absolutely stunning. Then, if seeing Joe's handsome face and physique were not enough of a turn-on, his apartment was absolutely beyond, beyond. It had huge floor-to-ceiling windows that wrapped around three sides, eastern, southern, and western views with a huge terrace. Wow, I was completely blown away and couldn't hide it.

"Joe, your home is absolutely stunning!"

"Well, I can't take credit for it really. It is mostly my wife's doing. She chose it and decorated it. I just forked over the money."

I was stunned. Billie had not mentioned that he was married and since we met on a Friday night at his home I just figured he was single. I had no issue with Joe being married, most men who hire prostitutes or keep sugar babies are married. But I was terrified to be in their home in case their wife or children showed up. I shot a fearful glance to Billie.

Billie got up from the couch, came up behind Joe and hugged him. She said, "Yeah, our sexy married man doesn't want to leave his wife."

"Because no one else would have her." Joe replied. Billie and Joe laughed and kissed one another sideways.

He went on to explain, "You can't leave a woman in her 70s, the mother of your children and grandmother of twelve to live alone. It's just not right. I'm one of those old-fashioned nice guys, I guess, I never did well with women in my younger days because they wanted bad boys. But seems like women start looking for good guys when they get older."

I piped in, "Yes, that is definitely true. Let's toast to good guys like Joe!"

"Oh boy, wait just a minute. I am not that good. I didn't get you a drink yet, young lady. What would you like?"

I saw the Champagne chilling in the bucket but I honestly was not a big fan. I asked, "Do you have chardonnay?"

"Ah, I do believe there are a few chards in the refrigerator. Would you like to come with me and look?"

I absolutely adored this man already. I told Joe, "Yes of course kind sir. I will go anywhere with you."

He shot an approving glance to Billie. Little did I know that his favorite activity was traveling with his sugar babies.

Joe gave me his arm and off we went to the kitchen and into our new life together. Joe became my only source of income from that point foreword, paying me between $4,000 and $6,000 per month. Not only was it a relief not to have to chase new johns, but also I genuinely enjoyed Joe's company. He was smart, chivalrous, kind, thoughtful, adventurous, loving, and funny. We always started the evening with dinner at a local restaurant and then back to his place. His wife spent most of her time in Florida and England, where some of their children and grandchildren lived. Joe became not only my financial support, but he became my emotional support as well. For in the next few months my mother continued to spiral downwards. My mother was dying.

Chapter 49

Mom's Decline and Death

Though Mom could take guided baby steps from her bed to the wheelchair, she never walked again. The doctor explained that once an Alzheimer's patient suffers such a severe break to the leg or hip, they rarely bounce back. Mom had been an intensely active woman, even through all her stages of Alzheimer's. It was painful to see her stuck in a wheelchair. In the next few months Mom would be hospitalized for a urinary tract infection and a colon infection. On her last visit to the hospital, the doctor gave us some devastating news.

"Your mother's kidneys are shutting down. There is nothing more we can do."

Everyone at Mom's assisted living was absolutely amazing and supportive. They told us she did not need to go to a nursing home to die, they would assign her a hospice nurse and Mom could die peacefully with Dad and all of us by her side.

The next few months were terribly trying and extremely sad. I stayed at Dad's house over night and spent the days with them at assisted living. I would travel back to New York a few days a week to change clothes, see Rebecca and Ananta, and of course to see Joe, the new sugar daddy who was fueling this rough ride.

We were getting super close, Joe and me. On one of my trips I completely broke down about the imminent loss of my mother.

Joe looked at me sweetly, "You know what I like about you my precious Shanti, beside your obvious beauty and brains? You are real and you are a beautiful person inside."

I smiled for a brief moment and then cried some more.

Then I asked Joe, "What if you get very sick one day or worse, what if you die? How will I know? Who will let me know? I don't know anyone that knows you except Billie."

"Oh, somehow I think you will know. I will wink at you from above, or below, depending on my report card."

We both laughed uproariously. There is something incredibly intense about a belly laugh after a good cry. The joy almost hurts as much as the sorrow.

Mom finally passed the night of July 25, 2011. I was alone with her for half an hour before she left us. She was resting peacefully though her breathing was labored and shallow. The warm bright light from the sunset was streaming through the blinds and I opened them fully so the sun could bathe her cheeks. Her eyes were closed and had been closed for most of the day.

I told Mom, "The light of God is coming for you soon that is brighter than this sun. Go into that light with great joy Mom for you are about to have the most glorious journey of your life. I promise you. It is time for you to go home to God."

Then I got up on the bed with Mom, spooned her and held her tight. I kissed her back and started to cry as I spoke.

"Mom, thank you for my precious gift of life and all the sacrifices you made. Please forgive me for not loving you more and for holding resentments towards you. I could have done more to care for you if I wasn't so angry with you. I'm sorry. I know you were not happy for much of your life. You didn't get what you wanted. I know that. You will have a chance to come back and start over again in a new body. I want you to promise me that you will go for what you truly want next time. Promise me. Promise yourself."

Then one of Mom's eyes popped open wide and I came around to look at her. She was clearly focused on me. I called Dad into the room, "Dad, come in here!" He was waiting in the lounge for me to join him for dinner.

I said, "Mom? Hi Mom. I love you so much Mom."

And I kissed her goodbye on her now sunken cheek.

"What?" Dad asked. "I'm hungry. Can we go to dinner now?"

"Dad, say good-bye to Mom."

"I don't need to say goodbye to her. We're coming back here after dinner."

I told him, "We never know when it will be her time Dad. Best to say good-bye anyway."

Dad leaned over and touched her arm, "Okay honey. See you after dinner."

Then we went downstairs to the dinning hall. Dad entertained the troops as he always did, I'm sure my social butterfly comes from him. A gorgeous sunset poured into the dinning hall, as it had in Mom's room. Just as we finished our meal, one of the attendants came and crouched down next to Dad's chair. I knew exactly what she was going to say: "I'm sorry Mr. Owen. Your wife has passed."

We spent the next few hours with Mom in her room as various assistants and hospice care attendants came in to offer their condolences. Though Mom's spirit had left her body, it was comforting to look upon her face, though tired and worn, the face of my beautiful mother.

Chapter 50

My Very Empty Nest

My sister Janet left Mom's bedside two days before she passed. Janet was angry with Dad about something he said over lunch and left us, said she wanted to be with Mom. Then I received a text from her, "I said my good-byes to Mom. I'm going home. This asshole is all yours."

Though I felt a moment of abandonment, I knew that if the shoe were on the other foot and Dad was dying and Mom was working my last nerve, I might have jumped ship too. But now what? We planned to stay with Mom to the end and do all the funeral arrangements together. So here I was, comforting Dad, writing Mom's obituary, and contacting family and friends. It was heart-wrenching. There was no way I was about to plan her funeral. I just took that off the list. Mom wanted to be cremated anyway, so we could organize a memorial later. Dad was a total mess and needed attention. He talked about going back to his house but the director at the assisted living suggested otherwise.

She said, "Jim, why don't you stay here for the next month so you don't have to worry about anything? You'll be surrounded by people you know that care about you. This is not a time to be alone. We all know exactly what you are going through here."

Dad barked, "Nah, why do I need to spend money I don't need to spend? I have a house that is paid for."

I said, "Dad, remember, I need to fly out to California in a couple weeks to get Rebecca settled at college. I've got tons to do to get her ready. So I really won't be able to be here for a while. I think it's a perfect solution. Everyone has gotten to know and love you here. They will be sad to see you go and you will miss them too."

That was it. Tell Dad he is needed and he will go and do anything. That used to drive my Mom crazy. He was always helping out all the neighbors. For now though, this trait was working in my favor. Knowing Dad was taken care of was a huge burden off my shoulders. I spent a few more days with Dad, handled Mom's cremation and obituary announcements, then headed back home to New York. I had been away nearly two weeks, dealing with all this. I was completely burnt.

When I arrived at Port Authority, Ananta was there to greet me. I thought it odd that he wanted to pick me up. He had never done that before. But then again, my mother had never died before. When I saw him he was full of enthusiasm, he picked me up and swung me around.

"Excuse me," I said, "Have you seen my husband?"

I was actually serious about my question but I don't think he got that. Ananta had gone through several months of deep depression, he even began taking anti-depressant meds. He spent much of his days like a zombie and when he wasn't depressed he was still a low-key guy. So his extreme enthusiasm really threw me.

"My Bunny, my Bunny, I am so happy to see my Bunny!" Ananta shouted from the top of his lungs.

I contemplated, "Does happiness appear over the top since I just went through such an intense loss?"

I told him, "Honey, I never thought I would say this to you but could you turn it down a notch on the enthusiasm? I am completely wiped out right now and need some calm."

"Sure Bunny. Anything my Bunny wants, my Bunny gets."

Have to get him to stop calling me Bunny. It is tolerable when it comes out sweetly, but with enthusiasm, it makes me nauseous.

We took a cab home since my working relationship with Joe allowed me to relax about finances. As soon as we got through the door I lay on our love seat and Ananta removed my shoes and started massaging my feet. He wanted to know everything that happened surrounding my mother's death but I didn't want to talk about. I just wanted to vegetate.

He said, "I understand Bunny. Would it be okay if I told you about my adventures while I make you dinner?"

"Hmmm, dinner too?" I replied, "picking me up at the bus station, foot massage, and dinner too? Someone is extremely happy. Did you get a job?"

"No, but I did get someone to help with my new resume. You remember our friend Tracy from Rochester? She used to be a recruiter and she came here a couple of times and gave me some really great tips."

"Tracy is not my friend. She is your friend," I clarified.

"Oh yeah but you met her at the wedding. She loves you. She thinks you're great," Ananta replied. He continued, "Then I went over to Billie's a couple of times and she made me dinner. I was surprised she was such a great cook and then she taught me a couple of new yoga poses that I could barely do of course"

"Ananta, are you high on cocaine?" I asked.

"No Bunny, don't be silly. I don't do coke, you know that."

"Then why do you seem high and why can't you stop talking?" I asked. "You never talk this much."

"It's just that I'm so excited to have you home and share my adventures with my Bunny," he beamed. Then he asked, "Can I tell you the other fun thing that happened?"

"Sure," I said with some reluctance.

He continued, "Cherie, the wife of the guy who owns that swinger club from Philly, she asked me to help them redecorate their space so I drove down to Philly with her."

"Did they pay you?" I asked.

"No, but we get five free passes to their next swinger events." Ananta said with joy.

All of a sudden I got a lightning bolt of an intuition. "Stop!" I yelled.

When Ananta stopped talking the apartment was completely still. I broke the silence: "All you have been sharing with me is about these hot women you have been hanging around with these past two weeks. Were you sleeping with them?"

306

Ananta's face dropped. His hyper-activity subsided. He looked at the ground. "Only one of them," he said.

"Oh, only one of them. Like that is supposed to make it better? Who was it?" praying it was not my girlfriend Billie who had set me up with Joe.

"Tracy," he said.

"Tracy, the girl you have had a crush on for ten years now." I reminded him.

He explained, "Bunny you said I could have a side relationship if I got a sugar mommy or sugar daddy."

Slowly jostling my memory banks, "Okay, that's true. Sorry if I misspoke. How much did she pay you?"

Enthusiastically he replied, "She didn't pay me in cash but she paid me in resume coaching."

I came back quickly, "That does not pay our bills and that does not constitute a sugar mommy! I was taking care of my dying mother and you were having a great old time fucking your heartthrob. How nice. I knew something was weird. You were covering up that you cheated. Fuck you! I just lost my mother, and I'm about to lose my daughter. I should kick your sorry ass out of my life for good, but I won't be able to handle another loss."

So I did what I do best: I compartmentalized this fucked-up situation. I would pretend it didn't happen until I got back from California.

I was on a roll and I continued to Ananta, "Right now you get the fuck out of my apartment and go see your Mommy and Daddy. They will always cater to your every whim. Why do you think you can never get work? Because they always wipe your ass! I am going to rent this place while I am in California so you can't use it as your fuck pad. And if you think you might want to stay married to me, you better not fuck anyone else but yourself while I'm away. Clear?"

"Yes," Ananta said without addressing me as Bunny. That meant he was mad. Good, let him feel some of my rage.

Then I said, "And if you need some money, ask your parents. I am officially firing you as my pimp. You get no more money from me for selling my ass and my soul. Maybe you will finally get a job. Please leave. I cannot stand to look at you another moment."

I knew I was being nasty and cruel but I didn't care. If discovering Ananta's infidelity the previous year was the angriest I had ever gotten, this was right up there. I wanted so badly to kick him out of my life forever but there was too much loss already going on. I wanted to focus on taking care of Rebecca and her needs for college, tuck her in over there with all my love and attention. My baby, my one and only child was leaving the nest. Such a huge loss, on top of losing Mom, it was crushing me. So I put this whole fucked-up situation on ice.

Chapter 51

Planning Mom's Memorial

I was happy and fulfilled supporting Rebecca into this big new chapter of her life as a young adult. I did not want to ruin her excitement so I mentioned nothing to her of what had transpired with Ananta.

However, while packing and prepping the apartment for renters she asked, "Hey Mom, where is Ananta?"

I lied, "Ananta wanted to give us time alone together. He is staying with his parents."

She replied, "Aweee, that's really sweet of him."

I hated giving him credit for anything, but smiled back at her to cover my lying tracks.

Rebecca's big California move came and went with tons of activity, great joy, some frustrations, and a few tears. At the airport heading back home I hugged her Dad, who dropped me off.

"We did a good job raising our daughter. Thank you for being such a good Dad."

Over the years we had our share of tension, her Dad and me. I think he was shocked and moved by both my hug and acknowledgment.

On the plane ride home, I flashed back to the plane ride home from my honeymoon in Paris with Ananta, only one year earlier. The situation was nearly identical. I put off handling Ananta's infidelity during the honeymoon, just as I put off handling Ananta's infidelity while moving Rebecca into college. Now it was time for me to confront his cheating ass, again.

I also had some much-needed down time on the plane to think about Mom's memorial. There were tons of details so I pulled out my notepad and made lists. What excited me the most was putting together a video of Mom throughout her life. We had footage dating back to the days when Mom and Dad were first dating, all the way up to one year ago at my wedding in Brooklyn. She had a blast dancing there, Mom loved to dance. Got that from Mom too.

The more I contemplated the memorial, the more I felt I needed to defer my confrontation with Ananta for one more month. I had no time to grieve the possible death of our relationship. I needed to stay focused on creating a space to gather and celebrate Mom. It would be my last gift to her.

Back in my apartment, I called Ananta at his parent's house, "Hey, can you come here? It is time to talk."

I could hear the fear in his voice. I had not contacted Ananta or returned his calls the entire time I was with Rebecca in California.

When Ananta walked through the door I saw a broken man. Part of me wanted to hug him, the other part of me wanted to slap him. I did neither. We sat down.

I launched right into my thoughts. "After giving this much contemplation, I have decided that I am not ready to deal with your infidelity right now. My mother's memorial service is in one month and I've got a lot to do. I don't have the wherewithal to handle us too."

He looked visibly relieved and said, "Okay, what would you like me to do?"

I replied, "Great question to which I don't have the answer." I continued, "I need a week to myself, that I do know. So please, return to your parent's home."

"Sure," he complied.

"My sister and I need to book the reception space in Massachusetts and contact everyone. You cannot help with that." Then I looked at Ananta to consider what he could possibly do to help.

I asked, "Do you know anything about creating a movie? I want to put together a movie for the memorial of video clips and still photos of Mom."

"Ummm... I don't know too much about that but I know some things. My father knows a lot about this, he made a movie after his mother passed."

"Oh yeah, well, can you do some research in the next couple of days, to find out how? I am sure the technology has changed.

"Yes Bunny."

We sat staring at one another in silence. Then I broke it. "Ananta, I can't open my heart to you right now. I am full of grief, anger, and loss over how to proceed with us. I think it best you stay at your parent's house right now."

"I understand. But I want you to know that I do miss you, very much," he said.

"I wish I could say the same. The only person I miss right now is my daughter. I can't even say I miss my mother. She had a horrible life the last 12 years. I guess I miss my Mom from decades ago."

Ananta replied, "The memorial movie will bring those years back again." Ananta was a wise soul. He was a horny devil, but truly a wise soul. He started to leave and then turned around, "May I hug you?"

I just wasn't ready. I told him, "I can't right now. I'm sorry. But, thank you for the sweet gesture. I'll call you in a couple of days."

Chapter 52

Yom Kippur Epiphany

Mom's memorial service took a full month to create and carry off. Janet and I put it together like a wedding. There was the church service and then a huge reception at the country club. I was delighted that Janet could put aside her anger towards Dad to make this happen with me. I thanked her profusely.

But she reminded me through her tears, "I'm not doing this for Dad. I'm doing this for me and you and Paul and everyone that loved Mom."

When Mom's Memorial was over that Saturday, September 24, 2011, Ananta and I returned to New York and we stayed together in our apartment for the first time in over a month. I took a few days off to sleep and do nothing. But when I received a call that a former boyfriend from Massachusetts lost his brother to suicide, I headed back to Amherst to be with his family as they had been there for mine. Seemed my roots were calling me.

Finally back in New York I began to prepare for Yom Kippur, October 7th and 8th that year. I participated fully and fasted, as I had done for the past eight years, since studying Kabbalah. Yom Kippur is the Day of Atonement when our sins can be purified. This holiday was all about cleansing our negativities and judgments. So I found it incredibly annoying that all I could think about for the first half of the services was my lifestyle with sugar daddies and johns.

"Was this negative behavior?" I kept asking myself.

Part of me knew that it was indeed negative behavior but it was also paying the bills. But did I believe the end justified the means? My sex-for-hire lifestyle escalated when Mom got so sick and Dad's abuse became apparent. But I promised myself that I would stop after Mom died. Yet, I had to see Joe a couple of times after her death, I needed the money. How would I survive without prostitution and sugar daddies? I was convinced the economy was still crippled.

But then I thought, "Maybe it is me that is crippled?"

This thought hounded me all day. Finally, when I took seriously the idea of leaving prostitution, leaving my sugar daddies, I felt my heart explode with joy.

I told myself, "This is it. This is what you have to do. Leave this lifestyle for good. Your heart knows all the answers."

For the remainder of the Yom Kippur services I felt light and full of love and joy. That is how I knew it was the right decision.

That night I met up with Ananta and his friends at a house party. I was excited to break my fast with delicious food and friendship. I was also excited to share my Yom Kippur epiphany with Ananta.

When I found a quiet moment, I declared to Ananta, "I am leaving the world of sex for hire forever. You get to be my only sugar daddy now!"

Ananta seemed shaken. I knew he had issues surrounding employment but I also knew that I was enabling him by bringing home money and not expecting him to do the same. I had no idea how we were going to generate income but I stopped trying to control it. I would allow Ananta to come up with solutions for once and made no suggestions. This would be a first for me.

One avenue that was still ripe was renting my apartment for short-term stays. We could make upwards of $1,200 a week. In a couple days we had tenants arriving so needed to clear out for two weeks and stay with his family. We spent the next two days cleaning the apartment, washing bedding, and packing. Monday night, October 10, 2011, would be our last night alone for a while. Ananta suggested we make it a romantic evening. Our sensual connection had been nearly non-existent in recent months, mainly because I was angry about his infidelity. However, I decided to forgive him, though I had not yet told him. So I was looking forward to our romantic evening. We agreed that I would prepare dinner and Ananta would be home by 8 p.m. with a bottle of wine.

At 7:50 p.m. I lit the candles and played sexy Turkish music. I was already dressed in a beautiful silk teddy and robe that I had not worn since our honeymoon in Paris. This was the night I would let go of my resentments. I felt happy, joyful, and sexually excited. 8:15 p.m. rolled around but no Ananta. I texted him at 8:20 p.m. when there was still no sign of him.

I thought, "He must be in the train with no reception."

By 8:30 p.m. with no Ananta and no message, I started to vacillate between worry and anger. I don't mind when people are late. It happens, but call or text. I sent him another text message.

I stopped reaching out to Ananta at 9 p.m. At 9:25 p.m. he walked through the door.

"Hi Bunny! You look so beautiful!!"

Here was that eerie enthusiastic persona again. I knew immediately that he had to be hiding something. I asked calmly, "What time did you say you would be here?"

"Eight, I think. What time is it?" he asked.

Sharply I replied, "It is nearly nine-thirty. Where were you?"

Ananta began his explanation with gusto: "Well I got on the bus heading up First Avenue to come home and then I remembered that it was Poly Cocktail Night so I jumped off and decided to say hello to a few peeps. I ran into everyone! It was so much fun and they all asked about you, of course. Sandy brought a whole crew of newbies with her and she was flirting with everyone, you know how she does. Then..."

"Enough!" I yelled, "You were an hour and a half late for our romantic night, without calling me, because you had to get your fix from your kinky polyamorous community. I should have guessed you were up to something sexually sneaky because you put on your 'Hi I'm such a good boy' mask. Get out! Get out of my face and get out of my life forever!"

I ran into the bedroom and slammed the door. I couldn't stop pacing, my adrenaline of anger was running high. I kept pacing and thinking, "This is it. I will never ever take this man back, never again. Oh my God. This is the end. It is finally over. I can't believe it."

I changed out of my sexy sleepwear into yoga pants and a tank top. I ejected the Turkish music and blew out the candles. Ananta was sitting on the love seat staring straight ahead, frozen.

He finally spoke, "Bunny, I am sorry."

"No Ananta, you are not sorry. You are only sorry that I do not accept your lies, manipulations, and infidelities, like your mother does with your father. Well you get to do whatever you want now. We are over."

"Bunny, I..."

"Get out of my life!" I screamed, "I never want to see you again!"

I walked to the front door and opened it. I had no control over the powerhouse voice coming out of me. It was like it came from someone else. I could even hear the thoughts of my frightened self. I remember distinctly thinking, "I can't believe I'm doing this. I'm kicking my husband out for good."

But Ananta remained on the couch.

"I, I don't want to leave," he eked out.

I screamed, "I could care less what you want! We lived this insane relationship the way you wanted. Now we are ending this insane relationship the way I want. I am done. Three strikes and you're out! Now get out!"

Part VI: **Recovery!**

How did Shanti not see her sex/love addiction smashing her in the face all these years? After her mother's death in 2011, Shanti is finally able to remove the blinders of denial. Yet recovery is a slippery slope. Shanti only truly gets sober when she finds a sponsor, four years later.

Chapter 53

The Aftermath of Leaving Ananta

My decision to banish Ananta was abrupt and enveloped me in shock, quickly followed by intense rage, extreme fear, deep sorrow, and then relief, all within the first five minutes. Later I would revisit these stages for weeks and months at a time. If being in love felt like sipping a dopamine cocktail, then falling out of love felt like drinking a cyanide shot. In the 12-step program of sex/love addiction they call this detox phase "withdrawal" and like a drug addict, I found withdrawal to be miserably painful.

I decided to move in with Dad for a while and continue to sublet my place for income. Dad was grief-stricken and I was full of rage. We made a great pair. But we needed one another to help heal our wounds. I slept in Mom's room, which my sister thought was creepy. It was comforting to me though. Every day I would go through another chunk of Mom's clothing, jewelry, trinkets, and note cards, trying to piece together the woman I never really understood. She had to be in pain much of her life if she was always that angry. I feared I was becoming just like Mom.

Mom's death stirred many deep emotions within me and ultimately began my process of coming out of denial. Somehow it felt safe to see and tell the truth after her passing. Maybe this was because my original abuser was gone? I don't know. But I do know that I had no more room for bullshit in my life. First at bat, I wanted to know the truth about Ananta's secret sexual life. After all, I was leaving him for his lying and infidelities, better find out if I was being overly sensitive or had true reason to stand my ground.

I started my investigations by doing Internet research on the behavioral signs of lying and lo and behold, Ananta had one of the traits down pat. This trait was referred to in the world of psychology as overcompensating. Someone who is lying often overcompensates by giving out too much information, often unrequested. Their elaborate tales are a sure sign that they are trying their best to convince you that their story is in fact true. He did this right before I discovered his first infidelity, then again when I returned from my mother's deathbed and again the night I ultimately kicked him out for good. I referred to it as his over-enthusiasm but I now see that it was him spinning his tall tales, his overcompensating. Not looking too good so far but I still didn't trust my instincts.

Within a few short weeks I rounded up some allies in the polyamorous and kinky communities who were quite disturbed to hear the extent of Ananta's lies. Several of the women came forward and confessed that they had been sexual with Ananta because he told them that we had a completely open relationship. Interestingly enough, many people in these communities had quite a strong sense of integrity. If they were having multiple sexual relations they wanted to be honest and open about them. I admired that.

I also found out that Ananta attended an orgy while I was at the funeral of my ex-boyfriend's brother in Amherst. He never mentioned anything about that. Next I did a little investigating on Fetlife. Fetlife is like the Facebook for fetishists, kinksters, and those involved in BDSM, Ananta and I each had an account. His friends' feed revealed that he recently contacted a gay man so I contacted that man too. I wanted to know if Ananta preferred men. Whenever I found him watching porn it was usually gay male porn. That strong suspicion had been sneaking up on me and if that was the case, I might let him go more easily.

I asked this man, "If you wouldn't mind letting me know the tenor of your conversations because I want to know if my husband is on the down low."

The down low describes men, often men of color, who live a heterosexual life outwardly but secretly enjoy sex with men. Oddly enough, it was Ananta who told me about these poor men living on the down low that suffer in silence while he gets to have his kink openly online and occasionally at sex parties. The gay man from Fetlife agreed to keep me informed if indeed Ananta contacted him.

The next day he sent me a copy of Ananta's recent pornographic invitation for sex.

He closed the email, "Sorry. I am sure this hurts. Blessings to you sister. May this help you find closure."

I was stunned by the extent of Ananta's graphic homosexual invitation, not angry, just stunned. I emailed Ananta my findings. I told him, "If I wasn't sure before, I am 100% sure now that this relationship is over for me."

I cited all the women who came forward to share their sexual relations with Ananta that he hid from me, the orgy he attended without my knowledge or permission, and then his connection with this gay man on Fetlife. I accused Ananta of being far more gay than straight. I had no issue with gay men, had a ton of gay friends, but I did not want to be married to a gay man and I told that to Ananta.

His response, "My heat is for men but my TLC is for women. Does that make me gay?"

"Yes that makes you gay!" I replied

This was the piece of information that ultimately freed me to let go of Ananta for good. Why I did not see this truth years ago is still a mystery to me, most likely it was my love addiction that didn't want to let him go and be alone. Being alone was akin to death. Craig's list personal ads from gay men and the Manhunt gay website were regularly open on Ananta's computer screen and he quickly minimized them when I'd walk in the room. Like I never noticed? But he said he was only sex chatting with these men, not meeting up with them, which I accepted. I even thought the sex chatting and cyber-masturbation would keep him away from doing anything in person. Looking back, I'm surprised that I was so cool with this. I guess because Ananta accepted my promiscuous past, including liaisons with women, not to mention my current career as a courtesan.

Whatever was my reasoning, my love for Ananata made me want to cut him some slack and not judge too harshly his promiscuous fantasy present. My own experiences gave me great pathos for his sordid Eros. Fantasy I could deal with. But I later found out from Ananta himself, months after kicking him out, that his fantasies often became realities. He told me, after I asked for full and honest disclosure, that he occasionally ordered in men when I was out, or he'd make a special delivery of himself when I was home.

I wasn't sure I understood what he meant by the "special delivery" so he gave me some examples.

"Bunny, I'm going to the Bronx to help Mom with the Christmas lights, the shoveling, the gardening, the groceries..."

The lists of chores to do in the Bronx for his mother were endless. Sure he would go to see his momma, but he would also stop off for a quick man-hit first. This information hit this wife hard but I was grateful that he was finally honest with me.

I had to ask, "How long had this been going on with men?"

"Pretty much since we first met," he replied.

I held my head in my hands.

"I'm sorry Shanti."

He called me Shanti, no more Bunny. I knew we were finally over from his side too.

"Please tell me that you used condoms?" I asked.

Ananta replied, "Yes, of course."

"Well you lied about so much, how do I know you are telling the truth now?" I begged.

"I have nothing to protect any more. We are over, you deserve to know the truth about everything. I am not lying to you about anything any more. I hope this helps ease your pain. You are right to not be with me. I need to discover who I really am."

I responded, "You know, you told me when we first met that you didn't know who you were. But I didn't want to believe you. Guess this is all my bad in the end."

"Shanti, you are not bad. You were my greatest love and I will be forever grateful to you for this amazing journey we took together. I am only sad that I have hurt you so deeply."

We both cried in one another's arms. It was the beginning of our road to letting go and healing. In that embrace I allowed myself to feel my love and gratitude for my husband again.

Husbands on the down low, the tell-tale signs we prefer to ignore. They were glaring at me with high beams blazing, but when we are in denial we are blind.

I thought, "Thanks for the amazing grace, Mom. I truly was blind but now I see. So why am I still so angry?"

When I discussed all of this with one of my mentors she recited a quote made popular by Gloria Steinem, "The truth will set you free, but first it will piss you off."

Swimming in piss right now.

Chapter 54

Seeing My Sex/Love Addiction

Though I was clear Ananta had a major sex addiction, he continued to deny it. I was also clear that I did not want to stay married to a sex addict, straight or gay, that was not interested in being sober. Gone were the days of threesomes, foursomes, swinger parties, orgies, constant sex chatting and pornography. Gone was the discomfort of finding my husband in the throes of seducing some woman at a party or waking to him jerking off to male porn. I was done with his sex addiction. Several months later we were divorced. I did it online and I did it fast.

After leaving Ananta and living with Dad for a couple of months while we both healed our abandonment issues, I announced to Dad, "It's time for me to go back home."

Dad replied, "But you are welcome to stay here as long as you want."

I could see Dad wanted me to stay. It was so endearing. And in many ways I wanted to stay too. We had a blast going over our family history together. I learned tons about Dad's life, Mom's life, my grandparents' lives and it helped fill in some of the missing pieces in my psyche. But I couldn't avoid the work I knew I needed to do. I wasn't sure what that work would be but I knew I would find out by going home.

I began to cry, "Awweee, Dad. Thank you for making me feel so welcome," I said, "it's just that I have to get my life back together. You know? It is so sweet being here with you but I need to get back to work. I don't know what I'm going to do for money but I have to figure it out. My life is in New York. I need to go back home Dad."

Within a few days I returned to my apartment. There were photograph of Ananta and me everywhere. The apartment was a shrine to our love. Now it made me cry. Everything made me cry or rage. There was rarely any joy or laughter during that year. I remember soon after I moved back home I invited my dear friend Eliot Tanner over for tea.

After hearing me rage for about 20 minutes Eliot remarked, "Shanti, I have never seen you so angry before. What happened to my Shanti?"

I told him, "Your Shanti is dead. This is what pain looks like Eliot. Life is not all about laughing and fucking."

"Wow Shanti, I really am worried about you."

"I am worried about me too." I replied. I could see how uncomfortable Eliot was in my presence. "Eliot, why don't you go home now? I am tired and don't have much to offer, I'm afraid."

When Eliot left I sat in my living room thinking about what a mess my life had become and yes, how angry I continued to be with Ananta. I just couldn't understand why he didn't see his sex addiction that was so clear to me. It was everywhere in all of his activities. Why wouldn't he want to get sober, if not for himself, for me? I was in constant pain vacillating from grief to rage, anger to sorrow, and numbness to depression. Feeling paralyzed with pain one day, I decided to stop everything and meditate. I had rekindled my meditation practice that I abandoned, for the most part, after 9/11 and it was helping me enormously. Meditation is not an instant high like a shot of tequila. It is more like a warm cup of tea on a cold rainy day. It felt soft, cozy, safe, and sweet.

I tried emptying my thoughts during meditation but one question kept gnawing at me that day, "Dear God, why did I attract this sex addict into my life? Why?"

Instantly this voice arose from deep inside: "Because you are that."

"What?!" I asked.

And in that instant I saw my entire sensual life flash before me, from childhood to the present, and I saw that I was indeed a sex addict as well.

I ran to the bathroom to throw up but since I had not eaten in days, nothing came out. I dry-heaved for quite some time. Then I lay on the bed in total shock. Soon visions of my sexual life began to play in my head. From my fascination with playing doctor as a young girl in the 60s, to cheating on all my boyfriends in the 80s, to repentance by marrying a man I did not love in the 90s, to embracing promiscuity after my divorce in the New Millennium, to a string of unsuccessful polyamorous and monogamous relationships, and finally, to meeting a fellow sex addict and spiraling out of control with swingers, orgies, BDSM, Tantra massage, sugar daddies and ultimately, prostitution in 2011. There was no doubt about it. I was a sex/love addict. How could I have missed that for 52 years?

Chapter 55

Healing and Recovery

In the days that followed my deafening wake-up call, I researched 12-step programs for sex addicts and sex/love addicts. Initially I went to a meeting nearly every day. It was eye-opening to be around others that were like me and to see how similar our journeys had been. My first instinct was to attend the all-female meetings and I followed that wisdom. One day, however, I thought I'd try a co-ed meeting. Not for me! Not for me at that point anyway. The men stared at me like they wanted to eat me alive. It was extremely disconcerting.

As I walked home from the meeting, I contemplated where I had seen such a gaze before. It seemed familiar. I was sure I had known such a gaze in the past, but where? All of a sudden I saw Ananta's face staring at me the first time our eyes met in the spring of 2004. I used to refer to his initial gaze as "lust at first sight." It was so intense. Imagine I just left a room full of men with that gaze. For me, who was trying to heal and get sober from a sex addiction, it was terrifying.

Initially I shared this newfound awareness of my sex/love addiction with only a few close friends. I felt ashamed, especially since I was a relationship coach. Clearly that career needed to be put aside, at least for a while. Who was I to give any sort of relationship coaching advice? I was a sex/love addict.

Though I had distanced myself from the majority of my kinky friends, as most of them I knew from Ananta, I still had a few in my circle and they were suspect of my newly self-diagnosed sex/love addiction. I chalked that up to it hitting too close to home and didn't take it personally. But my more conservative "vanilla" friends, they got it. They had seen me spinning out of control but

325

felt powerless to stop me. Adriana, my dear friend Adriana, former wild child herself, was one of those who abandoned me. We didn't speak for all the years I was acting out with Ananta. After all, she married an Orthodox rabbi and was a mother now. But once I got sober I reconnected with her. We were never the same again, never that close. Yet it felt beautiful to have her back in my life, even in a remote way.

I stepped up my therapy sessions to twice a week for a couple of months because I really needed the intense support of my beloved therapist, Ala. I could barely afford it but she gave me a discount and we did very deep work during that period. I had kept much of my licentious and lawless life away from Ala until I got sober. So there was much work to be done.

I returned to my Kabbalah classes and attending Shabbat services regularly. Amongst my Jewish friends I was teased that I, this Catholic-born woman, was more Jewish than they were. It was sweet. Between my return to meditation, Shabbat, Kabbalah classes, and prayer, I was reconnecting to the deep spiritual roots that I abandoned while joining Ananta on his hedonist journeys. Abandoning ourselves for others is a classic co-dependent trait and love addiction is a branch of co-dependency. It felt wonderful to get back to me, and what I truly wanted.

Exercise and yoga became a new part of my daily morning routine – hatha yoga, meditation, exercise, and then breakfast. This new morning ritual set me up for the day. I usually awoke with sorrow that Ananta was no longer by my side. However, after my morning ritual was complete I felt optimistic about the day ahead. It truly was one-day-at-a-time for quite a long time.

Now that I was starting to get my emotional and spiritual houses in order, it was time to get my finances in order. I had already gone through most of the money I earned from my liaisons with johns and sugar daddies. I never declared to Ananta the full scope of my earnings, because I was angry that I needed to do such work to pay our bills when he contributed nothing. Yet soon enough the funds would be depleted and I feared homelessness. Since I desired the stability of staying in my home and abandoning the gypsy life, I put out an ad for a full-time roommate. Mr. Italy came knocking at my door.

Renato was an art history professor from Florence, Italy. He accepted a position at Columbia University in January of 2012 but his wife and teenage children could not come until the summer. Therefore he searched for a small temporary space that was furnished to tide him over until his family could settle in. At first it was strange having a roommate that was not my daughter or husband or father. It had been decades since I had a non-family roommate. On top of that, Renato was a bit timid, which made me uncomfortable, in-your-face kind of gal that I was.

But one day he asked the question, "Excuse me please. But what does it mean to be a real New Yorker? I hear this phrase a lot. Could you please explain?"

I took this as my ticket to bust through his artificial properness.

"Sure, I'd be fucking happy to explain. A real fucking New Yorker doesn't ask stupid fucking questions first of all because we fucking New Yorkers know everything. You get what the fuck I'm talking about?"

Renato's face contorted and I wasn't sure if he was going to laugh or scream until he replied, "Well then fucking okay!"

We both burst out laughing and laughed often during his six-month stay. If it weren't for Renato and my 12-step fellows, I would likely have stayed by myself that year. For I made the decision to write my memoirs about my sex/love addiction, and writing is a hermit's trade. The reason I was so committed and passionate about writing my memoirs was because I found almost no information on women with sex addiction. Love addiction, yes, but not sex addiction. Sex addiction is thought to be more of a male addiction. Well, clearly I had this "male" addiction and I was outraged that there was next to nothing written for women.

I was certain that women acted out sexually in a very different fashion from men and I could address this in my memoirs. My goal was to give voice to women, like me, who have suffered in the shadows with this debilitating addiction that had no name for most of our lives. I wanted to change that.

Many of my friends and family members had similar reactions to my larger-than-life commitment to write my memoirs. "That is quite a noble endeavor, but how are you going to fuel the ride?"

"I have no idea," I'd reply and I would add, "I'll figure it out as I go."

Clearly finances needed to be handled. My roommate helped cover a third of my bills, now to tackle the other two-thirds. I did not want to go back to a full-time corporate position, as there'd be no time to focus on the memoirs. I spent weeks researching part-time positions that I was both qualified for and that appealed to me. I was well aware that I needed something that was not bloodletting for I had just come through a major emotional battle. Healing would take time.

While researching income streams, I met up with Lulu, a good friend and mentor I had not seen in years. She told me of a dear friend that had five-year-old twins who needed four to five hours of care after school. It was a perfect fit financially and emotionally. I adored caring for these delightful and feisty five-year-olds. They challenged my will and filled my soul. With my daughter away at college, it was heavenly to give and receive love with these little angels that could turn into devils in an instant. But even with their devilish sides, I loved them dearly.

Finances now handled, emotional, spiritual, and physical well being now flowing, what about sensuality and romance? I decided to take it off the roster of needs to be fulfilled that year. It was not hard to do. I had no inclinations in that direction anyway. My entire life used to revolve around sex and romance, and it clearly bit me in the ass over and over again. It was time to see what life had to offer without my fix.

Chapter 56

Dating in Recovery

Though completely celibate for nine months, Aaron Berger, the kind and generous CEO of a major financial firm, kept in touch with me. We met through a mutual connection, hoping Aaron might find me a part-time position at his firm. Oddly enough, Aaron was actually the one who encouraged me to stay away from corporate work.

During my interview with him he told me, "You don't want to work here or any other corporate giant for that matter. Your memoirs are too important. But whatever job you choose, make sure it is not a bloodletting job."

I laughed, "Those are exactly my thoughts."

He replied, "Yeah, you don't want to work here. But if I think of something, I'll let you know."

After that we'd meet about once a month for dinner. He was fascinated by my story and wanted to support if he could. He introduced me to a friend in the music industry, hoping to find a connection to the publishing world. With each dinner, Aaron came up with a new brainstorm for getting my memoirs financed and published. I really enjoyed his company but one night he had a tad too much to drink. He became effusive with me and I got clear that he wanted more than to help with my memoirs. He wanted me.

"Aaron, can we talk about the pink elephant in the room?" I asked.

Aaron looked up at me like a lost child. He did not speak.

"Aaron, I know you like me, and not just the 'good guy trying to help a friend' kind of like. I like you too. But I'm celibate right now."

"I know that, so what's the problem?" he asked.

"The problem is that I won't be celibate forever," I replied.

Aaron asked, "How many months do you have left?"

I smiled, "I have three months until my one-year anniversary of being sex-sober.

"So that's great. It's not that far away. What's the problem?"

"The problem Aaron is that you are married. I don't date married men. The only married men that I slept with in the past were johns and sugar daddies. Okay, plus one guy in the law firm. Anyway, I can't go there again. That would clearly not be sober sex or sober dating."

"So what are you saying?" Aaron asked.

"I think we should stop seeing one another," I said.

Aaron got quiet. I could feel his pain. I was starting to open my heart to him too and I didn't like the thought that our monthly dinners would come to an end.

"Shanti, I am going to be honest with you. I have been married for 35 years. I have three amazing children that are all successful in the world, thank God. Everyone in my family is happy except me. I stopped sleeping with my wife ten years ago. We live together like roommates. You are the first woman that has given me hope that I can have passion again in my life and I am not willing to let you go. Our dinners have been the highlight of my life."

"Awwweeee, I have enjoyed them very much as well, really. But Aaron, I am not going to date you while you are married."

"Fair enough. What if I tell you that my wife and I have been discussing divorce."

I replied, "Well, I would say that is fine but I don't want you leaving your wife for me. I don't want that responsibility."

"Shanti, believe me when I say this has been in the works for years. We wanted to wait until all our children graduated from college. It is time, it is way overdue and we both know it."

"Aaron, it is late and you are drunk. Let's meet next month and see how you feel then, okay?"

"Okay but I know my feelings are not going to change. As a matter of fact, I am going to start looking for a place to live. How about that?"

I told Aaron, "You do what is good for you Aaron. But please, do not leave your wife because of me. I am totally fucked up about romantic relationships. I have no idea which end is up right now so betting on me would be very risky."

"I am a gambling man. How do you think I got to be where I am? I know a good bet when I see one."

It was a beautiful summer night and Aaron took me home with his driver. Aaron was the Mr. Big in my life. When we got to my place he told the driver to wait while he took me to my door. There, in front of his driver, in front of my neighbors, Aaron kissed me for the first time since we met. It was a sloppy drunken kiss, but his passion showed through and my heart melted.

Though I tried to keep my commitment to one-year of celibacy, I soon fell prey to Aaron's charms. We met in hotels and took trips together while he was still living with his wife. Though we had great discussions in public places, when alone we were constantly having sex. I just assumed it was the backlash from nine months of celibacy but I noticed that Aaron was instigating all of our sexual contact. If I did not know better, I would guess he might have a sex addiction himself.

In between lots of sex we looked at apartments. His taste was exquisite so finding a $10k a month apartment that looked like $20k was challenging. He did not want to buy anything just yet, wanted to rent for a year first. One afternoon, while looking at a $15k a month rental apartment, I said to Aaron, "I could never fathom spending that much money on rent. Seems so wasteful."

He replied, "I like nice things. I want to live in a home that makes me happy. What's wrong with that?"

I replied, "Nothing wrong with that. It's just that, I think about how many starving people you could feed with that money."

Aaron looked at me intensely in the empty apartment and without taking his eyes off me, asked the real estate agent to meet us downstairs.

"Shanti, I know how much you struggle around money. Let me help you."

"No, Aaron. I told you before. I can't let you do that. That brings up all my sugar daddy stuff. I don't want money to cloud our relationship. I can't go there."

"You are tough," he said and then got quiet.

He came back with, "Tell you what. Let me pay you what you make from babysitting and not a penny more. I know how important your memoirs are to you. I want to support you in getting them done. At this rate it will take you ten years. You're so tired after being with those twins that you pass out, you basically only write on the weekends."

He was right. Once I took on caring for the twins I wrote significantly less and then, spending time with Aaron, the writing was nearly non-existent. With hesitancy and fear, I accepted his offer. I immediately told the twins' mother, letting her know I would stay on until they found someone they liked.

Within two weeks I was writing full-time and loving it. I was putting together the pieces of my broken past by connecting dots I could never have seen if I were not sex sober. I was clear when I began writing, in January of 2012, that these memoirs would heal me and perhaps many others who suffered in silence. But now, I was crystal-clear and my conviction fueled my passion.

However, after a month of writing bliss in September of 2012, I ran up against another block. It was not a writing block yet a block nonetheless. I was growing more and more uncomfortable around Aaron. He was going through hell with his wife begging him not to leave. Though I was having a wonderful time with Aaron, I was not in love with him and was not happy that I was the cause of his wife's pain. No matter how much Aaron told me that he was planning to leave her anyway, he chose not to leave her until after we met. If I was in love with Aaron and saw our forever future together, I might have been able to handle the guilt. However, I was not in love with Aaron, not yet anyway. I was also becoming more and more uncomfortable with how much sex we were having. We started as two people having deep conversations but once we became lovers, it was all about sex. This was bringing up my sugar daddy issues, tons of sex and getting paid a monthly salary. I told Aaron how I felt. With a tear and a hug, Aaron excused himself and we broke up.

Now that Aaron was out of my life, so was the income. I thought about taking another part-time job but could not deny how much more writing got done when I focused on it full-time. In a bold and insane move, according to many of my friends and family members, I decided to not take a job. With excellent credit and no debt, I joined the ranks of the American debtors. Because of my pristine credit rating, I was offered upwards of $60,000 at 0% APR that would extend for nearly two years. Surely my memoirs would be done by autumn of 2014. Then I would search for a literary agent or publisher to sell them.

Seven celibate months later, in the spring of 2013 with a good chunk of my memoirs written, I was feeling more secure and thought I could handle a bit of instability. I contacted Aaron. Addicts, especially sex/love addicts, thrive on drama and intrigue. I met Aaron for dinner. I shared with him my success in writing and he shared with me his success in taking steps towards leaving his wife. He said he had had several meetings with attorneys and mediators and they were working out property settlements. He was sleeping in the guest room. I felt encouraged to rekindle our flame, knowing that with no contact for seven months, I was not the motivation for his divorce. We planned a trip to Paris to see my daughter Rebecca, who was studying there for her semester abroad. Paris in the springtime, oh yeah!

Paris was amazing. Nothing could be better. I spent a great deal of time walking the streets of my beloved city with Aaron, showing him all my favorite spots and discovering new ones. I got to be with my daughter, some dear friends from Paris, and was treated to incredible food, presents, and Aaron's company. My heart was opening to him and I was beginning to see our lives merging. Then we returned to New York and I did not see him for weeks. Aaron cited his busy work schedule, and his annual conference in Las Vegas.

Something told me not to ask the burning question on my tongue for I knew it could pull me from the bliss of denial. I asked anyway. "Did your wife attend the conference with you?"

Aaron looked down at his plate.

I asked, "She did, didn't she?"

Aaron replied, "Yes, she did. But listen, it was not like you think..."

Aaron spoke but I heard very little of his explanation. It didn't matter. His wife was still very much a part of his life. I finally got it. It reminded me of Ananta's enthusiastic explanations when covering his lies and I knew that Aaron too was over-compensating for lies. When I pressed him with more questions about his wife's time at the conference, he got angry, another sign he was lying. Aaron also had a very hot temper. But I was willing to overlook the temper, his possible sex addiction, and his alcoholism. However, I was not willing to overlook the lies about his marriage. Aaron was still married and had no intention of leaving his wife any time soon. This was a deal breaker.

Though I finished dinner in relative calm on the outside, I was anything but calm on the inside. I rejected a ride home from Aaron and took a cab. I told him I was not feeling well, which was the truth. But my pain was mental and emotional, not physical. I was feeling abandoned and betrayed.

I thought during the cab ride home, "Is this what it feels like to be a mistress? Does the man continually promise to leave his wife and never does? I felt like the last on his list of priorities. Work came first, then his kids, then his wife, then me if he had any time. I did not sign up for this ride yet I still found myself sick from the motion.

As soon as I got home I crawled into bed, hoping desperately to forget my thoughts and realizations. Yet when sleep eluded me by 4 a.m., I knew my conscience needed to be heard. I wrote a Dear Aaron email. My fantasy of a relationship with Mr. Big just died. We had only been back together for two months but, this break-up was far more painful than the first. This time, I had opened my heart to him. My withdrawal symptoms began the instant I knew this relationship was over and the Dear Aaron email opened the withdrawal floodgates. Intense loneliness, grief, fear, anger, and hopelessness enveloped me completely.

Instead of falling deeper into withdrawal, the next day I went onto the Internet, searching for men. Clue number one that this was a non-sober activity – looking to medicate the pain. But I told myself I was not looking to hook-up so I fooled myself into thinking that finding a relationship would be a sober activity. Since the sex addict was quiet, the love addict got to go about her business. Ah, what we sex/love addicts will tell ourselves about our sobriety...

Chapter 57

More Dating in Recovery

I joined okcupid.com. Since it was a free dating site, I convinced myself that this exploration would not be too serious, dating lite. This would give me time to grieve my relationship with Aaron yet allow me to put my toe back in the dating waters. However, within hours of joining the site, a big fish bit my toe and he even apologized, in French!

Gabriel Gaspar was American-born of parents from the South of France. He grew up in New York but never much liked the city. He moved to "sleepytown," New Jersey soon after marrying his wife. They had a son and lived happily never after. He did what many couples with children do when they are unhappy, they stay together and tough it out. From what Gabriel communicated to me via the dating site, as his son prepared to leave for college, he felt it was finally time to leave the nest too.

We both had the empty nest syndrome in common, our recent divorces, and our college-age children in common as well. We were both tall, attractive, the same age, spoke French, and enjoyed one another. It all seemed very safe and easy-going until one day Gabriel sent me a link to a song on YouTube that sounded intensely tragic.

Unable to contain my intuition I asked, "Did you recently lose someone that you loved?"

"What? How did you know that?" he wrote.

"Ummm… the song told me that. It's a terribly tragic story of deep loss."

"Wow, I've sent that song to other women in the past and not one of them ever picked up on that."

"I'm sorry. I don't mean to pry. It is none of my business. But it feels like your soul is in pain."

He replied, "No, I do have to say something. I have been on this fucking okstupid dating site for nearly two years now and not once did anyone pick up on the meaning of this song or any other song that I sent. It's all very superficial la-di-da crap here."

I took the chance to express more of my intuition: "You sound a little bitter that you have not yet found anyone that holds your heart."

"My God," he replied, "I think I just did."

From that moment forward, our written communications became far more meaningful and intimate. We switched out of okcupid and into our personal emails. The content grew deeper, but so too did the length of our emails: seven to eight pages deep on any given day. My memoirs were taking a back seat but I didn't care. This was the first red flag, getting lost in love, a signal I ignored. I thought I had finally found a man who grabbed my heart like I had not experienced since meeting Yigal in 1999. Fourteen years was a long time to wait for such a connection and I let myself drown in it.

This is a classic love-addict pattern, getting lost in love. Also at work here was another red flag. We love addicts get intimate instantly and reveal everything about ourselves right at the beginning. We are terrified of rejection and abandonment, so best get it all out in the beginning so we don't get side-swiped later. Meeting Gabriel was no exception to my pattern. But I didn't notice it then because the love addiction is often co-mingled with the sex addiction. We clearly were not having sex, we hadn't actually met, so I felt I was being sober. We weren't even speaking on the phone yet, never mind flirting with one another. Why should my behavior feel suspect?

By week's end, I gave Gabriel the highlights of my life as a sex/love addict, from being a serial cheater in my 20s to being a swinger and a prostitute in my 40s and early 50s. I figured if he flinched, he would not be a good match for me. There was nothing I could do about my past.

Gabriel asked, "What did you do in your 30s?"

"I was a nun." I replied. "Well, not officially a nun but I might as well have been. I was on a deep spiritual quest, married, but had sex only once or twice every couple of years. My daughter was the Immaculate Conception."

He commented, "I think we had parallel marriages except I was not on a spiritual quest. My ex-wife just enjoyed rejecting me sexually and emotionally."

After exposing my dirty hand, Gabriel began to share the real reason he left his wife: he fell in love with a married woman at his office. He ignored her advances towards him for months but after nearly 15 years of no intimacy, attention, or sex, he caved in. He felt terribly guilty about the affair, yet his heart and soul felt nourished. Eventually their respective spouses discovered the affair, a rocky time for everyone. However, just when it looked like everyone was ready to leave their spouses and move in with one another, Gabriel's lover came down with ovarian cancer. She was in stage four. Though there was great tension, both Gabriel and his lover's husband took turns caring for her. Within nine months she passed away.

Gabriel was afraid to reveal his past infidelity to me at the beginning. He explained, "Advertising oneself as a cheater doesn't usually go over too well in the dating world."

I told him, "Advertising oneself as a sex addict only goes over well on hook-up sites."

From then on I stopped communicating with men, other than Gabriel, as possible romantic partners. I removed my profile from okcupid. Then, on a trip to Vermont to visit my dear friends Jim and Dina, Gabriel and I expanded our communications to include phone conversations. Every night, after Jim and Dina retired for the evening, I would spend hours speaking with Gabriel. None of our conversations were sexually oriented except for sharing my explosive past. We were getting to know one another on a deep emotional level. It felt totally sober to me.

One night, during a four-hour phone conversation, Gabriel expressed his fear of meeting me in person and getting closer to me.

He asked, "Can you guarantee that you won't fall back into your sex addiction again?"

I repeated the old adage, "Nothing's certain but death and taxes."

"Ha ha, very funny. But I'm serious," Gabriel replied.

"I'm serious too. There are no guarantees in life Gabriel. I can tell you that I stopped cheating on boyfriends in my late 20s when I lost the love of my life because of my infidelities. I have never cheated on anyone since. You have recently had an affair so I should be more nervous about you, no?"

I continued, "Look, I'm not about to sell my ass again if that is what you might be worried about. I made that promise to myself, no matter how tight my finances get. I am also not going to become a serial dater again. I already took myself off okcupid."

"Wow, you did?" Gabriel asked with excitement.

"Yes, I didn't want you to feel pressured into only communicating with me. I just knew that I wanted to get to know you and not pull in other men to make me feel safe in case you bounced. That was my old pattern. Gabriel, I hear your fear and I am 99% certain that I am not going to act out sexually any more. That is as close to a guarantee as I can give you."

We exchanged a few more words and hung up for the night. Then I cried, I felt as though Gabriel would not be able to handle his fear of me acting out again. I started experiencing my abandonment issues as I moved into withdrawal, and cried myself to sleep.

When I awoke I did not find even one of Gabriel's usual morning emails or text messages. I was afraid he was gone. I wrote Gabriel a long email thanking him for the beautiful deep connection of the past two weeks and what a gift it was. I also let him know that I could feel his intense fear of moving forward with me and although I was devastated, I understood and wished him well. I really cared deeply for Gabriel and was sinking into my intense grief-stricken withdrawal.

Five minutes passed, if that, when Gabriel called, "Shanti, no I am not pulling away from you, not at all!"

In a wave of tears I asked, "You're not?"

"No, hell no I'm not. I'm not going anywhere. Shanti, I am falling in love with you. God, I can't believe I said it out loud but that is exactly what is happening to me. I know it sounds crazy because we haven't even met in person yet but I am falling in love with you. Reading your email this morning killed me that you would be in such pain and that I might lose you. No, I am here, not going anywhere."

Crying and laughing at the same time I told Gabriel in French, "*Je suis tellement heureuse!*" I am extremely happy!

After this rollercoaster ride of a morning, our relationship took a dive into the waters of intensity. We were continuously professing our love for one another without ever meeting in person. There is a lot you can discover about someone in two weeks but to be this attached this quickly smelled of love addiction and I feared it was not merely coming only from my side. If two alcoholics usually end up passed out at the bar and two sex addicts end up at an orgy, two love addicts end up engaged within weeks of meeting. Yes indeed, that was Gabriel and me. I knew we were moving too far too fast. I couldn't stop it and had no interest in stopping it. I was completely high.

A week after leaving my friends in Vermont, I made a trip to visit my sister. I had no idea Gabriel lived so close to her. We planned our first face-to-face meeting. Though I found Gabriel very handsome in his photos and loved his voice on the phone, I found it difficult to synthesize our deep conversations with a body I just met for the first time.

At one point during the evening I told Gabriel, "I need to close my eyes and listen to you. I need to reconnect with your voice."

Within a few minutes I began to tear, "It is you Gabriel…"

Needless to say our first make-out kiss was among the best kisses of my life. The build-up had been so intense. But to Gabriel's credit, technically, he was an amazing kisser. He didn't shove his tongue down my throat from the jump, which guys often do, and he kissed with his lips for a long while, until our tongues could no longer be contained.

We continued to have great make-out sessions over the next couple of days and then we could hold back no more. For once in my life I made love with a man the first time we lay naked together, not just sex but love. It felt like a miracle. I slept in Gabriel's arms in total bliss. It seemed as though nothing could break this spell, until the light of day came a-calling.

Was it Gabriel's love addiction or my love addiction acting out? I did not know. But I was clear that we both had a hangover.

Gabriel started clinging to me, which I found unappealing, then Gabriel found me to be cold, which made him cling all the more - causing me to pull away even more. Oh, we were a tragic mess. After making excuses for pulling away I finally confronted Gabriel.

"Sweetie, last night was one of the most sacred nights of my life. It was a lot for me, from where I have come from. It was beautiful. But I need a little space right now. I'm going upstairs to write and will be down in a couple of hours."

I saw that Gabriel felt rejected but I knew that I needed to lay down my work ethic early on, or I would keep shoving my needs to the sides as I had in every previous love relationship. After two hours apart though, I was happy to make out with Gabriel again. That was a relief. Was starting to worry that my intimacy issues were rearing their ugly heads. Starting? They were already out in full force.

In the weeks that followed, our relationship continued to deepen but so too did my annoyance with the amount of time and attention that Gabriel desired from me. Those four-hour phone calls were not our special introduction to the relationship. They became our default setting. Between the four-hour phone calls at night and the three or four hours of email and text banter during the day, my memoirs were no longer being written.

At first I made jokes about how much time we spent communicating with one another but Gabriel would laugh it off as our puppy love phase. But at least a half hour before hanging up at night, I would attempt to disengage but Gabriel would pout and sulk. Though I knew for sure I had a sex/love addiction, it was now clear to me that Gabriel had the love addiction. It just wasn't normal the hours this man could spend flapping with me. He made me look love-sober!

One weekend in July, when my roommate was out of town, Gabriel came to stay with me. We went to my best friend Eliot Tanner's apartment for a cocktail party with Eliot's friends, many whom I already knew. It was a lot of fun. Gabriel seemed out of place. He was a self-professed introvert so I cut him some slack. But my critical mind was on over-drive after weeks of not getting through to Gabriel that I could not afford the luxury of eight hours a day in communication with him. It was a full-time job being his girlfriend and I was in no financial spot to afford this ride. I needed to get back to writing.

I drank too much and had a drag from someone's joint. I could barely walk home. Gabriel had a hell of a time getting me there. I passed out as soon as I hit the bed. I remember Gabriel making a motion to make out with me and I was not friendly in my response. I don't remember exactly what I said but it must have been nasty, for I do remember the shock on his face.

Still asleep I felt Gabriel tug at the sheets nestled around my neck. He was standing next to me, fully dressed with the sunlight barely raised behind him.

Groggy I asked, "Gabriel, what are you doing?"

"I'm leaving Shanti. I'm leaving for good."

"What?" I asked, now fully awake.

"Before going to sleep last night you said, 'Leave me alone!' You said it with such viciousness that I could not sleep all night."

I felt terrible. I could see how hurt he was.

"I'm sorry Gabriel but I was drunk, and stoned as well."

"*In vino veritas* my dear," he replied.

For the next hour I explained to Gabriel how deeply I cared for him but as the weeks progressed I found myself more and more resentful of his demands on my time. He was not aggressive in his demands but his pouting, anytime I could not speak with him, grew more and more needy. He ignored my requests for less communication, so I had to get more aggressive. That night after Eliot's party, my built-up defiance finally burst open.

Gabriel replied, "I was already married to a woman that rejected me. I cannot go into a relationship with another woman doing the same."

"If you were as needy with your ex-wife as with me then I understand why she rejected you. You have to look at your responsibility Gabriel. For me, I see that I let my love addiction carry me away, letting you think that I would be available to you 24/7. That was my bad. Gabriel, I will never be available to you or anyone 24/7. It is unrealistic and unhealthy. I need to have my own sense of self. It's being emotionally sober, togetherness is wonderful, neediness is not."

I could see that Gabriel did not understand his responsibility in any of this. All he could see was another woman like his ex-wife. I

341

guess I saw my ex-husband in Gabriel too, a man who did not take responsibility for his addiction. My ex-husband was a sex addict in denial. Gabriel was a love addict in denial. So when Gabriel told me he did not want to see me any more, I heard a man that was not willing to look at his shadow and I did not want to be with that kind of man again. I let him go.

For several days after Gabriel walked out on me I wrote and wrote, catching up on two months of pent-up realizations. Though I spent nine months in celibacy after my marriage with Ananta ended, I still attracted a sex addict to me in the form of Aaron Berger. Now I have attracted a love addict to me in the form of Gabriel Gaspar.

In all of this I was seeing how much more healing I needed to do in order to attract a man without these addictions. We attract what we are. It was a sad realization but I knew I would have to get to the bottom of this. In addition to my private therapy sessions with Ala Konopko, I went to 12-step meetings more regularly and read literature about love addicts and sex addicts, even though most of the sex addicts I read about were men. Men are often porn addicted as well, whereas women typically don't fall prey to that aspect of sex addiction. We are more often interested in intrigue, fantasy, and bantering with men over the Internet. That's women's preferred avenue for acting out on the Internet. It often takes the form of carrying on with multiple dating websites that can often lead to sex chatting. We like "real" attention, however fantasy oriented it may be. At least it is in "real" time and not a video as with much of pornography.

I made a commitment to myself not to date for at least a year. I needed to get to the root of my addiction, for it was abscessing and driving me crazy.

Chapter 58

No More Dating in "Recovery"

It made sense that I attracted Aaron to me after I left Ananta. My ex-husband is a sex addict, I am a sex/love addict, and prostitution, my most recent form of acting out, was sexual. So to attract Aaron, also a sex addict, made complete sense. Therefore, after leaving Aaron the first time, I spent the next six months dissecting and healing my sex addiction. If I had not done that, I would not have been able to see Aaron's sexual manipulations during our second round after those six months were up, and to leave him within a couple of months once I got clear. While un-sober I might have stayed with Aaron for years. I was making progress.

However, the fact that I jumped right into looking for another man the day after dumping Aaron was clearly un-sober. Yet my sex addict convinced my love addict that since this quest was for love and not sex, it was sober dating. These two addictions have been in cahoots all my life and with their slippery relationship so finely tuned, I missed all the red flags. That became evident to me when I understood that Gabriel was a love addict. Gabriel had it so bad and was so blind to it that he was like someone walking down the street with his arm cut off, not knowing why he felt faint. Ah hello, the blood is draining out of your body? It was so clear to see, why couldn't he see it? Yet I knew it was not my job to break through the denial of these men. I had to stay focused on my own denial, I had to get clear and get sober, so I could stop attracting these types of men.

But I also knew that there were no accidents. I attracted Gabriel to me because my love addict was not yet sober. I wanted desperately to fall in love again, whatever it took. So with a year to dig in deep, I dove into my memoirs, with more therapy and more 12-step recovery work. I spent a great deal of time grieving the loss of my original source of love, my mother. I was not grieving her

343

recent death but the death of our nearly non-existent bonding. I barely remembered a time when she was tender and affectionate with me as a child or an adult. With such a deficit, it was no surprise that I chased love wherever I could find it, and usually from those who could not give it, just like my mother. When I did find healthy men, their love was too unfamiliar and unappealing, I pushed them away or cheated on them. Such a sad and sorry love mess I created for myself.

I barely noticed that one year of celibacy was up as I was also busy healing my broken wrist from an exercise fall. For four months I had to speak my memoirs into a microphone. It was extremely challenging but it kept the writing going on a low-burner basis. My credit cards maxed out months back but with my broken wrist I could not even work. Without a book advance, I was at a loss of how to pay my bills so I did the unthinkable. No, not prostitution, that was a lesson learned for good. I liquidated my IRAs. Since I was not of retirement age I lost a significant amount of money. But it pulled me out of a big chunk of debt and allowed me to keep on keeping on with my memoirs.

Perhaps it was this financial ease or the summer breeze, whatever it was, I accepted the possibility of romance back into my life that August of 2014. A man that I had met while on a meditation retreat that summer asked me out on a date. Grigore was originally from Romania but moved to New York with his parents as a young teen. He was tall, attractive, my age, creative, and on a deep spiritual quest. We had much in common. But for some reason or another, either Grigore was out of town or I was out of town, it took nearly a month before we landed our first date. We did communicate after we met, and had begun to get to know one another. I was acutely aware of the amount of time we spent writing emails and talking on the phone. One hour on the phone was my limit and he was not put off if I was too busy and could not speak. Phew, he passed the love addiction test!

When we did finally meet for a vegetarian dinner, I had a lovely time. Grigore's deep spiritual exploration was as intense as mine, and I found this rare in a heterosexual man, especially in New York.

As we were about to say good-bye, I could see Gigore was uncomfortable as he said, "I'd really like to see you again."

Yikes! My stomach turned flip-flops and not in that sexually excited way. It was in a sexually repulsed way. I had to be honest with him.

"Grigore, I don't know. Really, I don't know what I want from a man any more or even if I want a man any more. God, I feel so awkward! I haven't dated in a year and I feel like I did in junior high school - geeky, uncomfortable, and not really interested in boys."

Grigore replied, "That's okay. I like you. If all we do is become friends I'd be happy with that."

"Really?" I asked.

"Really. Remember, I told you I went for ten years without a romantic relationship in my 20s. I think I can handle a friendship. Of course, if it turns into more, I'd be happy with that too."

Grigore kissed me on the cheek and I jumped into the subway. During my ride home I thought over our many conversations of the past few weeks. I was ecstatic to discover that not only was Grigore not a love addict, he was also not a sex addict. A sex addict could never spend months with a woman and not have sex with her unless he was getting it from someone else. We remained platonic friends. I wanted to get to know him well before we became more intimate, if we ever did. He was totally fine with that. It wasn't until a couple months passed that we kissed for the first time. It was less sexual and more romantic. I was starting to fall for him.

Originally I thought it was me that was avoiding intimate contact with Grigore but the closer I got to him, the farther he seemed to move away from me. It was curious. Then, after he canceled Thanksgiving dinner with my sister and me and cancelling two other events with me that week, I broke up with Grigore via text message. It seemed a cruel way to end our relationship but I felt he was being incredibly cruel to me by abandoning me three times in one week. Three strikes and you're out of my baseball league for good. I was hurt and angry.

When the painful dust settled I remembered a 12-step meeting on sexual anorexia and saw Grigore's sexual avoidance behaviors all over this aspect of sex/love addiction. Sexual anorexics are terrified of intimacy, they may go for years and decades without a romantic relationship. I laughed out loud in my bed as I had a tragi-comic conversation with myself.

345

"Woman, you have attracted the Three Faces of Steve to your bed since leaving Ananta. They are the three reflections of your own addiction - sex addict, love addict, and sexual anorexic."

When I stopped laughing I got quiet with the realization that I was indeed in my sexual anorexic phase. Shit, more work to do, oh well. I went to more 12-step meetings for sexual anorexia and learned my addictive nature was less about anorexia and more about sex and love. However, I could not deny that I was in a sexually anorexic phase. My desire for intimacy was nearly non-existent and my desire to protect my heart from pain was high. I couldn't afford a painful break-up, literally, as I had no savings to carry me if I landed in bed for weeks due to withdrawal. Sexual anorexia felt safe to me.

Back to therapy, back to 12-step meetings, and back to endless contemplations, meditations, and speculations. With six months of no dating, I finally accepted a blind date the night before my 2015 birthday with a guy that I had been avoiding for three years on Facebook. His name was Cosimo from Milano, Italy, and I was avoiding him because he looked to be the typical bad boy that always got me into trouble – tall, dark, handsome, tattoos, motorcycle and a foreign accent. He must have asked me out at least twice a year via Facebook. So why did I finally accept? I was vulnerable, it was my birthday, and he was sweet with me. On a private message he asked me the simple question that he must have asked a dozen times over the past three years.

"*Amore*, how are you?"

Usually I would not respond to his non-personal message or I'd give him a quick Ok. But on this night, I was vulnerable and spoke my truth.

I told him, "I am terrible."

He asked, "But why my beauty?"

I replied, "It is my birthday next week and I have run out of money and afraid I may become homeless."

"*Amore*, not to worry. Let me take you for birthday dinner and maybe I can help you find work. Okay?"

I was not thinking romance. I was looking for someone to save me from drowning financially. Maybe he would have a connection in publishing or fashion and entertainment. I was desperate and scared. We had hundreds of friends in common on Facebook, which somehow had me feeling safer about him. Nevertheless, I met Cosimo at a public art gallery opening in Soho. The instant we connected in person I felt safe. Though he was a tough looking guy on the outside he had an extremely sweet nature. Plus we discovered that we knew a few people in common at the gallery opening.

After taking in the edgy nightclub photos from the 70s and 80s, Cosimo invited me for dinner in Little Italy. Though I had difficulty understanding his English, it only added to his charm. When our dinner plates were cleared, he kept looking at his watch.

I asked, "Are you meeting someone later?"

"No, no," he said.

I excused myself for the bathroom. When I came out Cosimo was standing near the door. He pushed me up against the wall and kissed me passionately.

"Happy birthday *amore…*"

Wow, what a hot birthday kiss! So that was why he kept looking at his watch, he wanted to kiss me at midnight. Aweeee, he was too sweet my Cosimo. He took me home in a cab and got out with me.

I explained, "Cosimo, I told you before you jumped in my cab, you are not coming home with me."

"Why no?" he asked.

"It doesn't matter why no," I said, "it is No."

I saw how very sweet and sexy he was, a soft-hearted tough guy. Cosimo was a personal trainer with a black belt in martial arts. His body was built like a finely tuned machine and he was super hot. Before getting sober from my sex/love addiction I would have invited him upstairs in two seconds. Couldn't do that any more. But I was interested in knowing more about him before he left.

I said, "We can go to the park down the street and talk, okay?"

"Okay," and he gave me the hook of his arm. I loved his old world grace and charm.

We had a lot of fun talking, dancing, and making out. I did not know if this experience would go anywhere but I was grateful for such a beautiful birthday gift. *Gracie mille* Cosimo!

We tried keeping in touch by phone but Cosimo's English was so bad and his accent so thick that I never understood anything on the phone. In person I could guess some of the meaning via body language and facial expression. So we stuck to text messaging in between our dates.

"Houston, we have a problem," I said to myself after our third date walking through the park. Cosimo shared with me his financial challenges. We were two people teetering on homelessness. Actually, he already was technically homeless, living on his friend's couch. Every part of me said to run from this guy because he reminded me of Ananta: handsome, exotic, sexy, ten years my junior, and broke. But my heart went out to him. He probably spent his last few dollars to take me to dinner on my birthday. I couldn't just ignore him. Plus he prayed everyday. He was deeply spiritual. I decided to be honest with Cosimo about everything, my sex/love addiction, my finances, and my fear of falling for him, a guy with no money.

Cosimo replied, "*Amore*, life is hard in this world now. Why we don't spend time together make each other feel good. Is a good idea, no?"

"It's a good idea, I don't know," I replied.

"Anyway, you have roommate so I don't move in with you so you no have worry. But sometimes maybe when you roommate no home we can be sweet together, no?"

And he kissed me and kissed me and we went back to my place that night and made love. We cuddled after and Cosimo spooned me all night long and we played footsies under the covers. I don't think I had a guy play footsies with me since Yigal. Footsies are a very tender expression of love. He was so sweet and tender that I could barely sleep, wanting to soak it all in. I was falling for Cosimo but doing my best not to get too attached.

In the next few weeks Cosimo had a few private clients out of town and my sister gave me some temporary work landscaping for her clients in New Jersey. Therefore my time with Cosimo was extremely limited. But I remember one week when we were both in town and he had one thing or another to tend to, so we did not get together. Something felt off. Then I saw a photo of him with a woman on Facebook that week he was MIA.

I messaged, "Is this your new girlfriend?"

He replied, "LOL! No, she just a friend."

Cosimo added, "I am single and no ready to get into commitment relationship."

I was totally puzzled. All I could think about was how odd that he could text with me several times a day and play footsies in bed, yet he did not want to be in a relationship. I was shocked. I really thought we were heading towards a relationship. It felt more like love than sex even though the sex was super hot on its own.

Right after he made that Declaration of Independence speech he added, "*Amore*, I come see you next week when I get back."

I replied, "No Cosimo, you don't come see me next week."

"No? Why no?" he asked.

"Cosimo, I cannot date you any more." I began to cry. "I need to be in a committed relationship because of my sex/love addiction. It takes me to a bad place when I feel someone does not want to be committed to being only with me. Then I get crazy and start sleeping around and I just can't. I can't. I am sorry Cosimo. If you are not ready to be in a committed relationship with me I have to stop seeing you."

"*Amore*, we speak about this when I see you next week, okay?"

But I knew I could not see him if he would not change his stance. I cried myself to sleep. The withdrawal was beginning.

The next day I awoke with the most unfamiliar feeling. I awoke feeling happy. How could this be? I had just lost a lover, I was in withdrawal. But I felt this wonderful sense of self-esteem that I had never experienced after a break-up before. I did not feel bad that Cosimo chose his freedom over staying with me. I did not take it personally. It was just where he was at in his life. I enjoyed our sweet two months together and let him go.

Chapter 59

Am I REALLY in Recovery?

After my brief time with Cosimo I knew I had still more healing to do surrounding my sex/love addiction. Though I was able to quickly see that it was an unhealthy relationship for me, I still walked into it blindly. Aaron, Gabriel, Grigore now Cosimo were all short-lived relationships during my first four years in recovery. Yes, I was proud of myself for seeing the unhealthy and addictive nature of all four relationships and cutting them off quickly. However, I still walked into them wearing blinders. Though I had been sober from my bottom-line behaviors of promiscuity, prostitution and sex outside of a monogamous relationship since October 10, 2011, as of the summer of 2016, I still had no idea how to have a sober relationship. I simply did not know how to have a romantic relationship where my sex addict was not in the driver's seat and my love addict was not in the passenger's seat. Yes, I managed to stay sober off my bottom lines, but I was certain there were more behaviors that I needed to identify, isolate, and add to my bottom lines. Finally, after four years of regular participation at 12-step meetings, I was clear I needed to find a sponsor.

I had several excuses for never having a sponsor. Mainly, I didn't want anyone telling me what to do. I knew it all. "Look I'm sober off my bottom lines and I did it without a sponsor!" But I was in denial about several questionable behaviors and the last four years of unsuccessful dating made that clear.

Finding a great sponsor is never easy. It takes time to find someone strong in recovery and someone who gels with our personality. In the alcoholic-based recovery programs there are far more sponsors to choose from. These programs are abstinence-based. To stay sober, an alcoholic must abstain from drinking. Though staying sober from alcohol is not easy, we do not need alcohol to live. However, getting sober from a sex/love addition is not an abstinence-based recovery program, unless we plan to be a nun or a monk. Therefore, we need to find moderation within our sexual and romantic drives. Moderation is far more difficult than extremes. Ask those with a food addiction. Eat all the potato chips or eat none of them. But eat only a handful? That is tough.

Attending a meeting for alcoholics one summer evening in 2016, as I embarked upon my sobriety from alcohol and drugs as well, I had fellowship with a member after the meeting about how alcohol and drugs were often the gateway to my main drug of sex and love.

He told me, "I wish I had a sex/love addiction. Sounds like a great addiction to have."

I knew he was being facetious but I also understood that he had no clue how difficult is this addiction.

I told him, "Oooh, you have no idea just how difficult it is to stay sober with a sex/love addiction. Imagine you, as an alcoholic, have to have three shots of whiskey a week and not more. Could you refrain from jumping back in the bottle head-first?"

He replied, "I couldn't do that. I'd be drinking all day every day again."

We talked on and I explained that abstinence protects us from returning to the bottle. As long as we abstain we are good and the longer we abstain, the stronger we get in our sobriety, assuming we are working a steady program with our sponsor. However, sex/love addiction is not an abstinence-based recovery program unless we intend to stay celibate. But if we ever want romance in our lives, we have to navigate the waters of sex and love. Therefore the sexually-based 12-step programs are harm-reduction models of recovery. What we need to learn is moderation in our sexual and romantic lives by abstaining from harmful behaviors (bottom lines) and reducing as many triggers as possible.

As I began to wind down he said, "I take back what I said, not an easy addiction. I'm sorry I made a joke out of it."

Laughing, I reassured him, "No worries, I got my funny bone back a couple years ago. That's one way I knew I was healing and getting better."

I continued to feed him information, as he seemed eager to learn. "Sex/love addictions are similar to food addictions. They are also harm-reduction models of recovery for we cannot be abstinent and stop eating. We need to eat to live. Imagine an over-eater being confronted by food choices all day every day? It is not easy."

Shortly after this meeting for alcoholics I spoke with a Certified Sex Addiction therapist (CSAT), on the West Coast. She came highly recommended to me. I shared with her my frustration in finding a sponsor. After hearing my history she suggested I check out another sexual recovery program that had several phone meetings. She shared with me that her first sponsor had been a little old lady from Tennessee who she worked with for several years but never met in person. I was thrilled to know that my options in finding a sponsor just grew exponentially.

Two days later I attended a face-to-face meeting of this new fellowship to feel it out before trying a phone meeting. I came with a heavy heart since I spent the previous day searching for storage spaces - it was apparent that I would soon be homeless. It took a lot longer to finish my memoirs than I had anticipated. I went through my savings, my IRAs, and maxed out my credit cards. I looked desperately for work again as a legal secretary but months passed with not one job interview. A brave headhunter finally revealed to me that my online presence was too risqué to pass HR. I had written several articles about my sex/love addiction for the Feminine Collective, using my real name. My logic was that I had nothing to hide so why not use my real name? I soon understood why there was always an "A" after all the 12-step names. "Anonymous" was there to protect us because all addiction has stigma, especially sex addiction, specifically for women with sex addiction.

During this new meeting I shared my terrifying financial crisis and my desire to find a sponsor. A dynamic woman named Virginia shared after me and I was immediately drawn to her strength, her solid recovery, and her connection to God. I wanted what she had. At the end of the meeting I approached her and asked if she would be my sponsor. Virginia said she had several sponsees already but was willing to be my temporary sponsor to get me started. I was grateful for any guidance I could get.

I started working the steps with Virginia. She was curious how I had been able to stay off my bottom lines for four years without the support of a sponsor.

"How do you think you were able stay sober?" she asked.

I replied, "I'd like to take credit for my strong will power but it wasn't that. I crashed hard on October 10, 2011, completely disgusted with myself, so much so that I wanted nothing to do with the life I had been living for ten years. It was not the legacy I wanted to leave my 22-year-old daughter. I believe it was the intensity of my crash and disgust that began my sober journey but I am sure it was my return to a deep connection with God that was my true strength. I prayed and meditated each morning without fail."

"Aaah God. Good, you got much of our first three steps organically. I'll take you through the steps formally to go more in depth. In the 12-step process you will also discover parts of yourself that you have not yet surrendered."

My spirit soared to have Virginia's support. I began Step One that night, with the recommended readings she assigned from *The Big Book of Alcoholics Anonymous*. Though my main addiction was sex/love, it was easy to translate the term "alcohol" to "sex" or "love". Virginia also assigned readings from the *Green Book of Sex Addicts Anonymous*. Though I was still in a financially precarious situation, focusing on the steps helped me to stop obsessing. This in itself was a miracle.

Chapter 60

Working with Addicts

What happened next was mind blowing. Four days after going to this new S fellowship meeting and working the steps with Virginia, my new sponsor, I got a phone call that would shift my financial situation and alter my direction.

The voice on the other end of the phone answered, "Hi Shanti, it's Carol from Recovery Assistants. How are you?"

I was frozen in disbelief. This was one of the women I trained with five months earlier to become a recovery coach and sober companion. Since I couldn't get work due to the scarlet letter of my sex addiction, while praying and meditating I got the calling to look for work with addicts. Thank you God, that's something I do know about! Several years working as a dating/relationship coach taught me how to support and inspire clients who are struggling. So working with addicts as they struggle to stay sober was a perfect fit. Plus I understood an addict's struggle first hand.

Carol runs an agency for sober companions out of Philadelphia. I had tried on several occasions to elicit work from her. Finally, in a face-to-face meeting in Philly she told me, "Shanti, I've never had a client with a sex addiction. Maybe they have some sexual acting-out issues but their main addictions are drugs and alcohol and these are not your addictions. I really don't have clients for you."

I said, "Carol, it is true that sex/love is my main addiction. However, I have been sober from drugs and alcohol for over a month now."

"That's great Shanti but, you need at least a year sober from substances before I can work with you. I usually insist on two or more years of sobriety, depending on the companion."

When we had this meeting two months prior I took it as gospel and stopped reaching out to other sober companion agencies. Writing about my sex/love addiction cost me a return to the legal field, yet I did not even have the "right" kind of addiction to work in the recovery field. I felt as if I was swimming in the quicksand of debt, awaiting my financial death while still praying for a cash crane to pull me out somehow.

So when Carol called I was shocked but did my best to disguise it. She said, "Listen, I have a tough case that most of my experienced companions have burnt out on already. Just being upfront with you. I told her parents that you are new to substance recovery but have five years recovery from sex/love addiction. This girl is a heroin and meth addict who has been in and out of prostitution. Her parents think you could be a good fit, they are at the end of their rope. She's been to rehab twice but keeps relapsing. Lydia is likely bipolar or borderline personality disorder but we haven't been able to get her off drugs long enough to diagnose her properly. She is a handful. I'm telling you now. It would begin in four days for a few weeks in New York. Once she stays clean our goal is to get her to a sober living home. Are you interested?"

Was I interested?! Who was I to be choosy while facing homelessness? I was ready to jump without asking any questions but Carol went on to explain how difficult it would be to work with Lydia and to prepare. She told me to rest up.

Carol did not exaggerate how challenging it would be to work with this young woman. Lydia was in constant motion externally and internally. When we weren't racing about the city doing errands or shopping, we were flushing through her list of complaints, nothing was right in her world. But I liked Lydia. With all her emotional outbursts, belligerent defiance and constant threats to use drugs or go back to prostitution, I still liked her. Lydia had a big heart though she tried desperately to mask it. She took in stray animals and stray people, nourishing their bodies and souls until they were strong enough to leave. Then she would find them good homes. Lydia herself was a broken bird but I could still hear the song in her heart. I stayed with her until she was solid enough in her recovery to get to sober living.

This assignment led to another and then working with multiple agencies and more assignments. My bills were finally being paid and debts diminishing, nothing short of a miracle from where I was stuck. In addition to financial relief I had altruistic relief. Participating in volunteer work all of my life, I longed to find a career where my nurturing nature could be utilized alongside earning an income. Nursing was out because I couldn't stomach blood and guts, I tried that as a candy-striper in high school, dismal failure. My normal pattern was to work for several years then do volunteer work for several years and the pattern would continue. So working in the addiction/recovery field was a godsend to me.

I discovered a deep calling to support these poor souls struggling in their recovery, as I have struggled. Though I was not their 12-step sponsor I was their 12-step escort and often their caretaker, secretary, entertainment buddy and mental health support. At times I was their emotional punching bag and I had to learn to hold firm boundaries. I got to see them at their worst but I also got to see them break through and experience them at their best.

I often felt I got more out of working with them than they got from me. I have learned far greater patience and compassion, and let go of my need to control. Just try controlling an addict!

I found my calling and have been working in the addiction/recovery field ever since. While on an assignment I often get very little sleep, I'm emotionally challenged and have practically no personal time. Yet I know I am making a huge difference in the lives of my clients and their families. I am eternally grateful for this opportunity.

Chapter 61

Working with My Sponsor

No one was more shocked and delighted with my financial bailout than my sponsor, Virginia. She revealed to me, weeks after I embarked upon this new career, that when she heard me sharing my financial ruin, she made a note to pray for me several times a day. She is a strong believer in prayer and now I am too.

Working with my sponsor has revealed how far I have come. However, working with her has also revealed just how far I've yet to go. Though I was sober five years off my three bottom lines of promiscuity, sex outside a monogamous relationship, and prostitution, there were more sexual behaviors Virginia spotted that I needed to add to my list.

1) No dating married men (even if they are separated).

2) No dating sexually un-sober men.

3) No sex for several weeks into a monogamous relationship.

If those bottom lines had been in place when I left my ex-husband Ananta and started dating again, I would not have dated any of those men. Live and learn for sure but I was seeing how important it is to have a sponsor. Those sober outside eyes and ears are invaluable.

When I first met Virginia I shared that it had been a year since I'd dated. She felt that had been a good decision and asked me to abstain further from dating until I finished all 12 steps with her. I had no problem with that, especially since my main focus was working the steps, creating steady income, and digging myself out of debt. I really had no time to date.

That realization would never have come to pass while I was acting out sexually. I would have dated even if I was homeless or on my deathbed. Now I am aware how important it is for me to see

357

clearly before entering the dating arena again. It is a place where I need sex-sober eyes and enormous support.

There was another phenomenon that I was completely unaware of until I started working Steps Four and Five with Virginia: the state of being emotionally sober. She pointed out that I was sexually sober off my original bottom lines but that I was not emotionally sober. As soon as she suggested this concept, though I did not fully understand it, I knew in my gut she was right. Though my constant craving for sex and romantic love had diminished, my anger had not subsided, in fact it grew.

I was still angry at the world. I was angry that I fell so low that I prostituted myself with a teenage daughter at home. I was angry that my husband didn't earn income and was fine with me prostituting myself, in effect, he pimped me out. I was angry with my mother for creating the original traumas that got me into this sex/love addiction mess in the first place. I was angry with men for never giving me what I truly wanted. I was angry at the wealthy for their financial comfort. By God, at whom wasn't I angry?

An alcoholic who no longer drinks yet retains this much anger is called a dry drunk. The alcohol was taken off the table but the underlying anger, resentments, fears, and other character defects are still active and more ugly than ever. There is no longer the alcohol to numb the pain. Without the 12-Steps it is extremely difficult to purge these toxic emotions. I guess I was a dry sex/love addict.

When acting out I would have made a joke about this, "Hey gang, they think I'm a dry sex addict. What, no lube in the house?"

Steps Four and Five deal with these character defects and I felt 100 pounds lighter working through them. Though I was keenly aware of how much anger I carried, I was not aware of its weight on my soul. After finishing Step Five I cried frequently as I released a lifetime of pain and sorrow. It was a much-needed purge.

With Virginia's patient and compassionate support I was able to complete all 12-Steps and start sponsoring others as she had so lovingly sponsored me. For the first time in my five years of recovery I felt as though I was truly in recovery -- body, mind and soul. I could never have achieved this type of sobriety without the support of my sponsor. Thank You Virginia!

Chapter 62

My Journey to Sobriety

After five long years of writing my memoirs, my diligent practices of yoga, meditation, kabbalah, psychotherapy, 12-Step recovery, trauma work, volunteer work, and keeping the company of my beloved family and friends, I can safely say I am solidly on my journey to sobriety. I am quite happy to be single for the time being. To be happily single is a total miracle for me.

Even though I am sober today, I will always need to be diligent with intimate relationships. Losing myself over to my partner in love addiction, or getting lost in the lust of my sex addiction, are patterns powerfully etched in my psyche. I will need to be forever on guard.

Unlike an alcoholic or drug addict who never has to use the substance again, we sex/love addicts have the added complication of having to constantly monitor ourselves if we wish to be in an intimate relationship. Thank Goddess for the 12-Step programs! Their powerful support system and message of hope offers me encouragement that one day I will be in a healthy intimate relationship. For now, I am in a healthy intimate relationship with myself, a place I have never been before, and I am infinitely grateful for my journey to sobriety...

About the Author

Shanti Patty Owen has been studying and practicing various forms of transformational work, healing modalities, meditation, service, and following a deep spiritual path for over 35 years. Super model, actress, recovery role model, relationship coach, spokesperson, teacher, mom, and now author, Shanti has several books awaiting her focus. For more information and to get in touch, www.SPOwen.com.

CPSIA information can be obtained
at www.ICGtesting.com
Printed in the USA
LVHW111302050820
662450LV00002B/410